BEYOND THE BRIDGES

The Suburbs of Shrewsbury 1760-1960

[handwritten inscription: with the best wishes of the author.]

[handwritten signature: Barrie Trinder 24.5.06]

The Mount, built in 1797.

BEYOND THE BRIDGES

The Suburbs of Shrewsbury 1760-1960

BARRIE TRINDER

Phillimore

2006

Published by
PHILLIMORE & CO. LTD
Shopwyke Manor Barn, Chichester, West Sussex.
www.phillimore.co.uk

© Barrie Trinder, 2006

ISBN 1-86077-393-1
ISBN 13 978-1-86077-393-8

Printed and bound in Great Britain by
THE CROMWELL PRESS
Trowbridge, Wiltshire

Contents

Other books written or edited by Barrie Trinder

A Victorian MP and his Constituents (1969)
Drink and Society in an early Victorian Country Town [with Sir Brian Harrison] (1969)
The Industrial Revolution in Shropshire (Phillimore, 1973, 1981, 2000)
The Darbys of Coalbrookdale (Phillimore, 1974, 1978, 1981, 1992)
The Most Extraordinary District in the World: Ironbridge and Coalbrookdale (Phillimore, 1977, 1988, 2005)
Yeomen & Colliers in Telford: the probate inventories of Dawley, Lilleshall, Wellington & Wrockwardine [with Jeff Cox] (Phillimore, 1980)
Victorian Banbury (Phillimore, 1982, 2005)
The Making of the Industrial Landscape (1982, 1986, 1997)
A History of Shropshire (Phillimore, 1983, 1998)
Victorian Shrewsbury (1984)
Industrial Heritage of Britain (1988)
The Blackwell Encyclopedia of Industrial Archaeology (1992)
The Industrial Archaeology of Shropshire (Phillimore, 1996)
The English Heritage Book of Industrial England [with Michael Stratton] (1997)
Miners & Mariners of the Severn Gorge: the probate inventories of Benthall, Broseley, Little Wenlock & Madeley [with Nancy Cox] (Phillimore, 2000)
Twentieth Century Industrial Archaeology [with Michael Stratton] (2000)
The Market Town Lodging House in Victorian England (2001)
The Iron Bridge: Symbol of the Industrial Revolution [with Sir Neil Cossons] (Phillimore, 2002)
Thomas Telford's Holyhead Road: the A5 in North Wales [with Jamie Quartermaine & Rick Turner] (2003)
Barges & Bargemen: A social history of the Upper Severn Navigation 1660-1900 (Phillimore, 2005)
English Market Towns and their suburbs in recent centuries (Wolfson Lecture, 2005)

List of Maps and Illustrations

Maps

Illustrations

Illustration Acknowledgements

Author's collection, 13, 42, 121; Barrie Kelsall, 14; J. Nightingale, *The Beauties of England and Wales*, 31; Shropshire Archives, 47, 79, 82, 109, 115.
    All other photographs in this book are by the author.

Preface and Acknowledgements

This book is written in the belief that historians of towns have an obligation to help people to understand the landscapes in which they live, not just in Shrewsbury but further afield. I have attempted to put a vast quantity of data into an explicable form and to explain how from the viewpoint of 2006 the town appears to have grown over two hundred years. The study has evolved over many years and has taken many forms. It originated about 30 years ago as a hastily-organised evening map exercise in Belle Vue for summer-school students whose projected field day on the Stiperstones had been prevented by incessant rain. It continued in the mid-1970s as guided walks for members of the popular 'History of Shrewsbury' lecture series at College Hill House and the Gateway, and became part of an ambitious county-wide summer programme of walks organised by my then colleague Andrew Jenkinson. After government cuts brought an end to that programme, ten-week series of 'Shrewsbury Suburbs' walks continued every summer until the early 1990s, some attracting more than a hundred people. The concept then mutated into a radio series, and I am grateful to Lawrie Bloomfield, MBE who thought of the title that I have borrowed for this book, and to Chris Eldon Lee who wittily edited and presented the programmes.

The study also derives from adult education activity of another kind, a research class on 'Victorian Shrewsbury' that met in the local studies library from 1973 until 1995. Its members produced a book of essays in 1984, wrote articles that appeared in *West Midlands Studies*, the *Journal of the Tiles and Architectural Ceramics Society* and the *Shropshire Magazine*, while two members went on to take doctorates, and a third is now a successful archaeological consultant. My gratitude for work incorporated in this study is due to all members of that class, but particularly to Joyce Butt, Janice Cox, Marjorie Dunham, the late Connie Evason, Pat Frost, the late Philippa Gray, Donald and Iris Harris, the late Deidre Haxton, Barbara Jarvis, the late Joyce Lee, Paddy Marsh, the late Dick Marston, Pattie Price, Henri Quinn, the late Frances and Olive Richards, Mary Richards, Stella Straughan and Brian Webb. I am also grateful to have made some use of probate inventories transcribed at a research class in Shrewsbury that I tutored with Dr Nancy Cox in the early 1990s. Every work of local history owes something to librarians and archivists, but this one owes a huge debt to Tony Carr, local studies librarian in Shrewsbury for three decades until 2004, who encouraged the presence of the 'Victorian Shrewsbury' class in his library, and throughout that period was a source of information, encouragement and advice.

I learned much from students of the Ironbridge Institute between 1980 and 1985 during field trips in Shrewsbury, and several of them wrote dissertations that have been directly useful in this book. Another, David Worth, stimulated my thinking about networks from faraway Cape Town. I learned much about Ditherington flax mill and its environment from working with Mary Macleod and Michael Worthington during investigations by the Ironbridge Institute in 1988-9, and from Keith Falconer and colleagues at the Royal Commission and English Heritage. I am grateful to students and colleagues at University College Northampton, and to members of my seminars at the Oxford University Summer School for Adults for ideas that have found their way into my thinking about the way towns grow.

Shrewsbury's growth can only be traced through the patient examination of many sources: maps, property deeds, census returns, newspapers and reminiscences. Only limited use has been made in this study of property deeds, and of the official records of the corporation, leaving many opportunities for further detailed research. Much has been learned from fieldwork, the study of building materials, the exploration of alleys and footpaths and the re-tracing of old boundaries. This is the kind of study for which the range of sources is infinite, and after many years the time for publication has come. It is for others to take the themes further.

This study depends heavily on the work of other scholars. Bill Champion has generously made available his researches on property chains in Shrewsbury, chiefly in the early modern period, which has strengthened the foundations of the work in many respects. I owe much to medieval archaeologists, chiefly to Nigel Baker and his colleagues for their work on Shrewsbury Abbey, but also to Martin Carver for stimulating thinking about Shrewsbury's history in the 1970s. My debts to architectural historians, in particular to Madge Moran and Eric Mercer, are evident throughout the book, and research on place names by Margaret Gelling and the late George Foxall has been invaluable. Chris Warn kindly allowed me to see his research on bus services, and Donald Harris has passed on details of Dr Robert Darwin's property transactions. David Trumper has done much to conserve and make available photographic evidence of Shrewsbury's past, and I have made much use of his publications. David Pannett was involved with the map exercise that began this study, and has published a valuable interpretation of the Old River Bed. The *Victoria County History* volumes on county government and agricultural have been further sources of strength. I am grateful to David Cox, formerly editor of the Shropshire *VCH*, for allowing me to see a draft of his work on the Abbey Foregate, and to his former colleague, Paul Stamper, now of English Heritage, who has provided interesting thoughts on the history of gardens, and persuaded me that it was worth persevering with this book at a time when I doubted the value of the project.

Many other people have, knowingly or unknowingly, provided information that has proved valuable in writing the final version of this study. I acknowledge with pleasure help from Mr & Mrs L. Asbury, Tony and Sue Cooper, Barry Davey, Norman Davies, Les Dolamore, Barrie Kelsall, Ian Sanders, John and Christine Smith, Lawson Smith, Mr & Mrs G. Sproston, John Wall and Alan Wilding, as well as from anonymous householders I have met during fieldwork. Geoff Gwatkin has provided excellent maps, and I am grateful to Patrick Pakes for ensuring the smooth operation of my computers. I am particularly indebted to Tony and Kathy Herbert for advice on botanical and architectural ceramic matters, and for helpful comments on a draft of the book. Any errors that remain are entirely my responsibility.

This book cannot and does not provide a history of every house in Shrewsbury beyond the bridges. I hope that it does provide a context in which the development of the various suburbs can be understood. Nor does the book attempt to be judgemental on the current character of suburbs. In this, as in other respects, it is intended as an historical foundation on which others may wish to build.

My greatest debt is to my wife who has helped in many ways with this book, as with many others, and has always cheerfully accepted the eccentricities of a writer husband.

Barrie Trinder
Shrewsbury 2006

Conventions

The council that administered Shropshire from 1888 was called the Salop County Council until 1 May 1980 when it became the Shropshire County Council. References to that body before 1980 are to the Salop County Council.

Metric equivalents are given for precise measurements, the dimensions of buildings for example, but not for approximate distances between places or areas of properties. There appears no necessity in this study to give metric equivalents for Imperial tons and hundredweights, nor for shillings and pence.

Dates of birth and death of individuals are given, where known, in the index of personal names.

Maps 1-10 are designed as guides to the text. They do not indicate the state of the areas they portray at any particular date.

CHAPTER I

Suburbs

Shrewsbury stands on a red sandstone eminence, encircled by a horseshoe bend in the River Severn. A castle guards its landward approach; spires and towers punctuate its skyline. It is an archetypal 'city on a hill'. Yet Shrewsbury had suburbs recorded in Domesday Book and since 1760 most of its growth has been beyond its bridges. Historians have given relatively little attention to suburbs, the homes of large numbers, perhaps a majority of English people. The processes that have shaped patterns of houses, the chronology of growth, and changing social structures are understood in very few towns. This book takes as a case study one of 'the primary towns of England', and by examining its growth over two centuries attempts to pose and answer questions in ways that will illuminate the history of all English towns.

The word 'suburb' is sometimes taken to mean a self-sustaining part of a large city, with an identity of its own, as in a study of the early 1980s that analysed Acton, Ealing, Bromley and Headingley. Some published studies have been concerned with model communities, with Hampstead, Bournville and Victoria Park in Manchester.[1] Yet the growing edges of the smallest towns, where suburbs were certainly not independent in that sense, have characteristics that distinguish them from the centres of the communities from which they have sprung. In Margaret Oliphant's *Chronicles of Carlingford*, published in 1876, Grange Lane, a leafy resort of wealthy old ladies, flanked by allotments and paths cut up by wheelbarrows, lacked the excitement of a town centre, forever made lively by disputes between townspeople, the passage of troops or entertainers. The area had a character that was threatened when houses fell into the hands of such people as a dissenting butterman.[2] Small towns provide archaeological evidence of features that have shaped the suburbs of larger places. In Ludlow, a brick clay quarry of the kind that provided materials for building many 19th-century towns remains in New Road; the site of an archetypal suburban tea garden of the Regency period is recognisable in Sandpits Road, while Rock Lane is a rough suburb similar to Mixen Lane in Hardy's *Mayor of Casterbridge*.[3] Shrewsbury is larger than Ludlow, and provides evidence of aspects of suburban growth that cannot be observed there, but is not so large that evidence of significant developments has been obliterated.

The foundation of any historical consideration of suburbs must be the late

1   The seal of the borough of Shrewsbury.

H.J. Dyos's study of Camberwell.[4] Dyos portrays the complexities of the suburban economy and analyses the nuances of suburban society. His subtle analysis of suburban growth, and his awareness of the significance of architectural detail are as applicable in the provinces as in London. Maurice Beresford's study of Leeds is a rewarding analysis of a provincial city, although the author affirmed that he was concerned with urban expansion rather than suburbs.[5] Christopher Chalklin pointed out that in the fastest-growing provincial towns building on new land began early in the 18th century, in manufacturing centres, such as Manchester, Birmingham and Sheffield, in the commercial ports of Liverpool and Sunderland, in the dockyard towns of Plymouth and Portsmouth, and in the uniquely prosperous resort of Bath. He demonstrated that most English towns accommodated population growth within their medieval bounds until about 1760.[6]

Architectural historians have added to our understanding of suburban growth by drawing attention to the distinctive types of houses built in provincial towns before the bye-laws of the mid-19th century, the court houses of Liverpool, the back-to-backs of Leeds and Birmingham, and the two-storey flats of Newcastle. Andrew Saint has chronicled the first appearances of the terrace, the semi-detached villa and other house types in London.[7] Studies of the impact of local boards of health and of building by-laws, of the building industry, of freehold land and building societies, and of the activities of philanthropic housing associations, have also made explicable some aspects of 19th century suburbs.[8]

Suburbs have not enjoyed a good press. Aesthetes of the 1920s and '30s used military metaphors, suggesting that 'the inexorable march of bricks and mortar' was threatening spiritual values that were eternally English. Thomas Sharp, the planner, considered

suburbia as 'essentially selfish and anti-social' because it was continuously pushing the countryside away from the town. The architect of the Dome of Discovery referred in 1942 to mock-Tudor suburbs and ribbon development as 'one of the greatest evils … so also the crimes of our own century'. John Betjeman's prediction in 1937 that the homes of Metroland with their bay windows and leaded lights would soon fall into decay proved erroneous.[9]

The most important study of suburbs of recent decades was published in 1981 by Oliver, Davis and Bentley, who pointed out that the suburban houses of the 1920s and '30s have proved adaptable and popular, and that suburbs demand objective analysis.[10] The words 'suburb' and 'suburban' nevertheless continue to convey pejorative meanings, partly because the ways in which towns have grown over recent centuries are insufficiently understood.[11]

This book seeks to raise issues about English towns as well as to answer questions about the expansion of Shrewsbury.

2 Mahim, No 69 Monkmoor Road, which, when newly-built about 1910, became the rented home of Thomas Owen, railway official, and his family. The writings of his sons, Harold and the poet Wilfred Owen, provide insights into the ways in which a suburb could be perceived that would never arise from fieldwork.

It examines economic growth, and the extent to which that growth was dependent upon suburban expansion. It considers the ways in which the building of suburbs was stimulated by the development of industry, or shaped by new means of transport. It analyses the influence of wars in bursting the limits of built-up areas. It looks at the role of government, of entrepreneurs and of philanthropists, in shaping suburbs. It poses questions about the changes in landscapes as areas passed from agriculture to housing. It is also concerned with concepts like respectability and paternalism.

Understanding suburbs requires imagination as well as diligence. The meanings of landscapes change for succeeding generations, and suburbs today may reflect neither the aspirations of those who built them nor the perceptions of their first residents. For the urban historian, the Underdale area of Shrewsbury is a satisfying case study of Victorian and Edwardian suburban growth, with houses of various sizes and architectural styles built as speculations and through the agency of a land society, and a landscape influenced by a failed railway and a racecourse. To the poet Wilfred Owen and his brother Harold in the years before the First World War the area appeared both idyllic and threatening. To examine Underdale in the light of the Owens' letters and memoirs reveals much about Edwardian society, about the need for a railway bureaucrat's family living in a rented villa to distance themselves from the working-class residents of adjacent terraces, about limited educational opportunities, about deference, and aspirations to social mobility, about the joyous release offered by rambles to Uffington. Harold Owen described the family home from c.1897, the newly-built Wilmot House in Canon Street, as 'rather shabby ... in a long street of other mean little houses – all exactly the same'. 'Shabby' is a subjective term, but the houses in Canon Street display many variations. Harold feared the 'idle, blowsy, dirty and vindictively resentful women' in Cleveland Street, where Wilfred remembered an ugly little grocery shop.[12] No other Shrewsbury suburb is illuminated by such rich literary sources, but it is necessary to see others as they were perceived in the past, to envisage the open spaces of Longden Green as they appeared to infantrymen who had survived the Western Front, Springfield to a guardsman who had driven a tank from the Normandy beaches to the Elbe, Factory Yard to a refugee from the Famine in Co. Mayo, or Roseway to a steam lorry fitter in 1935 earning just enough to make repayments on a mortgaged house.

Concepts and Language

A part of this study interprets suburban growth as the growth of networks. Shrewsbury's corporation in the 19th century often considered the extension of sewers, street lighting and paving beyond the bridges. The isolated suburban houses of the early 19th century were to a large extent self-sufficient, with wells, cesspits and gardens. As suburban houses multiplied, networks of roads, ultimately adopted by the local authority, provided access, and cabs and subsequently motor omnibuses supplemented private carriages. Shops at corners and later in parades were terminals of networks that supplied food. Sewers, water and gas mains, and later electricity and telephone cables were laid along the main roads and into residential streets. Mission rooms were linked to town centre churches and chapels, public houses to breweries, pillar boxes to the Royal Mail's sorting office, patrolling constables to police stations, and delivery vans to bakeries and dairies. Some networks were extended temporarily. Standpipes provided water before mains were extended into houses. Service roads remained boggy morasses before they were adopted. Tin tabernacles and tents provided accommodation for worship. Mobile shops toured estates before the corporation built shopping parades. The concept of networks assumes that suburban growth was centrifugal, that systems spread from the centre, but growth can also be a centripetal process, caused by the movement of migrants from the countryside.

If the concept of networks can be enlightening, other metaphors are less helpful. Suburbs were not the result of impersonal forces akin to the movements of tectonic plates. The military metaphors used by some Victorian writers, in which villas are seen as cavalry and terraces as infantry, are not always enlightening. Such 20th-century terms as 'bungaloid sprawl' imply the operation of deterministic forces. While the historian's task is to search for patterns, and for appropriate language in which to describe them, the development of suburbs is the consequence of decisions by developers, architects, builders and residents, and by government, and is shaped by the legacies of previous generations, by topography and property boundaries and by the availability of craftsmen and materials.

CHAPTER II

Contexts

Topography

The rocky hill on which Shrewsbury stands comprises sandstone of the Keele Beds of the Upper Coal Measures of the Carboniferous period, that dip under the Permian and Triassic rocks that make up much of north Shropshire. The scattered mines of the Shrewsbury Coalfield extend in an arc from Preston Boats to Bragginton, and were worked from the 16th century until 1941. None was large, and it is doubtful whether they ever provided a sufficient supply for Shrewsbury, which for several centuries also drew fuel from the Coalbrookdale Coalfield, 12 miles to the east. None was close enough to the town to be part of the suburbs.[1]

Much of the landscape of the Shrewsbury area was shaped by the Devensian glaciation, that began about 80,000 years ago, and covered much of Shropshire with ice that began to retreat about 15,000 years ago. Several lakes were formed which joined to form an expanse of water, known to geologists as Lake Lapworth, that forced an outlet to the east through what is now called the Ironbridge Gorge. As the lake drained, the course of the upper Severn, which had previously flowed downstream to Welshpool, then northwards to the present River Dee, was reversed. The retreating ice left a hummocky landscape of moraine, clays, sands and gravels from which Shrewsbury's builders obtained many of their materials until the early 20th century. Some blocks of ice remained isolated, were covered by moraine, and on melting formed steep-sided lakes, some of which filled with clay and peat. These are 'kettle holes', significant features of the landscape of the Shrewsbury suburbs, whether they remain as meres, like that at Springfield, or lurk unseen to prove hazards to builders.[2]

The River Severn is joined at Shrewsbury by the Rea Brook, which originates in Marton Pool, 22 miles to the west, and powered several mills between Meole Brace and its confluence with the Severn by the English Bridge. The Rad Brook, which rises five miles to the west, powered no mills but shaped the western suburbs. The landscape to the north has been influenced by the Old River Bed, once the main stream of the Severn, which extended in the shape of a horseshoe from the present West Midland Showground to Cross Hill. After the main stream of the river cut across the isthmus, which borings suggest occurred between 4,000 and 5,000 years ago, the old bed filled with peat. The Bagley Brook follows the line of the old channel, and enters the Severn through a culvert beneath the Gateway.[3]

Agriculture and Horticulture

Property in Shrewsbury, as in most towns, was fragmented. In the 1840s there were 71 landowners in Castle Foregate, 24 in Coton Hill, 71 in Coleham, 58 in Abbey Foregate, 41 in Frankwell and 59 in the township of Meole Brace.[4] There were no great estates in the suburbs, although some properties belonged to substantial landowners. The most significant were the Earls of Tankerville, who gradually sold off their land in the Abbey Foregate during the 19th century. The 5th earl owned over 300 acres in 1843, and his successors, while absentees, retained a close interest in their remaining land into the 1930s. The Dukes of Cleveland, inheritors of the Shropshire estates of the 17th-century Viscounts Newport, held land in Coleham that was significant in 20th-century suburban development, but it totalled only 27 acres in the 1840s. The Burtons of Longner Hall held about 25 acres in Castlefields, with 200 acres at Shelton, while the Powys family of Berwick House held the Abbey estate in the 18th century, and about 240 acres in Coton Hill and 80 acres at Shelton in the mid-19th century. The only landowner to plan a suburban development was John Maddock who laid out streets on his 74-acre Greenfields estate in the 1880s.

Shrewsbury was surrounded by concentric rings of agricultural holdings, the largest on the periphery, the smallest nearest the centre. The outermost were the home farms of the gentry, most of whom at some time practised high farming. The Wingfields had Scottish cattle and White Berkshire pigs at Onslow. The Corbets bred Ayrshires at Sundorne in the 1860s, and Robert Burton kept Hereford and Shorthorn cattle and Yorkshire pigs at Longner in the 1880s.[5] On the fringes of the suburbs were farms characteristic of the wider agricultural region, mostly in excess of 200 acres, where farmers practised mixed husbandry, and accommodated some of their labourers, 'indoor servants', in their farmhouses. At Crowmoor in 1881, Edward Wilks farmed 210 acres with five labourers, one of whom was an 'indoor servant'. At Corner Farm, Bicton Heath, there were six male 'indoor servants' in 1841, four in 1861, and two in 1881. Some farms of this kind, Bank Farm and the Meadows for example, gave their names to mid-20th-century housing estates.

Within this ring of farms were smaller holdings, of between 10 and 20 acres, market gardens, nurseries and dairy farms. Some 'cow keepers' who managed dairy units resided on their holdings, but others lived at their shops. William Pratt, cowkeeper, trading from No 33 Longden Coleham in 1881, worked 12 acres that were clearly not contiguous to his residence. The 17-acre holding at Kemp's Eye was occupied in 1881 by Thomas Jones, a dairyman, and his dairymaid niece, and was later worked by the Wall family, purveyors of 'new milk'. Highfields Dairy of 1879 is the outstanding monument of the 19th-century milk trade. The 18-acre holding off Longden Road, kept for decades by Humphrey James and his family, became the Longden Green estate after the First World War.[6]

Nurserymen provided seeds, fruit trees and ornamental plants for suburban Shrewsbury. In 1798 Charles Bigg established a nursery near the Column, bounded by St Giles' churchyard and the London and Wenlock roads. His two assistants took over the business in 1849. One of them, H.J. Olroyd, soon controlled it, and subsequently vacated the site, but worked a nursery near Beckbury House, and the Portland Nursery, where he had 12 employees in 1861. Olroyd sold fruit trees, Scots firs, larches, deciduous shrubs, hothouse grapes and roses. The latter were the specialism of his successor, Edwin Murrell, who took over the business in 1885.[7] The nursery in New Street, sometimes called the Frankwell Nursery, already had a long history in 1827 when Messrs Grant & Harley marked their retirement with a sale. By 1850 the nine-acre holding was occupied by Robert Phipps. It passed to Pritchard & Son, who relinquished part in 1898, when their stock included 300 apple, pear and plum trees and 175 poplars, but kept the remainder, until it was sold to the council in 1947.[8] Henry Instone, was cultivating a nursery on Sutton Lane by 1833, where, in the 1870s, his son Benjamin supplied gigantic yews, hollies, Wellingtonias, fruit trees and vines. The Calcot Nursery at Bicton Heath offered Lombardy poplars, American and Hemlock spruce and red cedars in 1866.[9]

The smallest holdings, nearest to the town centre, were allotments, mostly cultivated by people who occupied dwellings without gardens. Some built summer houses on their plots. A writer in 1836 perceived allotments as a feature of every town, and saw gardening as a means of diverting labourers from public houses.[10] Hitchcock's map of 1832 shows at least 400 gardens of this kind, many of which were still occupied in the 1890s. Allotments probably produced higher rents than dairy holdings, and for long periods they preserved areas like the Hermitages and the Luciefelde estate from housing developments. By the 1880s even quite modest new working-class dwellings had gardens, and their cultivation was encouraged by horticultural societies, by the Ditherington Flower Show, first held in 1882, the Holy Trinity Cottage Gardeners' Club in Belle Vue established in 1883, and by the Greenfields & District Horticultural Society, formed in 1894. The chairman of one society remarked in 1884 that 'after a man had been shut up all day in a workshop, he could not be better employed than in the garden with his vegetables and flowers'.[11]

During both world wars the town council encouraged vegetable growing on allotments. In 1917 it brought into cultivation land that was subsequently covered by Underdale and Monkmoor avenues, Walter Vickery's building plots on Porthill, and the former football ground at Copthorne. Allotments were in demand immediately after the war, but by 1930 many plots could not be let.[12] During the Second World War senior aldermen set an example by digging up the Quarry. Land on almost all the building sites active in 1939 was brought under cultivation, on Sundorne Road, at Copthorne Park, and South Hermitage, and the wide open spaces of the Longden Green and Coton Hill estates were put to the spade, until there were more than 2,000 allotments in the borough in July 1942.[13]

A Chronological Overview

Shrewsbury in 1760 was the market centre for a hinterland extending across most of Shropshire and into Wales. Macaulay classified the town with Exeter, Worcester and Nottingham as 'the chief place of an extensive and fertile district'.[14] A count in 1750, that appears to have been reasonably accurate, revealed a population of 8,171.[15] The town prospered in the ensuing half-century, but the ancient trade of the Shrewsbury Drapers Company, the buying and finishing of woollen cloth made in Wales, and its despatch to London, was dwindling. The last formal market in the Square took place in about 1796 but while trading in woollen cloth continued – there were five flannel merchants in the town in 1834 – it declined in importance.[16]

The prosperity of the late 18th century was due to other factors. Shrewsbury was the centre of social life in its county, and for much of North Wales. The brothers la Rouchefoucauld in March 1785 found the better inns full of people attending the assize, and remarked on the theatre and public balls. Sir Richard Colt Hoare in 1797 was amazed by the concourse at the market.[17] The improvement of roads increased the town's role as a centre for professional services, retailing and recreation, as well as stimulating stage coach services. Through the enterprise of Robert Lawrence of the *Lion* hotel, Shrewsbury prospered as a town of thoroughfare, servicing coaches connecting Holyhead, Liverpool and Manchester with London, Bath and Bristol, and providing connections to Barmouth and Aberystwyth. Shrewsbury showed signs in the 1790s of becoming a town of resort, attracting residents spending locally their income from investments. In 1790 it was observed that 'the numerous elegant houses which of late years have arisen and are daily growing up in our streets bids fair to render the long allowed pleasantest town in the kingdom one of the handsomest'. Wealthy residents were served by bankers, land agents and lawyers, of whom there were 35 in Shrewsbury in 1840, and by specialist retailers, china dealers, portrait painters and makers of barometers and perukes. Large-scale industrial development, flax mills at Ditherington and Castlefields, and varied enterprises in Coleham, began in the 1790s. It was remarked in 1803 that the town had 'of late years made rapid progress in the taste and number of its buildings; and the flourishing situation of its rising manufactures promises a certain increase of honor, wealth and population'.[18] Shrewsbury, with a population of nearly 15,000 in 1801, stood 24th in the hierarchy of English towns, was slightly smaller than Chester, Coventry and Leicester, but larger than Oxford, Hereford, Northampton, Lincoln and Worcester.[19]

Shrewsbury's walls had nearly gone to decay by 1800. The town began to grow beyond its medieval limits in the second half of the 18th century and, as elsewhere, institutions led the advance into the countryside. Millington's Hospital was built in the 1740s, and the Foundling Hospital on Kingsland from 1760.[20] A writer in 1865 remarked that a foreigner entering a county town would usually see four large buildings, a hospital, a workhouse, a gaol and a lunatic asylum.[21] The county hospital remained in the town centre, but the Foundling Hospital served as a workhouse between 1786 and 1871, the gaol was built beyond the Castle in the 1780s and the asylum at Shelton in the 1840s. Shrewsbury's medieval suburbs – Castle Foregate, Frankwell, Longden Coleham and Abbey Foregate – impressed John Loveday in 1730 but they grew scarcely at all in the 16th and 17th centuries.[22] The town was ringed by ancient wayside hamlets

3 Shrewsbury saw substantial industrial development in the 1790s, most notably in the building of the iron-framed flax mill at Ditherington by Marshall, Benyon & Bage.

– Porthill, the Red Barn, Bicton Heath, Coton Hill and the Old Heath – but the first residences that were truly suburban were villas occupied by wealthy men more than a mile from the centre, those of the lawyers John Maddock, at Greenfields, and Joseph Loxdale, at Kingsland, and of John Probert, surveyor, at Copthorne.[23]

Working-class families were accommodated before 1840 in courts lining the burgage plots of the town's medieval suburbs, in cottages scattered on open ground as at Old Heath, by a few back-to-back terraces, and by terraces of through houses of which the 26 in Whitehurst Crescent, built before 1832, are rare survivors. Thirty-two cluster houses near the Ditherington flax mill comprised the only accommodation built specifically for factory workers. Wealthier people settled on the Mount, in Belle Vue and Abbey Foregate, chiefly in three-storey terraces of a kind exemplified by Rutland Terrace in Stamford, or 'The Terrace' in Mark Rutherford's Eastthorpe.[24]

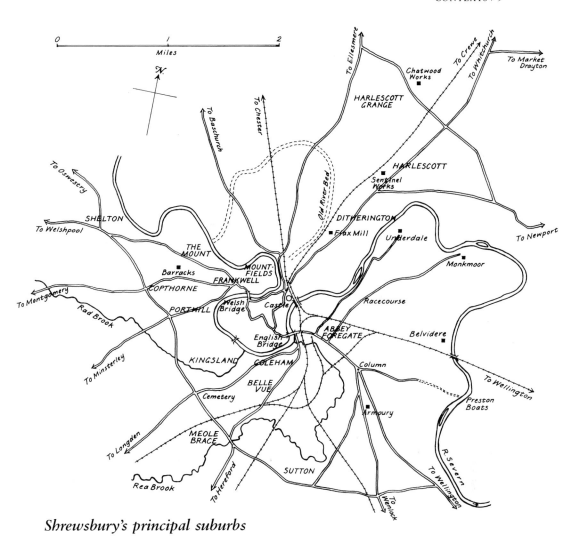

Shrewsbury's principal suburbs

A Welsh merchant remarked in 1825 on Shrewsbury's 'departed greatness as a commercial town' and the 'lonely quietude' that prevailed in its streets. William Cobbett observed in 1830 that Shrewsbury was a town where farmers came 'to sell their produce and [...] take in exchange their groceries, their clothing and all the material for their implements and the domestic conveniencies', yet found indications of decline.[25] The Castlefields flax mill was demolished in 1837 and textile manufacturing disappeared in the next half century. Distant railways drew away the Irish thoroughfare trade. A proponent of railways in 1838 saw in the town 'every symptom of a declining trade' together with the depreciation of property.[26] Richard Astley thought that the Grand Junction Railway had taken vitality from the town, sapping its economy and its 'sociability'. The town's population failed to increase during the 1830s, a time of rapid growth nationally, and it was acknowledged in 1841 that a decrease of up to 3,000 inhabitants was due principally to the closure of the Castlefields mill.[27]

4 One of the first buildings erected beyond Shrewsbury's medieval limits: the Foundling Hospital, designed by Thomas Farnolls Pritchard, built in 1760, and later used as the workhouse of Shrewsbury's united parishes, and, from 1882, by Shrewsbury School.

In the decade after 1848 Shrewsbury became an important railway junction. From 1852 until 1863 the mechanical engineering works of the Shrewsbury & Hereford Railway employed up to 200 men at Coleham, and subsequently the GWR had carriage shops as well as running sheds on the site. After 1863 the passenger station and three routes out of Shrewsbury were jointly managed by a superintendent acting for the Great Western and London & North Western railways, with many office staff. Railwaymen were one of the dominant occupational groups in the town, especially after the opening of the Severn Tunnel in 1886 made the Shrewsbury & Hereford line into the principal route between the North of England and the South-West.

Shrewsbury enjoyed relative prosperity in the mid-19th century – its population increased by 45 per cent between 1841 and 1881, compared with 24 per cent between 1801 and 1841. This growth was based on services, particularly on the professions and retailing, rather than on manufacturing. The foundry in Coleham relapsed into insignificance after William Hazledine's death in 1840, but its decline was matched after 1860 by the rise of Thomas Corbett's agricultural engineering business, and between 1877 and 1912 by the works of the Midland Railway Carriage & Waggon Co., both of which served international markets. Otherwise manufacturing in Shrewsbury comprised traditional market town trades – malting, tanning, milling, brewing, with several small engineering works of local significance. Carriers' carts made more than a hundred journeys per week into Shrewsbury even in the 1890s. Shrewsbury also benefited from the high levels of production and the fever of speculation in the lead mines of the Stiperstones region during the third quarter of the 19th century. Engineers like 'Captain' Arthur Waters made their homes in the town, and professional men like Richard Palin provided legal and financial services for mining companies.[28] The town was the meeting place for many organisations, including, in 1890, the Midlands District Union of YMCAs, and Shropshire associations of land agents, teachers and lawyers.[29]

Most of Shrewsbury's working-class houses from before 1850, with the exception of Whitehurst Terrace, were demolished under 20th-century clearance schemes, while most

5   Whitehurst Terrace, Copthorne Road, built before 1832 by John Whitehurst of The Mount House.
On a national scale this is a rare survival of such an early working-class terrace.

of those built subsequently remain. The pattern of development after 1850 was set by
the Freehold Land Society, and by the corporation as sanitary authority. Most houses
were of the tunnel-back type, a four-room house with a rear extension incorporating
a scullery and a third bedroom, built along streets with agreed building lines. Some
houses of simpler construction were laid out in the style of previous decades at right
angles to main roads. Shrewsbury's earliest tunnel-backs were constructed on the
Freehold Land Society's first estate in the 1850s and the type was built until the eve
of the First World War.

By 1901 Shrewsbury had fewer inhabitants than Worcester, Lincoln and Northampton, all of which had smaller populations a century earlier. The retiring mayor
argued in 1910 that it was impossible to 'fetch factories with smoky chimneys' to
Shrewsbury because the town did not appeal to manufacturers. Paradoxically, this
period saw intense building activity. A builder's merchant in 1894 referred to 'the
vast extension of cottage, house and mansion building that has prevailed during
the last 20 or 30 years', which 'gave a great impetus to all businesses connected
to the building trade', and in 1897 the owner of a joinery works referred to 'the
phenomenal activity of the building trade in and near Shrewsbury'.[30] In part this
reflected a movement of retailers and professional men from homes above their shops
and offices to villas in the suburbs, a tendency stimulated in part by the perceived
rowdiness of the streets adjacent to the brothels in Roushill.[31] From the 1840s most
upper middle-class suburban dwellings were villas rather than terraced houses, some
in exuberant Italianate or Baroque styles. Belle Vue and the Column were the most
favoured locations of the mid-19th century, but in the early 1880s a High Victorian
suburb was built on Kingsland, and in the 1890s the area between the old and new lines
of the Holyhead Road on The Mount was laid out in plots for substantial dwellings.
Some villas were semi-detached and of modest size, attracting retired retailers and
independent women living on modest invested incomes, but a few pairs, in Havelock
Road and on the Limes estate, were imposing.

6 Brewer's Baroque: the front elevation of The Hollies, Sutton Road, built by Thomas Southam in the late 1850s. Southam owned several surrounding properties, and his estate considerably influenced the development of the area between the Sutton and London roads.

After 1900 it was acknowledged that there was a shortage of houses for workmen, because wage rates in Shrewsbury did not enable householders to pay the minimum rents of 4s. or 4s. 6d. per week that made the holding of such property viable, and that building small houses for letting had ceased to be profitable.[32] The houses of that period include the last phases of the Whitehall estate, solidly-built tunnel-backs, in brick with stone dressings, laid out in straight lines with miniature front gardens, and the Lime streets, arranged in a similar pattern to the courts of a century earlier, but with trees, grass verges and gardens. Houses in the Garden City style, without the rear extensions of tunnel-backs, in spacious gardens and with neo-vernacular features, appeared dramatically in Shrewsbury on the town's first council estate at Wingfield Gardens in 1914-5, although the contrast between houses in this style and those of earlier generations is more marked in Copthorne Drive.

Shrewsbury's economy was radically changed by two world wars. The Sentinel Wagon Works moved in 1915 from Glasgow to a site at Harlescott, next to which the Royal Flying Corps (from 1918 the Royal Air Force) built a road transport depot, and also established a flying field at Monkmoor. In the inter-war period mechanical engineering became prominent in the local economy, while chain stores, roadhouse-style pubs, cinemas and the other characteristics of urban life of the 1920s and '30s developed in the town.

The borough council, with those in every other English town, began to build houses after the Armistice of 1918, and through many variations in government policy, constructed about 1200 dwellings before the outbreak of the Second World War. Private house building flourished quietly in the 1920s. Comfortable dwellings, detached and semi-detached, were constructed on the south side of the town in a style derived from the Arts and Crafts, while plainer houses appeared in St Giles's Gardens and Meole Crescent. Marketing was more flamboyant in the 1930s. To the south building was stimulated by the 1933 by-pass, and in the north by the extension of the borough boundary in 1934. In 1934 Fletcher Estates began to build on the former RAF camp at Harlescott, offering semi-detached houses at less than £500, and completed about 450 houses by the summer of 1939. Fletcher's houses had many characteristic features of the 1930s: windows that went round corners, bow windows with curved corners, and some stained glass. More flamboyant use of the same features can be seen in the sunshine homes in Monkmoor Avenue, or on London Road. In Copthorne two matching semi-detached pairs with flame motifs in the gables frame the entrance to the Madeira estate, and the characteristic feature of the Luciefielde estate is the display of overlapping rustic weatherboards in gables. Scarcely half-a-dozen suburban houses were

7 Service roads came into fashion in Shrewsbury in the late 1930s, but most of them were unadopted when war broke out in September 1939, and remained muddy morasses until the council began to surface them ten years later. This service road runs parallel to Wenlock Road and is part of the development that included Ebnal Road, and more houses on service roads alongside London Road.

built in the International Modern style, most of them designed by Frank Shaylor. In the mid-1930s building proceeded in prodigal fashion along the by-pass, with many domestic drives leading directly on to the trunk road, but towards the end of the decade service roads came into fashion. Fletcher Estates built houses on a road parallel to Whitchurch Road and short lengths were laid out on Shelton Road and on the London and Wenlock roads. Most remained unadopted in 1939, and became soggy morasses during the Second World War.

The military presence in Shrewsbury during the Second World War was overwhelming. Suburban houses were requisitioned, there were army camps at Harlescott, Greenfields and Shelton, and the Shropshire & Montgomeryshire Railway was taken over by the War Department.[33] Manufacturing prospered after the war, and in 1953 it was estimated that there were 3,000 engineering workers in Shrewsbury, most of them at Sentinel, Chatwood and J.C.R. Woodvine's machine

8 Studded doors in the medieval fashion were incorporated in some private houses built in Shrewsbury immediately before the Second World War, as in this example at No 14 Ebnal Road.

tool factory. The clothing firm that became Corset Silhouette originated in Cologne in 1886, moved to Paris, and was taken by George Lobbenberg, grandson of the founder, to London in 1936. Lobbenberg re-located it to Shrewsbury in 1940, at first to Beacall's Lane, then to the mission hall in Tankerville Street, and the waterworks on Coton Hill and the nearby Congregational chapel. The company moved to a purpose-built factory at Harlescott in 1956, and was so successful that production was revived at the waterworks.[34]

House-building resumed slowly after the Second World War, but in the 15 years after VE-day the council built more than 2,500 dwellings, some of them 'prefabs', part of the U.K. Temporary Housing Programme, and some permanent prefabricated dwellings, in steel or concrete. Slums, including overcrowded accommodation in the inner suburbs, were cleared on a large scale in the 1950s. Private building resumed in the late 1940s on some estates where work stopped in 1939, but developers were inhibited by difficulties in obtaining planning permissions, and by shortages of materials. The pace of building accelerated during the 1950s, and by 1960 private house construction was on the eve of rapid expansion.

This study ends when Shrewsbury was a booming manufacturing town. During 1958 Rolls Royce announced orders for engines for buses for Continental Trailways in the United States. Hall Engineering had work for the aircraft industry, and the labour force of Corsets Silhouette grew to 600. Expanding industry was absorbing workers from munitions establishments at Nesscliffe and Wem that were closing.[35] The service sector was investing in new buildings that substantially changed the town centre. This prosperity was reflected in further expansion of Shrewsbury's suburbs that is beyond the scope of the book.

CHAPTER III

Networks

Government

Shrewsbury was administered between 1760 and 1960 by overlapping authorities. The smallest units were the parishes. Four, centred on the churches of St Alkmund, St Chad, St Julian and St Mary, within the loop of the River Severn, pre-date the Norman Conquest. Their boundaries beyond the bridges were complex.[1] Most of the suburban area north of the Castle was in St Mary's, but the western side of Castle Foregate and the Greenfields district were in St Alkmund's, and there was an enclave of St Julian's around the *Golden Ball*. Most of the Harlescott area developed after the First World War was in St Alkmund's. Beyond lay the parish of Battlefield, which experienced ribbon development in the 1920s. The suburbs beyond the Welsh Bridge were almost entirely within St Chad's, but part of the settlement along the Welshpool Road was in St Julian's. The suburbs along the roads to Church Stretton and Longden were mostly in St Julian's, but merged into Meole Brace. To the east the parish of Holy Cross was undisturbed by enclaves, and beyond its boundaries the township of Emstrey in Atcham parish and the parish of Sutton experienced no suburban growth until the 20th century. Parishes influenced suburban growth through the building of schools and daughter churches, and through powers exercised by vestry meetings. A fading notice posted by the parish clerk of St Julian's, warning against committing nuisances, remains in Egland Lane. The sites of the parish pounds of St Julian and St Chad can still be identified. A pump in the Abbey Foregate, a parish responsibility in the 1870s, provided water for many householders.[2]

The borough of Shrewsbury was governed in 1760 under a charter of Charles I (14 Car I, 1630) by a mayor, 24 aldermen and 48 assistants, and extended over 14,680 acres, including part of Meole Brace. The Liberties of Shrewsbury included Sutton, the remainder of Meole Brace, and the distant parts of the four ancient parishes, as well as land in Broughton and Shawbury. The Liberties covered 9,940 acres in 1831, with a population of 2,195. The Municipal Corporations Act of 1835 enlarged the borough to include all the contiguous built-up area, while the outlying parts of the Liberties were transferred to other administrations. After 1835 the borough was ruled by a mayor, ten aldermen and 30 councillors. It retained its own commission of the peace and quarter sessions, and exercised its right to establish a police force. The powers of the corporation were limited – its expenditure in 1850 only just exceeded £3,000 – but it directly influenced suburban growth as the custodian of common lands at Ditherington and Kingsland. Improvement Acts in 1756 and 1821 scarely affected the suburbs but in 1853 William Ranger conducted an enquiry under the 1848 Public Health Act into the sanitary condition of Shrewsbury.[3] After the publication of Ranger's report and legislation in 1855, the corporation became, through its Improvement Committee, the sanitary authority for the town.[4] The legislative changes brought rapid results. The general cemetery came into use in 1856, after burial grounds in the town centre were closed. Orders were given in February 1856 for 104 new name boards for streets and for repainting 40 old ones.[5] In 1863 the corporation considered flagging the streets beyond the bridges, and the extension of water mains into Abbey Foregate and Coleham.[6] In 1868 the committee urged the numbering of streets.[7] After the publication in 1864 of critical articles in *The Builder*, there were demands for effective control of building developments, and the Improvement Committee appointed an inspector the following year.[8] Progress on other matters was less rapid. In 1862 a report on sewage disposal was commissioned from the highest authority, Sir Joseph Bazalgette, builder of London's embankments and outfall sewers, but it was not until 1901 that Shrewsbury's sewage was diverted from the River Severn.[9] The corporation took over the 16th-century water pipeline from the Conduit Head in 1853, and bought the rival water company in 1877. Thereafter councillors spent much time discussing 'the interminable water question', and it was not until the 1930s that a satisfactory system was established.[10] More success attended the Corporation's purchase of the town's electric light company in 1897. The gas company remained in private hands until nationalisation, although many of its directors were councillors.[11]

Even with an Improvement Committee, the corporation was only intermittently concerned with suburban growth. The council's agenda was dominated by the establishment of a central market, ultimately opened in 1869, the status and location of the town's grammar school, settled when the school moved to Kingsland in 1882, the water question and by such passing incidents as the appointment of an incumbent to St Mary's in 1853.[12] Few matters over which the corporation had direct responsibility in the 19th century were subjects of reasoned political debate, and councillors sometimes took pride in rejecting political labels. In 1920 a leading Liberal, during a presentation to Thomas Pace, commended a move away from party politics in municipal affairs, and there were cheers for the presence of Thomas Deakin, chairman of the Conservative Club.[13]

The responsibilities of the corporation gradually increased. Under the Education Act of 1902 it took over the duties of a School Board, established in the 1870s, setting up an Education Committee in February 1903.[14] The council installed a new sewage disposal system between 1895 and 1901, a waterworks in 1935, and developed Shrewsbury's electricity supply system from a few street lights in 1897 to a borough-wide network by 1938. It was slow to assume responsibility for housing, but its first estate, completed in 1915, was of high quality and, as in other towns, local government between the premierships of David Lloyd George and Margaret Thatcher was dominated by council housing.

Other authorities shared responsibilities for the town's affairs. In 1784 the four town-centre parishes with Holy Cross and Meole Brace established a union for the management of the poor, with a workhouse at Kingsland. Their example was followed by the parishes surrounding Shrewsbury, who built a workhouse at Cross Houses in 1793. The two groups of parishes, six in Shrewsbury and 43 in Atcham, became unions under the Poor Law Amendment Act of 1834, but the elected Guardians adopted contrasting policies. The Shrewsbury Union allowed outdoor relief to many paupers, and treated those who entered the workhouse with humanity. The Atcham Union under the chairmanship of Sir Baldwin Leighton was notorious for its pitiless severity to all who applied for assistance.[15] After deliberation, and against the wishes of Leighton, who died as the scheme was being implemented, the unions were amalgamated in 1871. The Kingsland workhouse was closed and its inmates transferred to Cross

Houses.[16] Legislation subsequently forced unions to remove children from workhouses, and consequently Besford House became a children's home in 1911. The Atcham workhouse was adapted as a military hospital during the First World War, but the guardians re-opened it in 1926, as Berrington Hospital for the sick poor, a use that continued after the union was abolished in 1930.[17]

The Atcham Rural District Council, established in 1893, was in part a successor to the union. It covered the same area, and its first clerk, Joseph Everest, 'brought up almost from childhood in the poor law service', succeeded his father as clerk to the union in 1864 at the age of nineteen.[18] In the 1920s the R.D.C. entertained plans for a new town at Harlescott. The council's influence diminished when the borough's boundary was extended in 1934, and it ceased to exist in 1974. Remains of the sewage works at Harlescott, and the houses in Shelton Gardens, inscribed 'ARDC 1921' are among its legacies in the suburban landscape.

County authorities, quarter sessions from 1760 until 1888, and Salop County Council thereafter, also shaped Shrewsbury's suburbs. Quarter sessions had responsibility for roads, and built two institutions in the suburbs – the gaol in the 1780s and the pauper lunatic asylum at Shelton in the 1840s. The county council, an elected body, abhorred party politics in its early years. Sir John Bowen-Jones said in 1913 that 'they had kept politics out of that chamber for 25 years and it was a great pity anyone should introduce them'.[19] The nepotism that had characterised quarter sessions – the county treasurer appointed in 1903 was the first since 1764 who was unrelated to his predecessor – was reduced. During the 1920s and '30s the council was notorious for its 'economy'. A more expansionist policy was adopted after the Second World War under Sir Offley Wakeman, chairman 1943-63, and G.C. Godber, clerk from 1944 to 1966, the year in which the council opened its new Shirehall at the Column.[20]

Under the Education Act of 1902 the county council was charged with the provision of secondary and technical education in Shrewsbury and for elementary education outside the borough. In 1931 the council built the school in Featherbed Lane, Harlescott, then beyond the boundary. The 1944 Education Act gave overall responsibility for education to the county council, but Shrewsbury was granted a Divisional Executive allowing devolved management, which continued until local government reorganisation in 1974. The county council implemented a vigorous programme of school construction in the 1950s.[21]

9 The turnpike tollhouse built at Copthorne in 1800-1, replacing one on the edge of the town in New Street, and the only one in the immediate vicinity of Shrewsbury that survives.

In 1760 turnpike trusts were responsible for the main roads through Shrewsbury's suburbs. The London Road was turnpiked in 1725, and those to Wenlock and Ellesmere in 1752. The routes over Coleham Bridge to Church Stretton and Longden and those beyond the Castle Gate to Newport, Shawbury and Preston Brockhurst came under the control of trusts in 1756, followed two years later by the Baschurch road and those crossing the Welsh Bridge.[22] The responsibilities of the trusts passed to the local Highway Board between 1871 and 1877. The trusts made improvements that changed the suburban landscape: the embankment over the Old River Bed and the cutting at Cross Hill on the Ellesmere Road,[23] the re-routing of Berwick Road, the cutting in New Street,[24] and Moreton Crescent that replaced the old road through Old Coleham.[25] To avoid conflicts with residents, the trusts moved several tollgates away from the town centre. The gate in Castle Foregate was re-located to Heathgates between 1790 and 1793, and that on the Montgomery road from New Street to Copthorne in 1800-1. The Mount gate was replaced between 1818 and 1821 by one at Shelton.[26] The Abbey Foregate, and the route from the Welsh Bridge to Shelton became part of the Holyhead Road, improved at government expense and under the supervision of Thomas Telford between 1815 and 1838. A road through the domestic buildings of the Abbey was opened in 1836 and between 1829 and 1832 a cutting eased the gradient of the road ascending the Mount, and the present road succeeded the route along Barracks Lane.[27]

The county council inherited the responsibilities of quarter sessions for roads. W.H.Butler, county surveyor from 1924-48, strove energetically to build by-passes, and Shrewsbury's by-pass followed those opened at Gobowen in 1926 and St George's in 1932. Its plan was approved in 1930, and contracts were let and the route was fenced off by March 1931. It followed existing lanes, Thieves Lane and Oteley Road, from Emstrey to Meole Brace, where, after crossing the Rea Brook on a concrete bridge, it climbed through a rectangular field to cross the Longden Road. It followed another existing lane to Porthill, from where a new route was built, crossing the road to Montgomery, to the junction of the Welshpool and Oswestry roads at Shelton. The road was opened on 23 May 1933, and parts were quickly lined with houses. Military vehicles were stored during the Second World War on Oteley Road, which was ceremonially re-opened on 22 September 1946.[28] Butler planned radical routes to divert traffic around Shrewsbury, but his objectives were not realised until the 1990s, and no significant changes were made to the town's road system between 1933 and 1964.

10 The influence of Salop County Council in the suburbs: No 89 Clive Road, the farmstead of a smallholding built just before the First World War, and surrounded by houses constructed during the building boom after the Second World War.

Salop County Council also influenced the suburbs by providing smallholdings through the Smallholdings and Allotments Act of 1907. Before the First World War the council acquired land at Crowmoor, where some homesteads remain, and its post-war programme included the purchase in 1919 of 427 acres at Emstrey on which 27 holdings were established. Six holdings of up to 49 acres were created at Harlescott in 1954.[29]

In 1930 the county council took over the welfare responsibilities of the abolished Boards of Guardians. It began to manage Besford House, the first of many suburban establishments sheltering the disadvantaged, some, like The Elms and The Hollies, adapted from homes of the wealthy, others, like Briarfields and Bromley House, purpose-built. The council appointed a part-time county medical officer of health in 1890, making his post full-time in 1897, began to provide health centres in 1919. and briefly took over the military hospital at Copthorne in 1946 before it was absorbed into the National Health Service.[30]

Utility Networks

In 1760 two systems provided Shrewsbury with water, a provision as ample as in any town of similar size. A pipeline from the conduit head in Mousecroft Lane terminated by the 1570s at a cistern on Pride Hill. In 1797 a reservoir was built in the Quarry. The system was improved through the 19th century, and in 1853 was purchased by the corporation. An alternative supply was pumped to cisterns near the top of Pride Hill by a waterwheel in one of the arches of the English Bridge, but there were complaints about pollution of the river by the carcasses of dead animals and dumped night soil.[31] The waterworks closed and the waterwheel was sold in 1830. Its replacement, built in Chester Street in 1827-32, used a steam-powered pumps, and was purchased by the corporation in 1877. Water supply was thereafter a subject for perpetual debate and continuous inaction. George Godwin described the water supplied to houses as 'of the colour and consistency of weak tea, muddy to the sight and slimy to the touch'. The county medical officer wrote in 1902, 'the system is so dangerous, dirty, and as to some respects of the plant, so decayed, as to involve a risk of serious breakdowns', and observed that Shrewsbury was probably unique in having unfiltered water from a river receiving sewage laid on to its houses. New pumps at the Conduit Head and a filters building at Chester Street were opened in 1909, and new engines were installed in 1912.[32] Not until 1931 did the corporation approve a new system, based on a treatment works at Shelton, which so caught public imagination that a replica of its water tower appeared in the carnival procession of 1934. The plant opened on 4 July 1935 and owed much to the determination of Charles Beddard, chair of the water committee from 1927, and mayor in 1935-6. He learned pork butchery in the Black Country, moved to Shrewsbury in 1912, and occupied his well-known shop at Nos 4-5 Mardol from 1916. The 80 ft (24m) tower at Shelton was, fittingly, called 'Charlie Beddard's pork pie'.[33]

Shrewsbury's sewers in 1760, and for the following 140 years as they were extended into the suburbs, poured waste into the River Severn, or on to its banks when water levels were low. The London engineers, Santo Crimp proposed radical changes in 1894. After a public enquiry on 7 January 1896, the Local Government Board sanctioned their scheme. The main tender was let in June and, with new gas mains being laid simultaneously, and the rebuilding of the railway station in prospect, Shrewsbury was 'given over to the navvy'.[34]

Under the scheme, sewage from existing outfalls was intercepted by a ring of iron mains, and lifted from a pumping station in Coleham to a gravitational sewer commencing in Whitehall Street, that extended 1½ miles to a treatment works at Monkmoor Farm. The work was subject to many delays – it was suggested in May 1899 that the scaffold poles had been in the ground for so long that they had started to grow. The pumping station began work on 1 January 1901, but the engineers faced problems caused by faults in old sewers, and by houseowners reluctant to make connections with the new system, and the system was not completed until the summer of 1904. Similar systems had been installed by many urban authorities they gained powers under the 1848 Public Health Act, and Shrewsbury in this respect entered the 19th century on New Year's Day 1901. A tunnel under the River Severn, completed on 31 May 1951, connected the Monkmoor plant with Harlescott, enabling the closure of the former Atcham R.D.C. sewage works.[35]

The shareholders of Shrewsbury's gas company first met on 13 January 1820, and began to supply gas from a works in St Michael's Street, on 8 September 1821. The works was enlarged many times, and in 1934 the company built a gasholder near the Abbey.[36] The company remained in private ownership until nationalisation in 1948.

Shrewsbury's electricity generating station at Roushill opened in December 1895 and the corporation purchased the Electric Light Company in 1897. Four arc lamps began to provide street lighting in 1899. A Bellis & Morcom engine and a Thomas Parker generator were installed in 1901, and by 1902 mains extended to Belle Vue. A new power station was opened in 1926. In that year the Electricity (Supply) Act put the industry under the direction of the Central Electricity Board, which began to develop the National Grid, enabling it to buy power from and sell it to local distributors. Legislation of 1919 enabled the creation of joint authorities authorised to provide power for particular regions. The appropriate body in Shropshire, the West Midlands Joint Electricity Authority, ran a 33 kv transmission line into a sub-station near the Comet Bridge in 1931, and an 11 kv underground line to the power station at Roushill. Conversion of supplies from direct to alternating current concluded in the summer of 1956, when the Roushill power station was closed. The W.M.J.E.A. bought the borough undertaking in 1938 and retained it until nationalisation in 1948.[37]

11 The interior of the Coleham Pumping Station during a school visit in 1968, about two years before the steam engines were replaced. The high standard of cleanliness, exemplified by the instruction not to touch the handrail, is abundantly evident.

Transport Networks

Shrewsbury's suburban transport pattern has always included means of crossing the River Severn. The English and Welsh Bridges succeeded medieval structures in 1768-74 and 1795-96 respectively. The Kingsland Bridge opened in 1882, but no other crossing for vehicles was built before 1960. A ferry near the Kingsland Bridge served the Kingsland Coffee House in the 18th century, and operated until the 1930s. The ferry near the *Boathouse* inn, depicted on early 18th-century paintings, was replaced by the Porthill suspension bridge in 1923. The Can Office ferry near Crescent Lane, disused in the 1820s, was revived about 1834. From the early 1850s it carried waggons from Burrs' lead works, and ceased when the works closed in 1893. A ferry crossed the river between Longden Coleham and St Julian Friars before the footbridge opened on New Year's Day 1880. The crossing that is now the Castle Bridge originated in 1809 when the trustees of the Severn towpath established a ferry downstream from the Underdale island, to carry towing horses. Residents in Underdale used the ferry after barge traffic ceased in the 1860s but it was inconveniently situated and a new crossing reached by the footpath alongside No 31 Underdale Road was inaugurated in November 1882. The ferry flourished during the Royal Show of 1884, but it was

12 The ferry in the Quarry linking the town with Kingsland, from an anonymous print of 1838.

13 The suspension bridge that between 1910 and 1950 linked Castlefields with Underdale.

14 The remains of Shrewsbury West station on the Shropshire & Montgomeryshire Railway, beneath the bridge that carries Belle Vue Road. The station had been closed for about four years when this photograph was taken on 3 September 1937.

not viable, and was replaced in 1910 by a bridge, that was succeeded in 1950 by the present concrete structure. A ferry from Smithfield Road to Frankwell was established in the 1860s to improve access to the county cricket ground, and was operating in 1916 when an inebriated inmate of Groom's lodging house was drowned when he tried to swim after using it. The ferry opposite Uffington Mill, where the footpath from Monkmoor joins the towpath, attracted walkers, but was not part of the everyday pattern of suburban transport.[38]

In 1760, and even 40 years later, it was possible to walk to the centre of Shrewsbury from the limits of the medieval suburbs. In 1800 the only suburban homes far enough away to require wheeled transport were a few villas occupied by professional men. Within the town, the wealthy travelled in sedan chairs. Thomas Yeomans, sedan chairman, born at Atcham in 1780, lived on Swan Hill. On 18 December 1828 he took the young attorney William How from College Hill to St Mary's Place for a fare of one shilling. Old ladies still travelled by sedan chair to matins at St Chad's in the mid-1850s, but Yeomans was then over 70, and when he died the sedan disappeared from Shrewsbury. Suburban villas, such as How's house by the Column, included stables and coach houses, and in 1854 carriages could be purchased for little more than £20.[39] Coach houses were customary appendages to the homes of the wealthy until the end of the century, and many remain.

Railways made no positive contribution to suburban growth in Shrewsbury. Few passengers used the Shropshire & Montgomeryshire Railway's halts at Shrewsbury West and Meole Brace, and only the privileged position of Thomas Owen, father of the poet, enabled him to commute from Cherry Orchard platform to his office at the station.[40] The opening of railways from 1848 stimulated road services. Omnibuses linked the station with the principal hotels and by 1851 six operators offered cabs for hire, some from suburban public houses. In 1852 the *Shrewsbury Chronicle* approvingly repeated the *Spectator*'s view that 'the omnibus is developing itself into a great social engine'. There were many passenger vehicles in the town by 1900. It was acknowledged at the rain-swept municipal election of 1903 that 'candidates with a good supply of carriages ... scored heavily [...] in the number of people they brought to the poll'. Motor cabs were introduced in 1911 by Arthur Crump's Shrewsbury Motor Cab Co., based in the coach house of Monklands, which operated 4-cylinder Humbers, and Henry Franklin of Swan Hill who took pride in his green Napier 15 hp Landaulette, equipped with a speaking tube for communication with the driver.[41]

Shrewsbury, a place where tramcars were manufactured, was one of the largest English towns never to be served by street tramways. The corporation rejected with some derision a proposal by a Birmingham solicitor in 1897 to promote a scheme.[42] There was no potential for an interurban link to a neighbouring town, as there was between Kidderminster and Stourport, Warwick and Leamington or Llandudno and Colwyn Bay.

Motor buses appeared just before the Great War and shaped Shrewsbury's growth for the next half-century, enabling the town to expand beyond the reasonable limits of walking.[43] The railway companies declined requests in 1912 to run buses to Meole Brace and Bayston Hill, but early in 1913 the landlord of the *Unicorn* began a service, apparently with one double-decker. The council, fearful of accidents, requested that passengers should not be carried on the top deck. The service ceased in August 1913, but in 1915 the London-based Allen Omnibus Co began to work buses to Abbey Foregate, Bayston Hill and Bicton Heath. On 3 May an open top double-decker, crowded with passengers, crashed into a shop when its drive chain snapped as it ascended Wyle Cop.[44] On 1 April 1916 the Birmingham & Midland Motor Omnibus Co. (the Midland Red) purchased the operation and in 1919 worked four buses from a garage in Roushill. The following year the company established a depot at Ditherington. Services within Shrewsbury were a Midland Red monopoly, although small private companies worked country routes through the suburbs. Routes were extended during the 1920s to the extremities of the growing town, to Battlefield, to Greenfields, to Underdale Avenue and Monkmoor Aerodrome, to Harlescott Crescent, to Meole Village, to the Cemetery along Longden Road. In May 1929 a conductor was fined for allowing 51 people on a bus with a capacity of only 37, and the company was prosecuted in 1937 for carrying 53 passengers on a 40-seater. The hub of Midland Red services was the Square, but in 1938 a station for services on the western side of the town opened in Barker Street.[45]

Numbers of bus passengers in Shrewsbury reached a peak after the Second World War. On weekdays in 1947 there were 99 departures from the Square along Monkmoor Road to Abbots Road, and 31 to the Column, some continuing to Weeping Cross, while 60 served Meole Brace, about half of which terminated at Bayston Hill, and 30 went along Longden Road to the Cemetery, some continuing to Kennedy Road. From Barker Street there were 53 departures to Copthorne, nine to Radbrook (Oakfield Road), and 15 to the *Grapes* at Bicton Heath. Greenfields was served by 32 departures from the Square, some of which went to Cross Hill. The Square was the starting point of 13 services that terminated at Sultan Road, and 27 that went to Sundorne Avenue, but most northbound services, some 84 departures for Harlescott and Battlefield, went from Barker Street. Demand was falling by the mid-1950s, and the Midland Red had given notice that it wished to reduce services when cutbacks, necessitated by the fuel shortage that followed the Suez crisis, took effect on 29 December 1956, and caused overcrowding.[46] In February 1950 services using the Square, where throbbing engines disturbed work at the Shirehall, were moved to St Austin Street. Many people complained, and the terminus was re-located in January 1952 to the car park alongside Rowley's House, where it remained in 1960.[47]

Aircraft flew regularly from the aerodrome at Monkmoor and from other fields in the suburbs between the two world wars. The Prince of Wales landed on 21 June 1932 at Battlefield, the site of air pageants led by Sir Alan Cobham in 1932 and 1933. The newly-elected mayor in November 1934 said that the town needed an airport, but while many municipal airports were built in the late 1930s, Shrewsbury never had one.[48]

15 The shop at No 19 Frankwell from which Edward and George Palmer operated their delivery-based bakery business from 1830 until 1896, when the premises were taken over by Morris & Co.

Economic and Cultural Networks

Retailing networks extended into Shrewsbury suburbs during the 19th century. Some shops were simply houses where tea, butter and other daily necessities were sold from front rooms. The Post Office extended its network of collection boxes, and by 1955 there were 15 sub post offices in the suburbs. Morris & Co. originated in the grocery shop at No 7 Frankwell, opened by James Kent Morris in 1869. The company opened branches at Castlefields in 1900, in Abbey Foregate in 1901, at Coton Hill in 1912 and at Meole Brace in 1913. Three shops were opened in the 1930s, and six in the 1940s, and in May 1950 the shop in Mytton Oak Road became Shrewsbury's first self-service store.[49] The Co-operative Society had four suburban branches in 1916 and eight by 1938. Another form of retailing network was the delivery-based business, exemplified by the bakery in Frankwell, established by Edward Palmer in 1830 and closed when his son George retired in 1896. In 1873 George Palmer's carts delivered bread and cakes as far as Bow Bridge, the Column and Sutton Lane.[50] In the 1950s Paddy's mobile shops took groceries to new shop-less estates. All four of Shrewsbury's cinemas in the 1930s were in the town centre and owned by Shrewsbury Empires Ltd, most of whose directors were local men, who probably considered it prudent not to expand into the suburbs.[51]

Elementary schools were managed in Shrewsbury's suburbs in the early and mid-19th century by parish churches, and by the British and National societies, but from the 1870s they became the responsibility of local government. As in Mark Rutherford's fictional Cowfold[52] and most other market towns, there were private boarding schools for pupils of both sexes. Most used large houses occupied by the families who built them only for a generation or two, such as Cadogan House, The Limes and Kingsland Grange. Millmead is a rare example of a purpose-built preparatory school.

Religious Networks

Shrewsbury was small enough in 1760 for suburban residents to walk to places of worship in the centre, enabling choices between brands of Anglican churchmanship or of Methodist, Baptist or Congregationalist practice, and providing a choice of sects, including, in the 1850s, the Campbellites, the Latter Day Saints and the Plymouth Brethren, or of languages. William Humphreys of Bradford Street, a corn merchant born in Machynlleth, for 50 years attended the Congregational church in Dogpole in order to worship in Welsh.[53] It is enlightening to look at the common characteristics of suburban congregations rather than to analyse ecclesiastical local history only in denominational terms.

Suburban religion catered both for those seeking theological or liturgical exactitude, and for evangelical Christians with ecumenical outlooks. Some congregations, the Wesleyan Reformers in Castlefields, and the Baptists in Castle Foregate resulted from schisms in town centre congregations. Others, some of them non-denominational, developed from missions. Charles Hulbert began a mission in his factory at Coleham in 1802, which moved in 1873 to a purpose-built hall that was taken over by the Salvation Army in 1920. The Frankwell mission of the early 20th century moved in 1929 to the chapel of the Belle Vue cemetery. Wesleyan Methodist services began in a tent in June 1890 at Greenfields, where the Revd Luke Wiseman opened a tin tabernacle on 18 September of that year and consecrated a permanent chapel in 1908.[54]

Methodists formed congregations in the early 19th century at Old Heath and Copthorne House, but the first significant extensions of the town's religious networks into the suburbs were places of Anglican churches serving the old suburbs of Frankwell and Coleham, and the industrial community around the flax mill in Ditherington. St George's, Frankwell, a chapel of ease of St Chad, was opened in 1830, St Michael, Ditherington, in St Mary's parish, in 1832, and Holy Trinity, Coleham, in St Julian's in 1837. Until 1836, only two services a year were performed at the ancient chapel of St Giles, but it became a parish church in 1857, and was rebuilt in 1860. The ancient parish church of Meole Brace was replaced in 1799 by a building that made way for Edward Haycock II's church of Holy Trinity in 1867-8. Mission churches were opened in Tankerville Street in 1884, Spa Street in 1886, Greenfields in 1892, Coton Hill in 1930 and Monkmoor in 1939.[55]

After the First World War the energies of successive vicars of St Alkmund's were absorbed in Harlescott. Services began in the Sentinel Works canteen during 1924, and a hut near the Harlescott crossroads was opened as the Church of the Holy Spirit in 1925. A small church on Roseway was consecrated in 1936, but growing congregations after 1945 rendered it inadequate and it was replaced in 1961 by an imposing building on Meadow Farm Drive.[56] The Roman Catholic church moved into the suburbs in the 1950s. St Winefred's, Monkmoor, was consecrated in 1956, and the church of Our Lady of Pity, Harlescott, was almost complete at the end of 1960.[57]

Religion networks extended into the Shrewsbury suburbs through patronage. The church of All Saints was a private venture of a Shropshire landowner, Bulkeley Owen, a heavily-built, bearded man, whose friends at Christ Church, Oxford, included the large and bearded Robert Cecil, later, as 3rd Marquess of Salisbury, prime minister. After his ordination Owen missioned to railway navvies and railwaymen. When he unexpectedly inherited his family estate, with the support of Archdeacon John

16 The Anglican mission church at Greenfields, where a congregation had been assembled due to the energy of the Revd Thomas Auden, vicar of St Alkmund's, and consecrated in 1892.

Allen, he built a temporary iron church in North Street in 1870, and led a team of clergy who lived, frugally, in Castlefields. The foundation stone of All Saints was laid in 1875. Owen had High Church inclinations, led processions of surpliced clergy through the streets, and enforced on parishioners the duties of kneeling on entering the church and respecting the altar. After the church was consecrated in 1876 he retired to his Tedsmore estate, but patronage from wealthy families, mostly from Severn Bank, continued.[58] There were parallels with the congregation at the opposite end of the denominational spectrum, which met in a gospel hall in John Street erected in 1880. It was founded by a dentist, Charles Gibbs Nightingale, who lived on Severn Bank, and was sustained by his son Charles, a qualified architect who spent most of his life as an unpaid minister.[59]

Similar patterns of patronage can be observed elsewhere. The Wesleyan chapel in Castlefields opened in 1837, was sustained by John Barker, timber merchant, who in his youth intended to enter the ministry. The Wesleyan Reformers in Castlefields depended on the leadership of William Phillips, tailor, magistrate and antiquarian.[60] Wesleyan worship began about 1846 in a room in Frankwell, rented by Thomas Brocas of Copthorne House. A chapel was built in New Street in 1870 after the death of Brocas's widow, and in the 20th century its 'lay minister' was John Williams, Superintendent of the Joint Railways.[61] The Primitive Methodist chapel in Belle Vue, opened in 1879, owed much in the 20th century to Alfred Bennett, a footwear retailer, Liberal councillor from 1929, and mayor in 1945.[62] The Woodall family, tailors, who maintained their allegiances with Congregational churches, were leaders of the mission hall in Coleham over two generations. The undenominational Radbrook United Free Church Bible School and Youth Club , a 'pleasant building decorated in cream and green' opened in August 1945 by the Revd Robert Newton Flew, the Cambridge New Testament scholar, was led by the Revd F. Morgan Ridge, a Primitive Methodist minister, born at Priest Weston, who retired to Shrewsbury in 1935.[63]

The Abbey Foregate Congregationalist Church, whose spire dominates the view from the English Bridge, was a different kind of establishment, founded by members of existing societies within the denomination to serve people from the southern and eastern suburbs. Opened in 1864, it originated as part of the bicentenary commemorations in 1862 of the ejection of Presbyterian ministers from the Church of England. Designed by the Wolverhampton architect, George Bidlake, it exemplified the kind of suburban Congregational church described by Clyde Binfield, expressing the Nonconformist Conscience, and providing a political and religious bed rock for tennis clubs, amateur dramatic, choral and literary societies.[64] The Congregationalist chapel at Coton Hill, in an Italianate style designed by A.B. Deakin and opened in 1909, was intended to fulfil a similar role for the suburbs along the Ellesmere and Berwick roads. Thomas Pace provided the site, and his daughter's wedding, two months after the consecration, attracted much interest.[65]

In October 1958 Baptists from the Claremont Street congregation opened a chapel at Crowmoor, in which charismatic worship became established in the 1970s.[66] This was part of a change by which suburban religion was adapted to a car-based society. There have been ecumenical ventures, like the co-operation of Anglicans and Methodists at Greenfields and the Emmanuel church at Harlescott Grange, but most of the suburban places of worship opened in the late 20th century cater for people of distinctive beliefs who travel from a wide area. Mormons worship on Mount Pleasant Road, Quakers in St Catherine's Hall, Christadelphians in Tankerville Street, and a Greek Orthodox congregation at St John Sutton.[67]

Recreational Networks

In the 18th century walking into the countryside was popular amongst Shrewsbury's townspeople, for whom coffee houses at Kingsland and at Belle Vue were regular destinations. Such establishments went out of fashion after 1800, but suburban taverns continued to draw custom. There were more than 30 public houses in Shrewsbury beyond the bridges in 1800.[68] Many were prosperous businesses doing rather more than satisfying the thirsts of local people. Almost all brewed their own beer, and many produced their own malt. Most had extensive stabling, used by country carriers in daytime, by stage coach operators overnight, and, in Abbey Foregate, by racehorse trainers during meetings at Monkmoor. Most guests were travellers on horseback or with vehicles, who preferred not to use coaching inns. Several suburban pubs were bases for cab businesses, while others were trade houses for such occupations as bricklayers and coopers. Pubs provided facilities for sports requiring space like football or cricket, as well as those like skittles or quoits that could be accommodated in yards. The *Pineapple* at Underdale and the *Grapes* at Bicton Heath were celebrated in the third quarter of the 19th century for summertime quadrille parties.

Suburbs in the 18th and 19th centuries were settings for rural as well as urban sports. There were hunting kennels at Ditherington in the 1820s and at Bicton Heath between 1855 and 1866. Battlefield and Shelton were venues for pigeon shoots, one of which in 1871 was organised from the *White Hart* in Mardol, with a fat pig as a prize.[69] The Shropshire Rifle Association in 1881 organised rifle-shooting at Berwick Park, and the Shrewsbury Shooting Club competed in 1881 on a range at Hencote.[70] The annual coursing meeting at Sundorne, established by Sir Andrew Corbet, reckoned 'one of the first in the three kingdoms', continued long after his death in 1855.[71] Until the 1880s Shrewsbury was famous for horse-racing. Meetings were held at Bicton Heath from 1729 until 1831, and from September 1831 until 1885 at Monkmoor. The former course reverted to agriculture from 1831, but the latter accommodated sporting and other events for three decades after racing ceased.

The Shrewsbury Blues Club played cricket on the Racecourse from 1839, and the game subsequently became popular. The town and county clubs amalgamated in 1862, and Samuel Pountney Smith designed a pavilion for their joint ground at Frankwell. Cricket Weeks in 1865 and 1866 proved successful.[72]

Benjamin Kennedy, headmaster of Shrewsbury School from 1836, encouraged the game that became association football, and acquired a playing field at Coton Hill for

17   Underdale House, the former *Pineapple Inn*, venue for celebrated quadrille parties and for a variety of sporting activities in the 19th century.

18 The cricket pavilion on the County Ground, Frankwell, built in the 1860s to the design of Samuel Pountney Smith.

the purpose. Many members of the influential Shropshire Wanderers club were Old Salopians. The game was being played by the 1870s on the Racecourse and nearby fields, at Copthorne and at Dorsett's Barn. Shrewsbury Town Football Club, established in 1886, played on the Racecourse and the adjacent Ambler's Field, then at Sutton Lane, at Copthorne between 1895 and 1910, and subsequently at the Gay Meadow.[73] Demand for pitches from amateur clubs has significantly influenced suburban landscapes.

Bowling was well-established in Shropshire by 1760, and in the early 19th century the game was played at several suburban inns, the *Peacock* on Wenlock Road, and the aptly named *Bowling Green* at Meole Brace. As late as 1937 a bowling green was provided at the new *Harlescott* public house. The council laid out several greens in the 20th century, and there were 17 clubs in the town in 1955. An American Bowling Saloon flourished at the *Boathouse* in the 1880s. Skittles and quoits were established summertime sports, and a quoiting league in 1905 included three clubs from suburban taverns. In the 1860s, the *Pineapple* at Underdale had facilities for 'the game of croquet [which] has now taken such a hold on society'.[74]

Lawn tennis, an archetypal suburban pastime, was invented in 1873 by a kinsman of the Wingfields of Onslow Park. By the mid-1880s members of rowing clubs played the game in winter, rackets, balls and clothing were sold by department stores, and mowers and marking machines by ironmongers. There were courts in Cherry Orchard and near Coton Crescent before the First World War, while after 1918 townspeople had use of facilities at RAF Harlescott, and the Evason family's courts on Sutton Lane.[75] The Shrewsbury Golf Club played for a time on The Mount before laying out the course at Meole Brace in 1891.[76]

Rowing was established as a formal sport in Shrewsbury in the 1830s, when Shrewsbury School held its first regatta, and the Pengwerne Boat Club was founded. The club subsequently faded away and was re-formed in the 1870s, when 'the healthy pastime of rowing on the Severn' was flourishing.[77] There were four clubs in Shrewsbury by 1879, bringing prosperity to the *Boathouse* and the *Crown* in Coleham. Most swimming around Shrewsbury until the early 20th century took place in the Severn, and nude bathing often offended Victorian susceptibilities. An indoor baths was opened on Coton Hill in 1831 and continued for about 70 years until the opening of the borough baths near The Priory.[78]

In Shrewsbury between 1760 and 1960, as in larger cities, 'the laborious and studious within its walls' were 'irresistably [*sic*] invited to relax from their daily toil by the surrounding enticements'.[79]

CHAPTER IV

Building

Building Materials

There are still buildings in Shrewsbury's medieval suburbs constructed between the 14th century and the mid-17th century that are framed with oak, and were infilled with wattle and daub and roofed with thatch or Harnage slate. Scarcely any ancient stone buildings remain, but blocks of red sandstone in boundary walls, cut from the Keele Beds, were probably re-cycled from the ruins of medieval structures. In the 19th century sandstone from the quarries in the Triassic measures at Grinshill, as well as stone from Shelvock and Red Hill, was used in suburban churches, and some prestigious houses. Stone from the immediate locality was rarely employed, and the 1831 census records no quarrymen in Shrewsbury itself. From the mid-19th century railways brought to Shrewsbury stone from Bath and Box that was used in some suburban buildings.[1]

In most towns before the end of the 19th century all but the most prestigious buildings were constructed of local bricks or stone. The pioneers of the Garden City movement around 1900 assumed without argument that materials for the developments they planned would be obtained locally. 'The business of the brickmaker', was said in 1821 to be 'carried on in the open fields and its mode of operation may be seen in the neighbourhood of most large towns'.[2] Locally-made bricks are part of the essence of Shrewsbury's suburbs. They were being made on the Old Heath before 1600. Thomas Tither, a brickmaker who died in 1684, left bricks, tiles, crests, gutters and quarries worth more than ten guineas.[3] In the 19th century there were brickyards on every side of the town. The brickmakers of Brick Kiln Lane, that led to the colliery at Preston Boats, may have burned their bricks with local coal. Most brickmakers used fuel from the Coalbrookdale Coalfield, delivered by road from Ketley, or after 1797

19 Evidence of brick-making in 19th-century Shrewsbury: Primrose Terrace, St Michael's Street, 32 houses built by the Williams family between 1886 and 1907 on a site that had previously been allotments and brickyards.

20 Bricks from the Randlay Brickworks, Dawley, used in No 76 London Road, built in the 1920s.

by the Shrewsbury Canal. Fifty brickmakers were working in the town in 1851. In April 1850, 150,000 bricks were available at a yard at Kingsland alongside the river, and four months later a riverside brick and tile works in Coleham was offered for sale with a bed of clay 20 yards thick. Brickfields extended along St Michael's Street near the canal, while the yard at Copthorne, worked in the 1870s and '80s by Henry Treasure, was linked by tramway to building sites on Kingsland.[4]

By the 1890s an increasing proportion of bricks used in Shrewsbury came from outside the town, although most originated within the hinterland. Field's Merchantile Co., established in the 1860s by William Field, partner of Thomas Brassey, supplied bricks from a works at Uffington in the 1890s. Thomas Kough established the Sarn brick- and terracotta-works in the 1860s near Westbury station, where it worked until the 1960s. Henry Treasure opened a brickworks at Buttington in 1896, with the purpose of 'making for Shrewsbury and district a good, hard-burnt, sound red common pressed brick, and a good red facing brick', as well as ornamental bricks and floor tiles. Some bricks came from the Coalbrookdale Coalfield, and examples of the creamy-pinky-grey Ironbridge Gorge bricks remain in Frankwell. Blue bricks of the kind made by the Coalbrookdale Company, flamboyantly displayed in the Coalbrookdale Institute, are evident in St George's Street, and white bricks, similar to those supplied by the Company for the G.W.R. station at Reading in 1867, contribute to the polychrome ornamentation of many Shrewsbury buildings. Lilleshall Company bricks were used in houses at Kingsland, and those from Randlay brickworks at Dawley, whose founder, Adam Boulton, spent his last years in Shrewsbury, appear in many early 20th-century houses. By the 1890s builders' merchants were offering blue engineering bricks from Staffordshire and fiery red bricks from Ruabon.[5]

Brickmaking in Shrewsbury ceased in the early 20th century. Thomas Pace observed in 1925 that the seven or eight yards working when he went into business in 1888 had all closed. Some bricks used during the house-building boom of the 1930s came from Buttington, Sarn and the Coalbrookdale Coalfield, but others were Flettons, from works on the Oxford Clay around Bedford and Peterborough. In 1946 bricks were said to be in short supply because Shrewsbury lay outside the delivery area of the London Brick Co., the principal firm in that region.[6]

The use of Welsh roofing slate was established in Shrewsbury by the 1820s. In the 1860s, the builders' merchants Tilston Smith & Co claimed to have been the first in Shropshire to supply Lord Penrhyn's Bangor slates in Shropshire, and Fields Merchantile Co. also advertised Bangor slates. In 1870 another merchant offered slates from Bangor, Caernarfon, Llangynog or Machynlleth. Some Shrewsbury architects favoured polychromatic effects in slate, using green slates that may have come from Coniston.[7] Fields offered ceramic tiles from Broseley tiles in the 1860s, and in the 1880s the 'strawberry' tiles, made locally by John Parson Smith, were esteemed. Many houses in the 1930s were roofed with tiles from Broseley, the carriage of which, on steam lorries, was a reason for the closure to traffic of the Iron Bridge in 1934. After the Second World War a councillor observed that Broseley could produce some of the finest tiles in the world, yet not one tilery was working there.[8] Some asbestos tiles were used in the 1920s, and the most common roofing material after 1945 was the concrete tile.

Imported softwoods or 'deals' were carried upstream to Shropshire on the River Severn by 1720, and Shrewsbury's timber merchants supplied a variety of imported timbers through the 19th century. Treasure's sawmills in Wood Street in the 1890s offered red and white deals, pitch pine, Oregon, Canary and yellow pine, Riga, Austrian, Stettin and American oaks, in the form of prepared floorings, match boards and turned balusters.[9]

In the early 19th century lime was carted to Shrewsbury from kilns at Lower Longwood on the road to Ironbridge, the Quina Brook terminus of the Ellesmere Canal, and from Loton Park. From the 1860s some came from kilns at Red Hill, and in the 1880s lime was brought by train from Nant Mawr. In many towns limestone and coal were burned in kilns near to the point of use, but there were no lime burners in Shrewsbury. By the 1860s Portland Cement was available for use in mortars, as well as Roman, Bath and London cements used in renders.[10]

Concrete building blocks were being made in quantity in Shrewsbury in the early 20th century by G. & W. Edwards who had a yard next to the *Quarry* inn by the Welsh Bridge and used the brand name 'Cyclops'. In the 1920s blocks were made at the works of the Shrewsbury Concrete Co. in Corporation Lane, and from 1937 in Building 84 on the estate of ex-RAF huts managed by Fletcher Estates at Harlescott.[11] Concrete blocks were of more significance in Shrewsbury than in most towns. They were used to build more than 100 houses, and as quoins in many more.

21 An advertisement of 1886-7 for the builders' merchant John Parson Smith, whose strawberry roofing tiles were particularly esteemed.

Shrewsbury lies 15 miles from large decorative tile works at Jackfield, and 25 miles from the terracotta factories of Ruabon. Encaustic floor tiles of one of the first patterns made by Maws at Benthall from 1850 decorated a fireplace in No 52 Belle Vue Road built in that year,[12] and Jackfield tiles appear in numerous porches. J. C. Edwards of Ruabon provided the terracotta panels on the Eye, Ear & Throat Hospital, and terracotta plaques adorn several suburban dwellings.

Ornamental lintels, sills and door cases were cast in concrete, artificial stone or terracotta, or made of stone by producers who distributed nationally, like the collieries at Robin Hood, near Leeds, where sandstone building components were despatched by rail.[13] Chimney pots probably came from local brickworks, but some surviving examples are cast in iron. A few houses have balconies or porches in cast-iron that were probably products of local foundries.

Prefabricated building systems were employed on a large scale in Shrewsbury only in the decade after the Second World War. The Air Ministry built 38 'prefab' bungalows

22 Houses built of concrete blocks in Lime Street just before the First World War.

23 A decorative terracotta panel on No 27 Underdale Road, probably from the Ruabon works of J.C. Edwards.

at Crowmoor in 1944-5, probably of the Uni-Seco type, and the corporation was allocated 167 of the aluminium type, part of the United Kingdom Temporary Housing Programme. Their kitchen units were made at the Sentinel works. In 1948-9 the council built 150 two-storey BISF (British Iron & Steel Federation) houses designed by Sir Frederick Gibberd, most of which remain. Atcham Rural District Council built several groups of the concrete houses designed by Sir Edwin Airey, just beyond the Shrewsbury suburbs.[14] Between 1949 and 1954 the corporation contracted with George Wimpey & Son for 150 poured concrete 'no-fines' houses, and with Messrs Wates for 212 of pre-cast concrete construction.[15] The corporation built flats in the mid-1950s, including five blocks of five storeys at Meole Brace built by George Wimpey and Co., but avoided the temptation of tower blocks. By 1955 local authorities throughout Shropshire were reverting to traditional brick construction.[16]

24 Decorative cast-iron at Milford Lodge, Sutton Road, a villa on the property of Thomas Southam, probably built in the 1860s.

The Profession of Architecture

The profession of architect emerged in Shrewsbury in the mid-18th century just as the town began to expand. The designers of Millington's Hospital in 1747 and the Foundling Hospital in 1760 were craftsmen who described themselves as architects. For more than a century afterwards the roles of architects and builders were mixed, and it was only in the late 19th century that recognised architects ceased to be involved in the practicalities of building. The development of the building trade was influenced by men brought in to construct the new St Chad's church and the English and Welsh bridges, and, after 1815, to undertake contracts for the Holyhead Road Commission.[17] Studies of some individuals illustrate the development of the architectural profession and the building trade.

Edward Massey, 'architect and carpenter', declared when submitting plans for Millington's Hospital in 1747 that he and his partner Richard Scoltock had 'for several years last past been very much employed in drawing plans of Publick and other great buildings and making calculations of the expenses of the building thereof'.[18] Thomas Farnolls Pritchard, also a carpenter, was, by 1760, co-ordinating the work of craftsmen, designing buildings in Shrewsbury and Ludlow, and revamping country houses, before designing the Iron Bridge. Pritchard's principal contributions to the Shrewsbury suburbs were the Foundling Hospital and his rebuilding of the Abbey Mansion. When he died the principal architects in the town were the brothers William and John Hiram Haycock, whose father had been apprenticed to Edward Massey. John Hiram Haycock, who retired in 1791, built an extension to Millington's Hospital in 1785-6, and the gaol in 1787-93. His son, Edward Haycock I, achieved national repute as the designer of

Millichope Park, was county surveyor from 1834 to 1866, and designed the churches of St George, Frankwell and Christ Church, Oxon. Edward Haycock II, of the fourth generation, built All Saints, Castlefields, and Holy Trinity, Meole Brace.[19]

John Carline I moved to Shrewsbury in the late 1760s as foreman mason on John Gwynn's English Bridge. He returned to his native Lincoln, but his son John II settled in Shrewsbury in 1780, built a house by the bridge, and with partners, John Tilley and then Henry Linnell, worked as an architect and stone mason from an adjacent yard. In 1791, when they employed about 70 men, Carline & Tilley took over the business of Alexander van der Hagen, the sculptor and mason who worked for T.F. Pritchard. Carline's son, John III, added a portico to the family home and built St Michael's church, but retired to Lincoln about 1850. His younger son Thomas designed Column Buildings and the grandstand on the racecourse, before leaving Shrewsbury in 1848.[20]

In 1786 or 1787 the 30-year-old Scots mason Thomas Telford arrived in Shrewsbury to rebuild the castle as a political base for his patron and fellow Scot William Pulteney.[21] Telford's architectural contributions to Shrewsbury's suburbs were Kingsland House, and his completion of the gaol, but as engineer to the Holyhead Road Commission, he transformed two of the principal routes into the town.

John Simpson, born in Midlothian, became clerk of works for St Chad's church in 1790, and in 1793 took over the business of the builder Jonathan Scoltock. Simpson worked with Telford as 'the accurate mason who erected the pillars' during the construction of the Pontcysyllte aqueduct, and was contractor, with William Hazledine, for the aqueduct at Chirk. He built the first apprentice house for the Ditherington flax mill, and became a substantial property owner in Shrewsbury. Telford regarded him as a 'treasure of talents and integrity', and acted as his executor.[22] Simpson was succeeded in his business by John Straphen and John Lawrence, son of the coaching entrepreneur. Straphen, born in Inverkeithing, was clerk of works for Telford's bridge at Dunkeld in 1809, and a contractor on the Holyhead Road. He built the memorials commemorating heroes of the Battle of Waterloo that adorn the road in Shrewsbury and at Llanfair PG.[23] When Straphen died, his business, based in St Julian Friars, was taken over from 1827 by Joseph Stant, who by 1851 was employing 48 men and had built about 200 houses in Shrewsbury. Stant's Court in St Julian Friars, Stant's Row in Coleham and Stant's Buildings in Mountfields are named after him. The Stants' yard was taken over in 1867 by Henry Darlington and William Bowdler.[24]

Samuel Pountney Smith, nephew and pupil of John Smallman of Quatford, moved to Shrewsbury in the 1830s, to practise as an architect and trade as a builder. He first worked from the Union Wharf but moved to live alongside a brick and tile works in Longden Coleham in 1844 and by 1852 had probably built Severnside House, Longden Coleham, part of the Limes estate that he subsequently developed. He was an ecclesiastical architect, but built suburban houses in Shrewsbury, whose distinguishing mark is a mixture of styles, combining star-panels with Gothic tracery and classical pediments, and incorporating features from older buildings.[25]

The architect Alfred Barnes Deakin was the brother of Thomas Deakin, and it was observed that 'much of the early 20th century residential property in Shrewsbury was built to his plans'. One of his early commissions was the Perseverance Ironworks, for his brother-in-law Thomas Corbett.[26] Arthur Edward Oswell RIBA, son of a vicar of St George's, visited the United States as a young man, and practised in Shrewsbury from 1881. He designed many suburban houses as well as the St Michael's Street School, Millmead, and the Sentinel Wagon Works.[27] His practice was taken over in 1923 by F. Milverton Drake who affirmed the values of the International Modern movement, and deplored sham half-timbering.[28] Drake's partner was Frank Shaylor who was born in Banbury, articled in Ramsgate, worked in London, and cycled through the Netherlands with Sir Edwin Lutyens before settling in Shrewsbury. He designed some distinguished houses including the Red House of 1899-1900, his own home, No 97 Copthorne Road built for his mother-in-law in the Queen Anne style, and Nos 31 Shelton Road and 21 Ridgebourne Road, which are unashamedly Modernist.

Some Builders

The aristocrats of the Shrewsbury building trade in the late 19th century were the Treasure family. John Treasure moved from Newport to Benbow House, Coton Hill, which he rebuilt, and from which he operated his business. His son, Henry, lived at No 4 Honiton Terrace in 1871, but moved to Benbow House, and then built Kingsland Grange in 1884. He employed 222 men in 1881, when he opened a drainpipe works and saw mills in Wood Street. At his depot at No 16 Chester Street he made joinery and sold timber, slates and cement. His yards at Copthorne supplied bricks for the barracks and for the building of Kingsland. He left Shrewsbury in about 1904 to live near his brickworks at Buttington.[29]

The builder Thomas Pace, Liberal councillor from 1894 until 1933, Lib-Lab candidate in the second general election of 1910, and a Congregationalist, rose from humble origins to exercise much influence in Shrewsbury's suburbs. He grew up at Brierley Hill, and moved to Shrewsbury in his teens. In 1871 he was living at No 8 Severn Square, Frankwell and working as a bricklayer. He was foreman for Treasures for 14 years, but set up his own business in 1888, and moved to Stockton Cottage in Greenfields Street. He built about 700 houses in Shrewsbury, many of them in Greenfields. By 1901 he was living, near his yard, at Sydney House, Coton Crescent. He was illiterate at the age of 13, but educated himself, making use of Sunday schools, and advocated the enlargement of educational opportunities for others, welcoming, at the age of 68, the improvements that had come in his lifetime, and reflecting that 'Some people have

25　The last home of Thomas Pace the builder: The Cottage, Pengwern Road, built on a plot on the new thoroughfare laid out by the town council in 1921-3.

cried for the good old times. They don't know much about it or they would not say that.' He spent his last years at The Cottage, Pengwern Road.[30]

Some builders acquired portfolios of property whose rents provided their incomes in retirement. Richard Lloyd Jones, whose office was at the Abbot's House in Butcher Row, retired on marrying in 1910, and moved to Lilleshall House, Porthill, managing the adjacent sandpit, and administering his many properties in Greenfields and Cherry Orchard.[31] Richard Price had three steam engines in his yard in Old Coleham, and spent his last years at Hazlehurst, a semi-detached villa in West Hermitage. He also owned its twin, Edenholme, 13 cottages and a corner shop in Bynner Street, two cottages in Betton Street and a semi-detached pair on Havelock Road.[32] James Reynolds reputedly built most of the houses in Cherry Orchard.[33] Samuel Smith of Column Buildings, who managed a timber business established by his father, was 'one of the largest if not the largest property owner in borough'.[34] Edward Parry of Berwick Road, manager of the Ditherington flax mill, owned 39 houses in the vicinity of the mill in 1901.[35]

Before the First World War most of the medium-sized and small houses designed by Shrewsbury architects and erected by the town's builders were for owners who let their properties for rent. This situation changed dramatically after 1919. Most of the dwellings built between 1919 and 1939 were either built by the council, or by builder-developers for sale to owner-occupiers. Many of the houses south of the town were constructed in the 1920s and '30s by the builder, W.A. Sherratt, or by J. Kent Morris who, after 25 years working for the Anglo-American Oil Co., established the oil business of Morris & Co. in the early 1920s, and was a Labour councillor for six years. He laid out Porthill Gardens before the First World War, and in the 1920s developed sites at Radbrook and on Roman Road.[36]

Houses for owner-occupation were marketed modestly in Shrewsbury during the 1920s. J. K. Morris drew attention to properties on his estates by tiny classified advertisements. Other builders advertised rarely. Sherratt used a show house in 1933, probably for the first time. Restraint ended in 1934 with the establishment of Fletcher Estates (Harlescott) Ltd. Roy Fletcher was partner with his father, Alfred Fletcher, in a Blackpool development company specialising in low-cost housing, and from 1929 they sought land in other towns. He visited Shrewsbury late in 1933 to examine a property that proved unsuitable, but noticed the disused RAF camp at Harlescott. The company purchased the site and in April 1934 began the first phase of an extensive estate.[37] Properties were marketed through show houses, floats in carnival processions, the promotion of mortgage facilities and vigorous advertising, emphasising the desirability of home ownership, sound construction and low prices. When the government was adopting protectionist policies Fletchers proclaimed that their houses employed 'British Labour, British Capital, British Materials'. When pilots were heroes they showed pictures of aircraft and the word 'progress' alongside the company name. When a model of a Fletcher house on a lorry won the Wellington Carnival they proclaimed 'to be first is no novelty to us'. Some advertising was directed at women: 'Clothes make the woman but Fletchers make the house'. By the summer of 1934 the company claimed that 'We have sold more houses in Shrewsbury in 10 weeks than have been sold before in a year', and completed about 450 houses in Shrewsbury before the Second World War.[38] Fletcher Estates Ltd resumed building on a large scale after the Second World War, first in Ebury Avenue, Sundorne in 1953-4, then on the fringes of Old Heath, and on the large Mount Pleasant and Heath Farm estates.[39] Regional and national developers, like the Alverley Co. and George Wimpey & Co., began to build in Shrewsbury in the late 1950s.

Land and Building Societies

The concept of the freehold land society originated in Birmingham, when Liberals realised that creating estates of owner-occupiers could increase the numbers of 40-shilling freeholders with votes in the Warwickshire constituency. James Taylor promulgated the idea in other Midlands towns, and freehold land societies considerably influenced the development of Northampton, Kidderminster, Banbury and Leicester. Taylor spoke at the *Lion*, Shrewsbury on 27 October 1851, when a society was formed whose inspiration was Richard Marston, builder, dissenter and temperance advocate.[40] By 1853 the society had its first estate, the allotments called Benyon's Gardens behind the prison, where 71 plots were distributed by ballot on 4 April 1853, when roads and sewers were in place. Members took formal possession of their holdings on 9 June 1853, meeting at a tea party in a marquee, serenaded by a Yeomanry band. The 71 plots materialised into Victoria Street, Albert Street and the south side of Severn Street. The plots of the society's second estate, centred on Benyon Street, were distributed on 3 October 1854.[41] The streets of the Castlefields estates were quickly filled with houses, but the society's third venture, the Holywell Cottage estate in Cherry Orchard, that became Union Street (Bradford Street), acquired by 1854, developed slowly. By 1858 the society considered that demand for the kind of housing plots it provided had been satisfied in Shrewsbury itself, and its fourth and fifth estates were in the countryside, at Grinshill and Wytheford.[42]

Holdings on the sixth venture, the Oakley Cottage estate in Belle Vue, were allotted on 3 April 1860.[43] Plots on a small development in Wem were distributed in April 1866, by which time the society had purchased Dorsetts Barn, adjacent to its estate in Castlefields, where more than 100 plots went into a ballot on 28 February 1867. Some plots remained vacant in April 1868, but sufficient had been taken up to repay the outlay on land and groundwork. Responsibility for the streets was taken over by the borough council after road surfaces were metalled in 1869. The remaining plots, particularly those on the estate's 'front row', Severn Bank, proved difficult to sell.[44]

In the autumn of 1871 Richard Marston expressed concern about the society's high management costs, and members made complaints about the secretary, Thomas Weatherby, who was suspended in 1872, and died soon afterwards. He was found to be bankrupt, and to have stolen £1,930 from the society's funds. The society subsequently disappeared from the public view, but its influence was profound.[45] It provided plots for about 400 dwellings over two decades, but the presence of houses on its estates in the portfolios of Shrewsbury's principal property owners suggests that it was a vehicle for speculators rather than a means of developing a property-owning democracy.[46]

The Freehold Land Society was one of several organisations encouraging house-building in Shrewsbury in the second half of the 19th century. Most were concerned only with finance, providing money from subscribing members or investors that enabled others to build houses. A terminating building society, having been successful for 18 years, was wound up in 1866. A meeting called in 1865 to form a branch of the Queen's Building Society was addressed by James Taylor. The Shrewsbury Star-Bowkett Building Society, a terminating organisation established in 1882, was successfully wound-up in 1913.[47] The only other body that built houses was the Salopian Society for Improving the Condition of the Industrious Classes, formed in 1853, with support from gentry and Anglican clergy. Its objectives were to erect public baths and wash houses, and to build model lodging houses for single men, and model cottages for families. The society's architect was Thomas Tisdale, who probably designed the four polychrome

Model Cottages in North Street, the Gothic terrace forming Nos 5-8 St George's Street, and four houses in Darwin Street. The society was receiving only £96 pa in rents in 1871, and was wound up in 1875-6, its members acknowledging that other bodies were fulfilling its objectives.[48]

The Local Authority as Builder

As in all English towns the town council was the principal provider of housing in Shrewsbury between 1919 and the 1980s. Local authorities were enabled to build accommodation for families from the 1890s but the legislation was permissive. Some councils, such as Northampton, built houses not significantly different from those erected by speculative builders, and found it difficult to let them at economic rents.[49] Local authorities were obliged to provide housing from 1919, following promises to build homes for returning servicemen in the election of December 1918, but there remained scope for local initiative or lethargy.

Pressure on the council to provide housing grew in the first decade of the 20th century, at the perception that private enterprise was failing to meet the town's housing needs. Expectations were increasing, and it was believed that bad housing bred social disorder. The *Shrewsbury Chronicle* commented in 1900:

> It is unfortunately true that there are far too many small houses in Shrewsbury, which are not really fit for habitation. Shut in squalid courts, with little light and ventilation, these tenements are calculated to breed dirty habits if not to slacken morals, and it would be a great boon to the town if they could be swept away and replaced by modern cottages in open street.[50]

Alderman T.P. Deakin observed in 1919 that the building of small houses for letting ceased to be profitable between 1900 and 1914, although houses for rent were built in Lime Street and Cherry Orchard in that period. The appointment of medical officers of health created an 'inspection effect' that increased public awareness of bad housing, but led to changes that actually reduced the supply of accommodation. Some insanitary houses were condemned and demolished, while privy blocks displaced some court houses, and back-to-backs were converted into through houses. In 1911, 62 houses were cleared as unfit and just over 70 new ones were constructed. The ideas of the Garden City movement gained currency, leading to the formation of the Shrewsbury Housing Reform Council in February 1911. The corporation responded by constituting a Housing Committee. The Reform Council organised visits to the Harborne Tenants' Estate in Birmingham and Fallings Park in Wolverhampton, to the School of Civic Design at Liverpool University and the garden suburb at Wavertree. On 29 February 1912 Raymond Unwin, prophet of the Garden City movement, spoke at the Music Hall. A garden suburb at Porthill was proposed and rejected, but the council agreed to build houses for Shrewsbury's working class. It applied the name 'garden suburb' to the 63 houses built in Wingfield Gardens in 1913-5, and with some justification, for this was accommodation of higher quality than any hitherto provided by the private sector for rent.[51]

The corporation sought land for further housing projects during the First World War, and gained new powers under Christopher Addison's legislation of 1919. In December 1918 it acquired the 19-acre Wynns Cottage dairy holding on Longden Road, and in March 1919 accepted an offer from the Berwick estate to sell nearly 38 acres at Coton Hill.[52] The mayor said that the council 'could not grapple with schemes

26 'Homes fit for heroes': houses on Shrewsbury Borough Council's Longden Green estate completed in 1922.

of this kind without state aid'. Thomas Deakin acknowledged that '… they had men coming back from the front who had served their country faithfully and there was nowhere for them to put their heads'. Deakin became an enthusiastic advocate of social housing, acknowledging that he had been appalled by knowledge of the town's slums, gained through his connection with the Shrewsbury Town Mission. His fellow Conservative Alderman W. M. How forecast that the provision of houses at public expense would deter private builders from erecting dwellings. He was perturbed that houses at Coton Hill and Longden Road cost over £1,000 each, and that their designs were taken from the manual by Raymond Unwin that accompanied the Housing and Town Planning Act, deploring the influence of 'certain faddy architects in London'. Deakin argued that 'the ship should not be spoiled for a happorth of tar'. Arguments arose over the allocation of tenancies and levels of rent during which Thomas Pace insisted that residents should be allowed to keep cats.[53]

The Longden Green scheme was completed in 1922 and the first stage of Coton Hill, after many delays, in 1923, but in May of that year a councillor claimed that council houses had not relieved the privations of the poor, since rents were higher than many families could afford, and proposed plainer terraced houses costing no more than £300. The councillor's views reflected government thinking, after the Lloyd George coalition was replaced by a Conservative administration in 1921. The next development comprised 70 houses on Sultan Road, of simple design, for people from overcrowded parts of the town centre. The first 24 were completed by the end of 1924, and the remaining 46 during 1926. Parlour-type houses cost £390 and non-parlour dwellings £372. Councillors took as much pride in this low-cost housing as in Wingfield Gardens, and the estate favourably impressed visitors from the the Institution of Municipal Engineers.[54]

On 20 June 1925 the council purchased the 56-acre racecourse in Monkmoor that had long been on the market, and announced plans for 204 council houses, building of which began in 1926. Most contracts were for relatively small numbers of dwellings, in accordance with requirements for grants under various pieces of legislation. By the autumn of 1928 some 180 houses had been built, and all the scheduled council houses were complete by January 1929.[55] The pattern of provision was varied by partnerships between the council and other bodies. Some plots on Monkmoor Road were sold to private developers, while 12 houses were constructed for the council by a local builder in 1929, and sold under the terms of the Housing Act of 1925.[56] In March 1926 the churches drew attention to housing problems by establishing the Shrewsbury Housing Trust, to encourage the re-housing of people from the town's worst dwellings, and observed a Housing Sunday in April 1927. By working with the Trust the council obtained a subsidy that would otherwise not have been available, and purchased two acres between the railway and Crowmere Road, where 16 plain two-storey houses were built during the summer of 1929. The Bishop of Lichfield inspected the houses after he laid the foundation stone of Monkmoor School, and 12 more were built in 1932.[57] The council provided the British Legion with land for a semi-detached pair, built in 1928.[58]

The emphasis in local authority housing in the 1930s, in Shrewsbury and nationally, was on slum clearance. The medical officer of health in 1927 defined the town's slums as 'small, isolated groups scattered throughout the town, in the form of small houses huddled together in enclosed and shut-in courtyards, approached through a dark alley leading off the main street'. Pressure was increased from 1926 by the Shrewsbury Housing Trust, whose emotive slogan was 'Save the Children'. Councillors who visited slums in Coleham in 1929 and 1936 argued that what they had seen showed the need for an acceleration of house-building. Such views were not universally shared. Alderman Charles Beddard asserted in 1928 that there were no slums in Shrewsbury, and that it would prove impossible to collect rents from re-housed families.[59] Nevertheless, through the 1930s the council continued to buy land in the suburbs, to build houses partly financed by government subsidies, and to move to them people from insanitary houses in the town centre and inner suburbs. The council completed its thousandth house, in New Park Close, in March 1937, but demand was unabated. It was estimated early in 1939 that there were 221 unfit dwellings in the town, and more than 1,000 families were on the waiting list.[60]

When the Racecourse estate was complete, the council announced in 1931 a plan to build 100 houses at Judith Butts west of Monkmoor Road. They were nearing completion a year later.[61] In 1933-5, 24 houses were built between Hafren Road and the Mount, most of them tenanted by people displaced by road-widening in Barker Street.[62] Council house numbers were boosted in 1934 when the corporation purchased 38 houses that had been the married quarters of the Harlescott RAF base. The 54 houses in White House Gardens adjacent to Wingfield Gardens were built in 1934-5. The next project, completed during 1937, was a group of 40 houses in New Park Road and New Park Close, next to the Sultan Road estate. A contract for 120 houses in Wingfield Close was let in January 1937, and all were occupied by November 1938.[63] Late in 1936 the council acquired land between the road to Whitchurch and the railway to Crewe on which the 86 houses comprising the Heath Lodge or Old Heath estate were built in 1938-9. Early in 1937 the council proposed to buy 27 acres at Crowmoor where it was planned to construct up to 140 houses and a junior school, but the following year it had to seek compulsory purchase powers, and development was halted by the outbreak of the Second World War.[64]

The council built more than 1,200 houses between 1914 and 1939, and a leading councillor suggested in 1948 that 'by 1939 the better-paid workman had very nearly been catered for'. Many insanitary dwellings in the town centre had been cleared and their inhabitants re-housed in spacious suburbs. Some families were still too poor to pay council house rents, and some courts judged as insanitary in the 1850s, Fairford Place (formerly Pipe Passage) with 29 houses, Britannia Place with 12, and Coal Wharf Square with 10, were still inhabited. In 1940 the council gave authority for 52 condemned dwellings to be re-occupied to ease the accommodation shortage.[65]

The politician who did most to shape Shrewsbury's suburbs between 1910 and 1935 was Thomas Pidduck Deakin. His Salopian credentials, acknowledged when he became mayor in 1898, were impeccable. His father, also Thomas, was a baker and confectioner at No 60 Wyle Cop. His sister married Thomas Corbett. His brother Alfred Deakin was one of Shrewsbury's leading architects. His uncle, Thomas Pidduck, attended Shrewsbury School with Charles Darwin, practised as a doctor for half a century, was a Whig in politics, supported the Mechanics' Institute and the British Schools, was a member in turn of three dissenting chapels, and a patron of the Coleham Mission. Deakin married when he was 20, and took over his late father's business. He played bowls, belonged to the Pengwerne Boat Club, presided over the High Street Literary Society, and chaired the finance committee of the Shropshire Horticultural Society from 1913. He was a churchman, and supported the Shrewsbury Town Mission. He was elected to the council in 1890, defeating two sitting members, and was supported at an election meeting by James Kent Morris, later a Labour councillor. Deakin regretted the intrusion of politics into council affairs and, while an unashamed Conservative, enjoyed cordial relations with such Liberals as Thomas Pace, and took a pragmatic attitude to most issues. He became chair of the council's Gas, Water and Lighting Committee in 1895, a member of the School Board in 1901 and the Education Committee from 1903. In 1912 he was appointed chair of the finance committee, and made his twenty-first and last 'budget speech' to council in 1933. In 1910 he purchased the *Clarendon Hotel*, and lived his final years at Egerton House in Havelock Road. He considered in January 1912 that private enterprise could meet the town's housing needs, but became convinced, perhaps by Raymond Unwin's lecture on 29 February, that only the municipality could alleviate housing problems. He chaired the Housing Committee for 23 years, and advocated the replacement of slums with quality housing until he retired from the council at the age of 84 in 1935.[66]

Shrewsbury Corporation, like every other local authority, faced formidable housing problems after the Second World War, although its housing stock was unaffected by enemy action. In the autumn of 1945 the council's officers estimated that the town needed 2,000 new houses, and forecast that rising standards would lead to the condemnation of 800 houses judged unfit for human occupation.[67]

The demand for housing, more strident than after the First World War, was expressed most forcefully in the occupation by squatters of military accommodation, at Harlescott, Monkmoor and Shelton, and, outside the town, at Atcham, Merrington Green and Sleap. The council resumed housebuilding slowly, but in the eight years after VE-Day it erected 1,185 dwellings, 95 per cent of the number built in the 26 years before 1939.[68]

Harry Steward, who was mayor throughout the war, declared in November 1944 that housing would be the first priority in peacetime. The concept of planning was accepted locally as it was nationally, but progress was impeded by bureaucratic delays, by shortages of building materials and problems in their distribution, by a lack of skilled labour, and by obstruction from landowners seeking high prices for their properties. In 1944 the council was allocated 100 aluminium prefabs, one of the four principal designs made available under the United Kingdom Temporary Housing Programme.[69] Sites were provided at Crowmoor, alongside some built in wartime for the Ministry of Aircraft Production.[70] Three prefabs were delivered daily from April 1946, and they could be erected in two days. The 57 built under the first contract were occupied by the end of June 1946, and the remaining 43 were erected in the autumn.[71] The council

27 Simple, unpretentious houses of traditional construction built immediately after the Second World War on Clive Way.

extended its property in Crowmoor but progress with conventional houses was slow. A contract for 100 dwellings was signed with Kent & Sussex Contractors Ltd in May 1946, but the company had built only 70 by April 1949. After complaints about the award of contracts to non-local firms, nine Shrewsbury builders agreed in August 1947 to erect 49 permanent houses at Crowmoor, but only 27 had been finished in April 1949.[72] The Ministry of Health allocated to the council for erection at Crowmoor a hundred British Iron & Steel Federation (BISF) houses, designed by Sir Frederick Gibberd, two-storey semi-detached dwellings, sometimes called 'Alice in Wonderland houses' because their panels were installed downwards from the steel frame of the roof. Construction began early in 1947.[73] By the spring of 1951 almost 500 houses had been built at Crowmoor, but the estate exemplified the housing problems of the early post-war period.

Some of Shrewsbury's aluminium prefab bungalows were built at Harlescott for employees of the Sentinel works, and a further 50 were constructed in 1947-48. Thirty prefabs were built during 1947-8 near the Golden Ball Farm, St Michael's Street, forming an extension to New Park Close. Another small group, on the site of Morgan's Houses in Old Heath, were the first houses built by the council specifically for old people.[74] The council planned an estate at Bicton Heath but abandoned the project in 1947, and decided to build at Crowmeole. Construction began in February 1948 of 50 BISF houses, which, with 104 traditional homes, were complete by October 1951.[75]

In March 1949 attention switched to Harlescott, and by July of that year negotiations were in progress with Wates of Norbury for the construction of permanent dwellings from concrete components. In August 1950 the council purchased The Meadows farm, and revealed plans for the Meadows estate in the autumn of 1950. The estate totalled 624 houses, 212 of them of the Wates concrete type, when it was completed in 1954.[76]

In December 1948 the council purchased the Springfield estate between the Wenlock and Sutton roads. Groundwork began the following summer, and construction commenced in December 1949 of the first of 329 dwellings of which 150 were No Fines houses, made by pouring concrete made without sand or other fine aggregate – hence 'no fines' houses – built by George Wimpey & Co., who built similar estates in Cardiff, Coventry and Walsall. By the beginning of 1952, 266 houses were occupied but building of old people's bungalows continued in the summer of 1954.[77]

The council's principal housing scheme of the mid-1950s was at Meole Brace where the first houses on a 50-acre estate west of the main road to Hereford were completed in the summer of 1954, 238 were occupied by the autumn of 1955, and more than 400 in June 1956. The council began to build flats, old people's bungalows and parades of shops on its estates.[78] The first purpose-built flats to be completed were traditionally-built three-storey blocks with hipped roofs at Sundorne, occupied from September 1956, but at Meole Brace eight blocks were built by George Wimpey & Co. during 1957 on a poured concrete system.[79]

Slums were cleared with vigour, and the demolition of the former back-to-back houses in Canal Buildings was applauded in September 1955. Three-storey blocks of flats similar to those at Sundorne replaced Cadran Place, once the apprentice house of the Castlefields flax mill, and the remaining cluster houses near the Ditherington flax mill. There were complaints during 1959 that areas cleared of housing in Mount Street, Derfald Street and Crewe Street were dangerous. A public enquiry was held in November 1956 into the council's proposals to clear almost all the housing on the Old Heath, Ditherington, some 62 dwellings, all more than 80 years old, only three of which had baths. Demolition was sanctioned in September 1957. The council had already built some houses to accommodate those about to be displaced, while the former heathland settlement was being surrounded by houses built by Fletcher Estates.[80] Clearance proceeded in Frankwell, where Bakehouse and Plough passages were demolished in 1958, and replaced by flats and maisonettes above flood levels. Maddox's Buildings were felled in 1959, and plans were announced in 1960 for the clearance of the 'island' formed by Frankwell, Chapel Street and New Street. The council undertook in December 1955 to clear 794 unfit dwellings within six years, of which 515 – 371 in clearance areas and 144 individual houses – had been demolished by January 1960.[81]

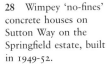

28 Wimpey 'no-fines' concrete houses on Sutton Way on the Springfield estate, built in 1949-52.

In July 1956 the council announced plans for a 105-acre estate of up to 800 houses at Harlescott Grange, between Ellesmere Road and the railway to Crewe. Contracts for groundwork were let a year later but government spending restrictions impeded progress, and Shrewsbury was one of only two local authorities in Shropshire to continue building houses during the post-Suez recession. Councillors hoped to build up to 300 houses during 1958, but the Ministry of Housing restricted Shrewsbury's allocation to 150 houses.[82] The first tender at Harlescott Grange, for 102 houses, was let in July 1958, but in November came the 'go' of the stop-go economic policy. The 'Never had it so good' election of 1959 was in sight. Spending restrictions were eased and construction accelerated. Work began on the second contract, for 100 houses, in January and the third, for 113 dwellings, was let in April 1959, while the first tenants moved in to No 24 Langford Green from a condemned house in Abbey Foregate in June.[83] The council offered to build houses to sell to families on the waiting list who could put down deposits of £50. The first of a contract for 36, on Little Harlescott Lane, neared completion late in 1958. The scheme was popular with purchasers, and with the council, since houses built for sale were not reckoned part of the authority's quota, and 50 more were authorised in 1959.[84]

Shrewsbury's thousandth post-war council house, No 1 Meadow Farm Drive, was occupied from November 1952, and the two-thousandth from June 1956, when the key of No 3 Woodcote Way was handed to the tenant, but the waiting list grew and by the autumn of 1958 exceeded 2,000.[85] There was nevertheless a swing throughout Shropshire from council to private building. By the summer of 1958 the council had built 2,382 houses since the war, and a further 857 were under construction or approved in tenders. Private builders had constructed 1,140, and were building 494 houses. It became easier to borrow money to buy houses, from building societies and banks. In August 1960, at the end of the period reviewed in this study, councillors were still calling for more local authority houses, but Harlescott Grange was to prove the last of the corporation's very large estates. Commercial developers had plans for 1,500 dwellings, and the 1960s and early '70s were the years of large-scale private building.[86]

It is fashionable to assert that council estates are drably uniform. George Orwell wrote in 1937 of 'the corporation building estates with their row upon row of little red houses, all much liker than two peas'.[87] Study of Shrewsbury's council housing – and the same would be true of any other town – shows emphatically that this is not so. The houses built by local authorities in six middle decades of the 20th century provide evidence of philanthropic temperaments, of miserly determination to curtail public expenditure, of the influence of national and local pressure groups, of experiments with non-traditional forms of construction. They reflect, perhaps more precisely than any other form of archaeological evidence, the ebbs and flows of thinking about the nature of society, the role of government and the architectural fashions of those years.

CHAPTER V

The Abbey Foregate

The Approach to the Abbey

The Abbey Foregate was an independent jurisdiction in the Middle Ages. It was the only suburb to be affected in recent centuries by a large-scale fire. Wealthy families lived in imposing dwellings in the area from the Reformation onwards, and from the early 19th century fashionable houses were built at its eastern extremity, but there were industrial premises in the Foregate, some work-a-day inns, and many small cottages that were replaced in the 20th century. The parish of Holy Cross extended over some 1,580 acres, bounded by the Rea Brook, the parish of Sutton and the township of Emstrey.

The Abbey Foregate is the route from Shrewsbury to southern and eastern England. The road to London crosses the River Severn at Atcham before joining Watling Street. By 1760 most travellers to the capital went through Shifnal, Wolverhampton and Birmingham rather than following the Roman Road. At the extremity of the Foregate is the junction with the road to Wenlock that crosses the Severn at Bridgnorth, and formed the principal route to Bath and Bristol, as well as offering alternative ways to London. Ribbon development along the two main roads, beyond the medieval limit of Abbey Foregate, began in the early 19th century, at the same time as the colonisation of the fields to the north along the lanes to Underdale and Monkmoor.

The Benedictine abbey of St Peter and St Paul was founded in 1083-87. Its medieval archaeology has been explained by Nigel Baker and colleagues, and must be the foundation for understanding the more recent history of the suburb. The medieval Stone Bridge over the main channel of the River Severn consisted of seven arches, and terminated on 'Coleham Island', where there was a junction with the road to Church Stretton. The island was bounded by the main stream of the Severn, and a channel to the east, that was joined by the Rea Brook, and by the channel that left the brook below Sutton Lower Mill and still in 1774 powered three mills that once belonged to the abbey.[1] The eastbound traveller crossed the 'Monks' Bridge' of 11 arches over eastern channel, skirting the area called Merevale. It continued along the present 'loop road' and through the 'Horsefair' before becoming the processional way that since 1816 has been terminated by Lord Hill's Column. The medieval structures were replaced in 1769-74 by a bridge designed by John Gwynn, which was widened, placed on concrete foundations, and rendered less steep in 1926.[2]

The Wakeman School, on the Abbey side of the English Bridge, was designed as Shrewsbury's technical college by the county architect, and opened in 1938. It replaced Abbey House, that served as a technical college from 1899, and was the home of John Carline I, foreman stonemason during the construction of the English Bridge. His son, also John, added a portico. Richard Carline sold it in 1862 to Richard Palin, a solicitor who promoted lead mines, whose widow lived there until 1887. It suffered a

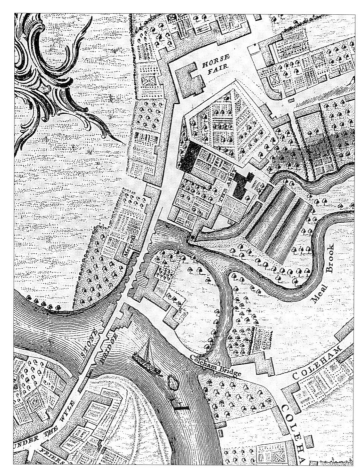

29 The medieval English Bridge, the Abbey, Coleham Island and the confluence of the Rea Brook and the River Severn, as they were depicted by Jean Rocque in 1756.

severe fire two years later. The adjacent Abbey Gardens were laid out in 1902 by the Derbyshire landscape architect, John Barron.[3] Outside the school until 1969 stood a timber-framed house called Merevale bearing the date 1601, flanking the approach to the Gay Meadow, home of Shrewsbury Town Football Club since 1910. On the opposite side was the Old Court House, a timber-framed tandem house, demolished in the late 19th century to make way for the three-storey houses and shops on the corner.[4] The adjacent pair of two-storey brick cottages, with a coach house and stable, probably accommodated staff from Abbey House.

Opposite the school stands the Abbey Foregate Congregationalist (now United Reformed) Church. It occupies the site of the *Victoria* inn, purchased in the autumn of 1862, which enabled the commencement of services in a temporary barn-like building on Sunday 5 October. In December a timber merchant from an adjacent yard sold his stock and moved to premises near the *Dun Cow*. The foundation stone of the church was laid in April 1863 by Thomas Barnes, MP, of the Quinta near Oswestry, a director of the Lancashire & Yorkshire Railway.[5] The imposing building, of white Grinshill stone, with string courses of red Grinshill stone and dressings of Box stone from Wiltshire, with a spire that rises to 114 ft (36 m), was opened on 31 May 1864. Most of the ancillary buildings were built in 1899 to the design of A.B. Deakin.[6]

The Abbey Precinct

A traveller leaving Shrewsbury by the newly-completed English Bridge in 1774 would have seen many remains of the Benedictine abbey. The range fronting Old Potts Way is known as the 'Old Infirmary', although archaeological evidence suggests that it was the lodging for the abbey's less eminent visitors, with a kitchen on the ground floor. In 1774 the building stood close to the millstream, but it had previously faced the wider waters of the eastern channel of the Severn. The 'Old Infirmary' was a malthouse in the early 19th century, and in the 20th century was used as a warehouse by a builders' merchant. The nearby mill consisted in the mid-18th century of two buildings, one timber-framed, the other a taller, rendered structure, with two parallel waterwheels between them. It was rebuilt about 1800, and about 1814 the two medieval fish ponds, on the site of the present car park, were amalgamated into one mill pond that was filled in during the 1860s, after which the mill stream was culverted. The mill worked until it was destroyed by fire on 16 August 1906, and in its last years powered a saw. Excavations in 1986-8 revealed a 4 ft 10 in (2.7 m) diameter, cast-iron pitch back waterwheel. The walls, footings and culverts were removed during the construction of the gyratory road system.[7]

The most prominent building, in 1774 as now, was the abbey church, that survives to about half its medieval length of just over 300 ft (276 m). When the abbey was dissolved the western bays remained as the parish church of the suburb, but the eastern part was stripped of its roof and any remains above ground had disappeared by 1760. The church was restored by Samuel Pountney Smith in the 1860s, and re-opened with a choral service on 28 July 1863. To the south stood a range of buildings that abutted on to the cloister, whose south-east range had been formed by the refectory, that was probably demolished around the time of the dissolution. Its pulpit remains, having been given to the parish, with the plot in which it stands, when the Abbey estate was sold in 1810. Archaeological evidence suggests that it is not on its original site, but that it was kept as a 'banqueting house', where the post-dissolution occupants of the Abbey Mansion would have dined with one or two associates, similar to the 18th-century gazebo at Tong Castle that replicated it, or the towers that remain at Eyton-on-Severn from Sir Francis Newport's mansion of 1607. The pulpit was a feature of the garden of the building called the Abbey Mansion or Abbey House, south of the cloisters, which probably accommodated the monks' eminent guests. Its owner in the late 1760s, Henry Powys, commissioned a new drawing room and fireplaces from Thomas Farnolls Pritchard. To the east, in

30 The refectory pulpit of Shrewsbury Abbey, that probably served as a 'banqueting house' where the post-dissolution occupants of the Abbey Mansion could dine with one or two guests.

line with the south transept of the church, lay the Abbot's Lodging. Early 19th-century evidence suggests that that it was then used as a coach house and stable and retained some medieval stonework. The precinct wall of the abbey also remained in 1774, a high, crenellated structure enclosing the whole of the monastic site.[8]

The principal new building erected within the precinct in the two centuries after the dissolution was the so-called 'Queen Anne House' (No 193), a two-storey, seven-bay dwelling of the early 18th century. Archaeological investigation shows that a kitchen stood in the garden to the south in medieval times, and a tannery in the 16th and 17th centuries. Between 1868 and 1881 the house was the home of the vicar of the Abbey.[9]

Traffic along Abbey Foregate increased after the opening of the new English Bridge with the growth of stage coach services to London, Bath and Bristol. The roads through Shrewsbury became the accepted route from London to Holyhead and Dublin. In 1815 the Holyhead Road Commission was established, with Thomas Telford as its engineer, and was granted government funding to improve the road. Telford hesitated to invest in the county town which he hoped to by-pass by constructing a new route from Wellington to Chirk. It was evident by 1830 that it would not be built, and a road through the ruins of the abbey's domestic buildings, contemplated in 1824, was one of the consequences. The Commission learned in 1837 that 'a new entrance has been made to Shrewsbury by carrying the road to the southward of the Abbey Church by which means the sharp angles and the old circuitous road has been avoided'. The road was formally opened on the king's official birthday in 1836, when 15 coaches from the *Lion* and two accompanying bands, forming the parade that traditionally marked the occasion, were the first vehicles to use it. Thomas Tisdale the surveyor laid out building plots at the eastern end of the new road before it was opened, and five two-storey cottages (Nos 183-87), with pedimented door cases, and five three-storey houses (Nos 188-92), called Abbey Terrace, were built soon afterwards. They were

31 The west front of the Abbey Church in the early 19th century, showing the lean-to building that was probably the one used for some years before 1841 as a savings bank.

probably designed by Edward Haycock I, who owned them in 1842 when he was living at the Abbey Mansion.[10]

The west front of the church was enhanced in 1841 by the demolition of the Old Savings Bank, a lean-to regarded as an eyesore. The embankment, bridge and viaduct carrying the Shrewsbury & Hereford Railway, opened in 1852, passed between the English Bridge and the abbey precinct, causing changes to drainage patterns, as well as disputes about rights of way. The original bridge, designed by Edward Jeffreys, was described in 1851 as a wrought-iron, 'box girder' structure. The first locomotive passed over on the last day of 1851. The bridge was rebuilt in 1932. In 1886 a 'drop station' was established nearby where trains stopped for passengers' tickets to be checked.[11]

East of the Abbey in the 17th century was an ornamental garden observed by

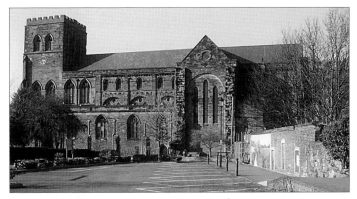

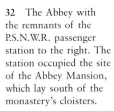

32 The Abbey with the remnants of the P.S.N.W.R. passenger station to the right. The station occupied the site of the Abbey Mansion, which lay south of the monastery's cloisters.

Celia Fiennes, 'gravell walks set full of all sorts of greens, orange and lemmon trees ... firrs, myrtles and hollys of all sorts and a greenhouse full of all sorts of Curiosityes of flowers and greens ... out of this went another Garden, much larger with severall fine grass walkes kept exactly cut and roled for Company to walke in'. The area was no longer so used by the late 18th century, but it remained behind the precinct wall, and about 1836 a public house was opened there, appropriately called the *New Road Tavern*. In 1839 a subscription was opened to enable the area to become a non-denominational cemetery. A house in the precinct was demolished in May 1840, and the fruit trees in its garden dug up and sold. The wall was removed in March 1841, and the materials of the *New Road Tavern* were sold two months later. The cemetery was consecrated and the first interment took place on 18 October 1841.[12]

The Potteries, Shrewsbury & North Wales Railway brought greater changes. In the autumn of 1863 its promoter, Richard France, acquired the Abbey Mansion, three other houses, orchards, pleasure grounds and ornamental waters, with six acres of meadow. The railway company opened a station in 1866 on the site of the Abbot's Lodging, demolished the Abbey Mansion, cleared its garden, for the station yard, and drained the mill pond.[13] The company failed to reach the Potteries or the Welsh coast, but linked Shrewsbury with Llanymynech in 1866, and with Criggion from 1871. Its trains were suspended between December 1866 and 1868, and ceased in 1880. No public services ran until 1911 when it was operated by Colonel H.F. Stephens as the Shropshire & Montgomeryshire Railway under a Light Railway Order. By the end of the First World War the area around the station was unkempt, and a female squatter occupied a bungalow adapted from a railway coach. Regular passenger services ceased in November 1933, but freight traffic and excursions continued, Bank Holidays trips proving popular. In 1934 the Anglo-American Oil Co. opened a depot, east of the 'Queen Anne House'.[14] The War Office took over the railway in 1941 and used it to supply an ordnance depot covering several thousand acres between Ford and Nesscliff. Trains bringing troops to Shrewsbury for rest and recreation terminated at the station, and there was disorder on Saturday evenings in the latter part of the Second World War as drunken soldiers were marshalled by military police. The War Office relinquished the line, and the last excursion train left Abbey Station on 20 March 1960, but tank wagons were shunted into the oil depot until the 1980s.[15]

Before the end of 1864 France developed the western part of his property, alongside the Shrewsbury & Hereford Railway, where he intended to establish a depot for coal, lime and similar materials, and an engineering works, to produce bridges, locomotives, wagons and construction equipment for railway contractors. He proposed to employ

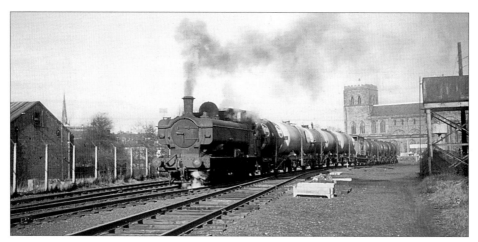

33   An ex-Great Western Railway pannier tank locomotive shunting tanker wagons into the oil depot at the Abbey Station in 1966.

skilled men made redundant by the closing of the workshops of the Shrewsbury & Hereford Railway whose plant was offered for sale in December 1863. The *Shrewsbury Chronicle* hoped that France's works would make Shrewsbury 'as it was in the days of Mr Hazledine, a great rival of the Coalbrookdale and Lilleshall companies'. France complained that the Shrewsbury & Hereford Railway refused to construct a siding into his premises, forcing him to unload two million bricks in Coleham, and that the company solicitor, J.J.Peele, was linked with his depot's direct competitor, the recently-formed Field's Merchantile Company. Neither business flourished. The workshops, fitted with two cupolas, heating furnaces, numerous smiths' hearths, two powerful cranes, lathes, shaping-, shearing-, drilling-, punching-, planning-, boring-, slotting- and plate-bending-machines, a saw mill, two weighing machines and four steam engines, lay disused. The machines, with the rolling stock of the P.S. & N.W.R., were offered for auction in 1869 but remained unsold until 1876 when the works was purchased and restored to operation by the Birmingham-based Midland Railway Carriage & Wagon Co.[16] During 1880 the company built railway coaches for New Zealand, South Australia and India, 200 air-braked vehicles for the London, Brighton & South Coast Railway, and tramcars for Southwark and Deptford. About 300 men were working at the factory in 1881, and more than 500 people went on the annual excursion to Blackpool in 1890. The works closed in 1912.[17]

During the First World War the factory was adapted as the Old Coleham Prisoner of War Camp and Remount Depot. Photographs show German submariners strolling by the boundary barbed wire, with smoking stoves, and laundry hung out to dry in the distance. The camp's huts, cooking ranges, barbed wire and timber were sold in 1919-20. The space between the carriage works and Abbey Foregate, the Midland Field, was a venue for shows. In May 1899 Lord George Sanger, 'the Monarch of all showmen', with 11 real gunboats 50-60 ft long, re-enacted Kitchener's journey to Khartoum. In October 1899 Lord John Sanger staged an exhibition football match between an ex-Shrewsbury Town goalkeeper and an elephant. Pat Collins, the celebrated showman, stayed on the field on census night in 1901, and was there in the spring of 1911 when he advertised the Joy Wheel, which had taken America by storm, and a scenic railway.[18]

The 'Loop' Road

The *Bull* inn (No 12 Abbey Foregate) stood on the site of the modern buildings built above flood on the old main road around the Abbey. It was the headquarters of the Tory interest in Shrewsbury and Benjamin Disraeli made a speech there in 1841. A well-known local politician Teddy (Double Ned) Edwards, a printer and bookseller, became landlord in 1843. The inn retained throughout the 19th century its reputation as the resort of 'fast' gentlemen, interested in the turf and associated sports. Sporting prints from the inn and a share in a painting of John Mytton and his foxhounds were offered for sale in 1847, and James Gardener, landlord until 1908, was remembered both as a Conservative politician and a lover of coursing. The *Bull* was de-licensed in 1937 and demolished in the early 1960s.[19] The timber-framed public convenience of 1935 adjoins two timber-framed buildings, each with three cruck trusses, with only six inches between the two. Dendrochronological analysis has given a date of 1408 for Nos 18/19 and 1430-1 for Nos 20/21. For about 70 years from the 1920s the range was used as a garage.[20]

An access through No 20 led to nine insanitary dwellings in Plowman's Passage. Two cottages behind No 21, owned by one Sarah Collier in 1878, lined Collier's Passage. Railway Road, known until the 1880s as Priddle's Passage, was the ancient access to fields called Lower Gay and Daniels Gay. In 1878 it comprised 17 recently-built houses, a coach house, two stables, a cow house, two slaughter houses and a workshop. Providence Grove, a terrace of nine two-storey red brick houses, was built by 1881. The two parallel terraces called Portobello were built before 1900.[21]

Beyond Railway Road, Nos 24-5 Abbey Foregate have a rendered front and side walls built with handmade bricks. Nos 26-27, distinguished by Dutch gables with stone globes on either side and Tudor-style chimneys inscribed 'JBM 1725', were occupied in the early 20th century by the Coleham Brush Factory, so-called because it had previously been located in Coleham. The inn, the *Crow* until the 1860s then the *Crown*, had 'a large and lucrative business' in 1903. In 1838 it included six bedrooms for letting, stabling for a dozen horses, and a brewhouse. Crown Court lay behind the inn until it was cleared in 1933.[22]

The Holy Cross almshouses, for 'decayed gentlewomen', were built in 1853 with money bequeathed by Daniel Rowlands in memory of his brother, for 34 years curate of the Abbey and later vicar of St Mary's. They were designed by Samuel Pountney

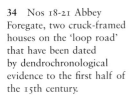

34 Nos 18-21 Abbey Foregate, two cruck-framed houses on the 'loop road' that have been dated by dendrochronological evidence to the first half of the 15th century.

35 The complex around the former *Old Park* inn near the entrance to the Horsefair, which includes an Elizabethan house with a later wing and a small Baroque mansion.

Smith in the Gothic style and built of Grinshill stone, with roof tiles from Broseley, and chimneys of specially-made bricks.[23]

The three-storey brick house on the corner of the Horsefair (No 32) replaced a timber-framed, jettied and gabled house, with two towering brick stacks, that was demolished in 1842, after being the subject of the oldest known photograph of Shrewsbury. It was the home of the Taylor family, maltsters over several generations, from William Taylor, born in 1756, to Richard Taylor who died in 1904. Malting prospered in this part of the Foregate. Mary Hampton, who died in 1662 leaving bread for the poor of the parish, derived her income from a malthouse, and in 1861 three maltmen lived nearby. A one-and-a-half-storey brick building, that was probably a malthouse, and a timber-framed barn-like structure remain behind the house. Ten cottages in the Horsefair were cleared as unfit for habitation in 1958. In the 1990s the Abbey Lawn offices replaced builders' yards and an industrial bakery of 1960.[24]

A Seventh Day Adventist church flanks the entrance to the Horsefair, beyond which is a three-storey brick range (Nos 33-36), erected by 1838, and once called Abbey Place. The adjacent group consists of a two-and-a-half-storey timber-framed Elizabethan building, with a later wing, and a small mansion in the Baroque style, and included the *Old Park* inn, which in 1862 had five bedrooms for letting, and newly-erected stables. The rest of the property comprised a nine-bedroom house, a shop and a public bakehouse.[25] Beyond the second entrance to the Horsefair until the early 20th century was an open space, the market place of the town created by the Abbey, and the location of fairs that continued after the dissolution. About 1860 the occupant of Abbeydale replaced the wooden fence enclosing the area with iron railings, ending its use as a children's playground. Park House, a three-storey building that has been a shop, with Selwood, Glyndene, Baschurch House, Alandale and The Gables, was built between 1902 and 1910.

Abbeydale, a seven-bay house of the early 18th century (No 40), stood in more than four acres of grounds and was occupied in the 19th century by minor gentry and army officers, before becoming the home of the builder George Bickerton, whose yard was in the Horsefair.[26] For many years it served as offices for the National Health Service, and it remains in commercial use. Abbey House, a three-storey, six-bay house, with a magnificent staircase, was built, by tradition, about 1698, by Thomas Jenkins, who had married Gertrude Wingfield, granddaughter of the builder of Whitehall.

Members of the Jenkins family lived there until 1831, and owned it until the 1850s. From 1839 it was occupied by the Revd Edward Bickersteth, curate of the Abbey, author of published memoirs, and Dean of Lichfield. He was succeeded about 1848 by the Revd Robert Lingen Burton, incumbent of Holy Cross and St Giles, and subsequently vicar of St Giles, who bought the house, probably in 1854, and spent the rest of his long life there.[27] The adjacent three-storey brick houses (Nos 41 and 42) have similar dentil courses and door cases but are of two distinct builds. The former retains the workshop, mentioned in sale bills as early as 1842, that was occupied for much of the 19th century by the house painter William Pugh. The three town houses of the 1960s (Nos 43-5) replaced two-storey cottages with broken pediments over their front doors.[28]

The Foregate

The 700-yard (650 m) straight road that extends from the Abbey precinct to Sparrow Lane has the appearance of a planned medieval suburb, with regular burgage plots, those on the southern side extending to the banks of the mill stream. Research has shown that the plots do not conform to a consistent module, and the settlement probably was shaped by existing field boundaries. The appearance of the street was changed in 1964 by the cropping of trees when it became part of the A49 trunk road.[29]

Many buildings in the Foregate, 47 houses, 16 barns, 15 stables and four shops over a distance of about 440 yards on both sides of the road, were destroyed by fire on 2 April 1774. The shells of well-constructed brick houses stood up amongst the ruins of lesser buildings, while homeless families were accommodated in the Foundling Hospital.[30] Cartographic evidence suggests that some plots beyond the corner of the 'loop road' remained empty for 70 years after the fire. Most of the area belonged to Sir Richard Jenkins in 1842, and appears to have been sold to Edward Haycock I, who built the three-storey houses that extend around the corner. Nos 46-49, with classical detailing

and not all of one build, were probably the first to be constructed. Monkswell Terrace (Nos 50-62), was built in at least four phases. Haycock offered to let Nos 3 and 4 in 1845, but the terrace was not completed until after 1851. Haycock was living at No 3 in 1861 and 1871.[31]

Linden Place (No 63), now Abbeyfield Court, replaced a butcher's shop in the 1870s. Most of the houses beyond (Nos 64-8) are of three storeys with classical detailing. A sale in 1880 of Nos 66-8 'attracted the notice of most of the speculative men of the town'. The corner property (No 69) was the *Angel* inn, an imposing five-bay building, with a pilastered porch, venue of the Holy Cross parish dinner in 1858, and location of Richard Stone's soft drinks factory from 1867. The inn closed in 1883, was the home for a time of Joseph Della Porta, the department store

36   No 52 Abbey Foregate, part of Monkswell Terrace, built by Edward Haycock in the late 1840s and early 1850s.

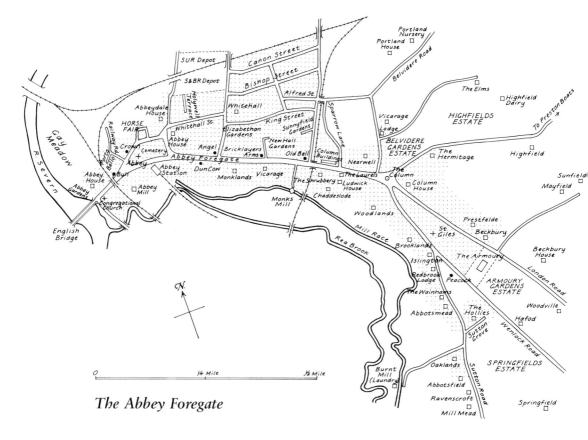

The Abbey Foregate

entrepreneur, and by 1901 accommodated the Holy Cross Institute. It was an hotel in the 1950s when its café served grills until midnight.[32]

On the south side of the Foregate, Cannock House Yard, lined by 20th-century buildings, was a base for taxis and lorries. The timber-framed houses extending round the corner into Brook Street (Nos 178-82) probably date from the mid-17th century. Behind them was Cold Bath Court, five mid-19th century dwellings, named after a bathing place on the Rea Brook. Brook Road was lined with 19th-century cottages, ten on the west, and eight on the east, until the former were demolished, with five properties on Abbey Foregate, to make way for Shrewsbury's first supermarket, opened by Safeways on 8 August 1964, closed in the 1990s, and replaced by the post-modernist Netto shop. Thirteenth-century pottery was found on the site in 1963. Buildings demolished included the *Barley Mow* (No 175), de-licensed in 1927, behind which extended Barley Mow Passage, also called Appleyard's Passage, after a 19th-century landlord.[33]

The *Dun Cow* (No 170) is a three-bay, timber-framed building, with a porch resting on classical columns. Dutch troopers from the army of King William III murdered the steward of Sir Richard Prince at the tavern in 1689. In the 19th century it catered for long-distance travellers and for country people, gaining much of its income during fairs, operating vehicles, making its own malt and brewing its own beer. When its spinster landlady gave up innkeeping in 1851, the sale included 20 feather beds, a handsome beer machine, pigs and poultry. Twenty-two horses were offered for sale during Shrewsbury's March horse fair in 1854. George Townsend, landlord in the 1860s, customarily held at ball at the inn in the first week of the New Year. Three racehorses were rescued from a fire in the stables in 1871.[34]

The much-rebuilt property to the east was concerned with the motor trade from the early 20th century, and in 1914, when owned by F.A. Legge & Co., supposedly had the first kerbside petrol pump in England.[35] The adjacent timber-framed range (Nos 164-6) probably dates from the mid-17th century. No 165 was a Ministry of Munitions hostel for girl clerks during the First World War, and 33 beds were sold after its closure. The office blocks extending to the Monklands boundary replaced a four-bay timber-framed dwelling, probably built as a farmhouse around 1500. No 163 accommodated the Shrewsbury Collegiate School teaching music, art and languages in the early 20th century.[36]

The house on the corner of Abbey Foregate and the eastern side of Monkmoor Road, until the 1890s the home of blacksmiths, was demolished in the 1960s. The houses beyond replaced a group that aroused the wrath of Richard Juson of Monklands who complained that 29 inhabitants had only one tumbledown, exposed and unusable privy, that the houses lacked water supply and drainage, and endangered the health of the neighbourhood. The timber frame visible in No 76 is evidence of the ancient settlement in this part of the Foregate. The old people's dwellings, Heath Houses, replace five cottages of that name. The *Bricklayers Arms*, rebuilt in the 1930s, was known in the 19th century for its stables, where race horses were accommodated, for the greyhounds and pigs kept by its landlords, and for its Russian bagatelle board.[37] William Scoltock, who owned the *Bricklayers' Arms* and an adjacent stone yard, probably built the 16 smooth-cast houses in New Hall Gardens in the 1860s. Nos 96-8 and 100 are one-and-a-half storey cottages, typical of many in the Foregate that were demolished in the 20th century. The Tudor Gothic Bushbury Villas, on the site of the *Black Lion* inn, were the home in the 1870s and '80s of William Phillips, hay and straw dealer, who operated a cab business. The three three-storey brick houses in Belgrave Terrace (Nos 109-11), with semi-circular headed windows in the Italianate fashion, were built not long before 1861 when they accommodated a widow fundholder, a flannel merchant and a traveller in a Manchester manufacturer's goods. Stanway Place, the adjacent two-storey terrace (Nos 112-14) named after Job Stanway, landlord of the *Old Bell* in the 1840s, is earlier, and in 1851 housed a land surveyor, a retired

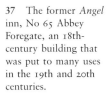

37 The former *Angel* inn, No 65 Abbey Foregate, an 18th-century building that was put to many uses in the 19th and 20th centuries.

bookseller and a widowed proprietress of houses. The *Old Bell* (No 115) in the 19th century included a malthouse, probably the building that remains at the rear, stabling for ten horses, and facilities for quoits. It stands on the corner of Bell Lane that until the 1980s had a wide verge on its eastern side that was the course of the link between the Potteries, Shrewsbury & North Wales Railway and the line to Wellington, used between 1866 and 1881. The 10 two-storey brick dwellings called Sunnyfields, with drip moulds over doors and windows, date from the 1870s. The Crowmere Gospel Hall stood on the east side of Bell Lane from 1936 but disappeared before 1962.[38]

The first houses beyond Bell Lane, Nos 117-18 are of brick, of two-and-a-half storeys, with dormers in tiled roofs. Their stacks suggest that they may date from the 17th century. The next pair (Nos 119-20) are three-storey brick houses that with Nos 121-4 were regarded as Column Buildings, or Column Terrace, built about 1840 by Thomas Carline. They were offered on 99-year leases in the summer of 1841.[39] The four dwellings in the principal terrace are of brick with a front of Grinshill stone. The terrace was home to some of Shrewsbury's richest citizens in the 19th century, including Samuel Smith, timber merchant and property owner, and the solicitors, Thomas Harley Kough, Charles Craig, George Wace and James Sprott.

Monklands, on the southern side, a three-storey, five-bay brick house, adorned with Venetian windows and a stone porch with Tuscan columns, is one of the most imposing houses in the Foregate. It was built in 1709 by Sir John Astley, who was related by marriage to the Prynce family of Whitehall. In the early 19th century it was the home of General Charles Phillips. There were nocturnal disturbances around the house in 1865 when the railway promoter Richard S. France lived there. It was sold in 1868, when there was a lake in the grounds with a Swiss arbour on an island, to Richard Juson, a Canada merchant who grew up at Meole Brace. After his widow died in 1899, it was adapted as government offices and was used for that purpose in 1960.[40]

The Cedars development occupies much of the grounds of Monklands, and Belgravia Court stands on the site of two garages of the inter-war period, one of which occupied its coach house. Bower's Court was approached between Nos 157 and 158, and was named after Thomas Bowers, a dairyman who worked from No 157. Caradoc House (No 155) is a four-bay, three-storey brick house with a pediment on the central bay. The former vicarage, occupied by a residential home, is a brick building of about 1900 with an elaborate doorcase in the Perpendicular style. Nos 146-9 comprise Monkland Terrace, or Monkland Place, three-storey houses probably of the mid-18th century, while Nos 143-4 are of later date, of Ruabon brick.

The *Old Bush* (No 141), may be timber-framed, and was already a tavern in 1749 when John Wyatt of Birmingham demonstrated a weighing machine on the premises. In 1869 it had a malthouse capable of wetting 40 bushels of barley every four or five days, a brewhouse, and a cellar stocked with port, sherry, claret, champagne, whisky and brandy. It included a skittle alley in 1888.[41] A bakery with a shed for a delivery cart occupied No 140 around 1900. The three-bay Mill House (No 139) has a pedimented doorcase and windows that suggest an early 18th-century date. It takes its name from the Monks' Mill (or Trill Mill) on the Rea Brook, approached along Mill Road. Brook House (No 133) is a five-bay building, sometimes called Waterloo House, the home in 1871 of 'Captain' Arthur Waters, the Cornish mining engineer, and in 1881 of Henry Rogers, partner in Richard Maddox's department store.[42]

Beyond the course of the former P.S.N.W.R. is the *Lord Hill* hotel, opened in 1964, incorporating The Shrubbery, a villa occupied in the late 19th century by John Bagnall,

38 Column Buildings, built by Thomas Carline about 1840. Only the fronts are of Grinshill stone. The side and back walls are of local brick.

a grocer, and by the corn merchant Alfred Attfield, and described in 1888 and in 1911 as 'one of the most important residences in Shrewsbury'.[43]

The lodge cottage (No 131) guarded the approach to another substantial villa, occupied in 2005 by the Community & Mental Health Service. Originally Hatton House, it was built before 1842, and was the home of Timotheus Burd, a land agent, and then of his son Henry. It was re-named Chaddeslode between 1901 and 1910, probably by its next occupant, Dr Henry Nelson Edwards, a kinsman of the admiral. About 1920 it was occupied by a home for unmarried mothers established in 1907, that remained there in 1960.[44] The land to the east was occupied until the 1850s by Burd's Cottages, eight dwellings all occupied by working men. They were replaced by twin houses that appear to have been built for Laurence Burd, whose portion was called the Laurels, and his brother Henry who lived in Ludwick House (in 2005 the Column Nursery). The former was purchased in 1956 by the Church Mission for Deaf & Dumb as a social centre for the deaf, and named after the mission's chairman, Canon John Brierley, rector of Wolverhampton.[45]

The Fields to the North

Two of the medieval common fields of Holy Cross parish, Barley Field and Clay Field, lay north of the Foregate. Beyond them were the pastures of Monkmoor and Crowmoor. The whole area was enclosed by consolidation and consent by the mid-18th century.

In 1800 Underdale Road and Monkmoor Road led through fields to the tiny settlements around Underdale Hall and Monkmoor Farm. Beyond the plots on the north side of Abbey Foregate was a rectangular enclosure called the Holywell Field, which was sub-divided and sold as building land about 1830. By 1832 Thomas Groves had constructed Holywell Terrace, and in 1834 Whitehall Street was laid out along the line of an existing footpath, that in 1748 was a tree-lined approach to the mansion from which the street derived its name.[46]

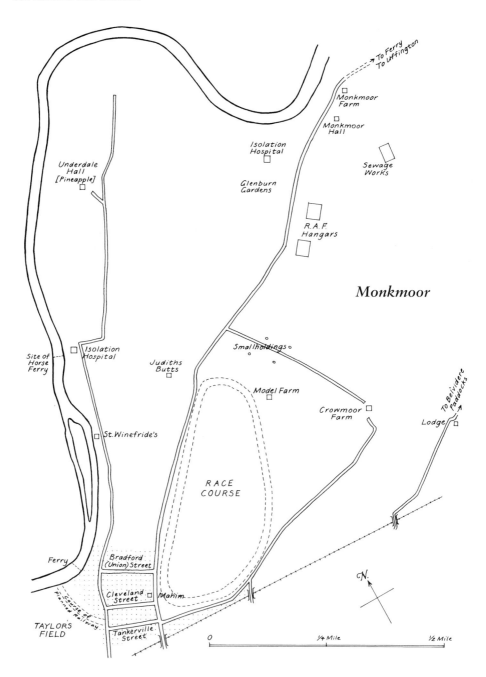

Whitehall Street developed slowly and was only adopted as a public thoroughfare in 1867. The properties at the junction with Monkmoor Road were part of the Whitehall estate, and the 20th-century shops on the northern side and houses on the southern side were the first buildings to be constructed there. The houses extending into Underdale Road, known as Stanley Place, several of which were demolished in the 1960s, were built about 1840 by Thomas Stanley, a brickmaker, and Nos 1-5 formed a single property with Nos 15-19 Underdale Road in 1903.[48] The opposite corner was occupied by Abbey House, and its gardens, beyond which is Whitehall Terrace, four three-storey houses built in the 1830s by Samuel Smith. Many of its 19th-century inhabitants were clergy or women living on invested income. Beyond the terrace Smith built the 11 two-storey houses with iron balconies that comprise Whitehall Place, which was also attractive to women of independent means. Tankerville Place on the north side of the street was built during the 1850s. Abbey Gardens, the two large pairs of houses at the eastern end, were built in the 1880s.

Holywell Terrace, consisting of 12 double-fronted, three-storey houses, with attics and basements, was constructed before 1832 by Thomas Groves, whose descendants lived there throughout the 19th century. For many years it was fashionable. In 1851 only eight of the houses were occupied, but all had resident domestic servants. Three householders lived on investments and among the others were a Baptist minister, a surveyor, and a railway agent. In 1861 the residents included a portrait painter, Jerome Goodrich, and three clergy, amongst them the vicar of the Abbey, who occupied two adjacent houses with his wife, five children and three servants. In 1891 all 12 houses had resident domestic servants, but ten years later there were servants at only two, and householders included a foreman pastry cook, a plasterer and a fishmonger's clerk.

Gayfield Terrace, a late 19th-century brick terrace, follows the original line of Underdale Road that led to a level crossing over the railway, which was replaced by the bridge over the dip in the road in 1872-3.[48] The property adjoining the line was occupied from 1849 by the locomotive depot of the Shrewsbury & Birmingham Railway that included a 'railway lodge', kept by William Thomas, a Welshman. Two Lancashire-born engine drivers stayed there on census night in 1851. The depot became a coal wharf but in 1871 William Thomas, then a signalman, still occupied the lodge which was demolished when the bridge was constructed. Beyond the bridge was the locomotive depot of the Shropshire Union Railway which by the 1860s was the Abbey Foregate Coal Wharf. The reservoir that provided water for locomotives remained into the 20th century. This was the location of a drop station, the Cherry Orchard platform, opened in 1886 and closed during the First World War.[49]

Underdale Road beyond the railway bridge developed gradually. The houses on the eastern side as far as No 46 were built with the streets running up the slope to Monkmoor Road. The open area to the west was Taylor's Field, purchased by the borough council in 1934 and, after much opposition, used for land-fill from 1957, which covered the earthworks of the northern extension of the P.S.N.W.R., dug in the 1860s, but never completed. In 1882 the photographer, James Laing, who settled in Shrewsbury in the early 1860s, built Ferndell (No 14), a substantial dwelling with Gothic detailing, whose cellars occupy part of the abandoned railway cutting. Laing also built the three adjacent houses on the corner of Cleveland Street.[50]

Sedgeford House (originally Goldstone Villa, No 27), on the western side, has ostentatious floral decorations in terracotta on its southern elevation. No 29 (Severn Villa) is a huge polychrome brick residence of the 1870s, with mock timber-framed gables. Alongside No 31 is the passage to the ferry that worked from 1882.[51] Nos 33a-39 form St Winifred's Gardens, a three-storey brick range with copious terracotta ornamentation. The site of St Winifrede's, once home of the landowner John Gough, was occupied by a house in 1832, but the present building is later. It is a three-storey house in buff-coloured brick, with Tudor chimneys, stained glass windows, and elaborate timber-carving in the style of the Shrewsbury carpenters of the 16th century, set within a classical pediment. A Gothic tracery window adorns the garden.

39 House built in Tankerville Street, with the polychrome decoration much favoured in Shrewsbury in the 1880s, but subsiding because they had been built on the filled-in cutting of the P.S.N.W.R. railway, and now demolished.

North of the junction with Underdale Avenue the road assumes the narrow, undulating character of a country lane, lined by 19th- and 20th-century houses. The metalled road ends by the site of the cottage built in 1809 by the trustees of the Severn towpath for the keeper of the horse ferry, which was moved upstream to accommodate passengers in 1882. From May 1893 the council used the cottage, enlarged to eight rooms, as an Isolation Hospital for smallpox patients.[52]

The lane formerly continued to Underdale House (or Hall), a celebrated centre of suburban recreation. In 1818 it was the centre of the Underdale Tea Gardens, and in 1837 Henry Pidgeon advised town centre residents to use the horse ferry to reach the 'quiet rural retreat'.[1] By 1840 the house was licensed as the *Pineapple*, and in 1845 the landlord offered tea and dinner parties, with strawberries in the summer season, and the use of a bowling green.[2] Through the 1860s and 1870s, when John Tudor was landlord, an invitation quadrille party, held annually in early summer, was a prominent event in Shrewsbury's social calendar. About 200 attended in 1863, when a marquee was erected and Mr Parry's band provided music for dancing by 'many twinkling feet'. In 1868 the attractions included a croquet lawn.[3] In 1869 the town's house painters and bricklayers gave a tea and dancing party for 200 members of their families.[4] Tudor's widow sold the inn to W.R. Gough in 1883, after which it became a centre for football, cricket, rowing and pigeon shooting, and a cinder track was provided for athletics and cycling. Underdale Hall now accommodates a golf driving range.[53]

Monkmoor Road in the 1820s led past Whitehall, through the enclosed fields of dairy holdings to Monkmoor Farm. The west side between Abbey Foregate and the railway was built up between the 1880s and the 1930s. The imposing Prynce's Villas (Nos 13-5), named after the family that built Whitehall, date from 1886, and mix traditional Shrewsbury timber-framing with classical elements. Nos 23-7 date from the inter-war period, and are part of the same development as the shops extending round the opposite corner of Whitehall Street. The Christadelphian Hall beyond the railway bridge was designed by A.E. Lloyd Oswell, and opened on 21 February 1884 as the mission room of Holy Cross parish. It was used for clothing production by Corsets Silhouette during the Second World War.[54] Nos 53-63 form the 'front row' of the Tankerville and Cleveland Street development. The houses beyond were built just before the First World War, Castlecote (No 77) in 1907, and No 69 about 1910. The latter, when newly-built, was rented by Thomas Owen, father of the poet, and named Mahim, after a coastal district of Bombay (Mumbai) where he had worked

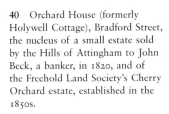

40 Orchard House (formerly Holywell Cottage), Bradford Street, the nucleus of a small estate sold by the Hills of Attingham to John Beck, a banker, in 1820, and of the Freehold Land Society's Cherry Orchard estate, established in the 1850s.

in his youth.[55] Nos 79-80 are detached houses, built on the Freehold Land Society estate, but, as the Art Deco glass shows, not until the 20th century. The *Abbey* public house, licensed in 1937, was built in the Italianate style in 1857, when it was named Ashley House, probably after Anthony Ashley Cooper, 7th Earl of Shaftesbury.[56] The Ice House, a much-rebuilt dairy farmstead, is difficult to date beneath its mock timber-framing. Beyond Ashley Street are three pairs of semi-detached houses built with concrete blocks in 1914-5.

Tankerville Street and Cleveland Street, linking Underdale and Monkmoor roads across Holywell Field, were laid out by 1880. Many of the houses were built by Edward Burley, of Burley House on Monkmoor Road. Tankerville Street was built above a cutting excavated in the 1860s for the Potteries, Shrewsbury & North Wales Railway that was intended to continue across the River Severn to Market Drayton. It was never used, and was incompetently filled-in. Thomas Bingley, who settled in Shrewsbury in 1856, remembered the earthworks in 1933 when he was ninety-seven.[57] The houses on the northern side by the junction with Underdale Road subsided, and were replaced in the late 20th century. Traces of subsidence can still be observed in the semi-detached pairs on the opposite side. Most of the houses in Cleveland Street display the polychrome brick ornamentation fashionable in Shrewsbury in the early 1880s, and four bear the date 1881.

In 1819 the banker John Beck built a villa in the Regency style, the present Orchard House (formerly Holywell Cottage), on a five-acre holding that he bought from Lord Berwick. The Shrewsbury Freehold Land & Building Society purchased the estate in 1854 and called it 'The Cherry Orchard'. The society laid out Union Street, between Monkmoor Road and Underdale Road, on each of which were several building plots. Members balloted for plots on 31 May 1855, but the estate was unpopular, and there were only five houses in Union Street in 1861. Holywell Cottage was then a dairy, but it became the home of William Parry, a Leeds-born commercial traveller for the Ditherington flax mill. The corporation took over Union Street in 1880 and re-named it Bradford Street in 1881.[58] The street bears traces of its chequered development. The numbering on the south side is irregular, reflecting the long intervals between building. The earliest houses have classical detailing. The semi-detached pairs, Abbeyville and Chance House, Stoneley and Walden, reflect the taste of the 1860s and '70s for the Italianate style and polychrome ornamentation. The five three-storey dwellings in blue and yellow brick comprising Brighton Terrace date from 1880. Avalon, a two-and-a-half-storey house in bright red brick with hanging tiles and a balcony between its bows, has a distinctive Edwardian appearance. Several houses date from the 1960s, and the names of two of them, Old Stables and the Coach House, reflect the street's history.

By 1902 building plots were offered for sale along Ashley Street, which also linked the Monkmoor and Underdale roads. Most of its houses are semi-detached pairs, with front elevations in Ruabon brick, side walls of dull red local bricks, ornate ridge tiles and flamboyant finials. Two pairs follow Garden City style, with brick and rough cast on the front elevations, and two are built of concrete blocks.

Underdale Avenue and Monkmoor Avenue were laid out on land used for allotments during the First World War, sold by the corporation in 1922. The former was taken over by the council in 1928, and building was in progress on the latter in 1935-7. Some houses in Monkmoor Avenue (Nos 46-52) have curved corners on the ground-floor bow windows and tiled roofs extending to form porches, and were probably the 'Sunshine Houses', offered by Harry Simpson for £675. Monkmoor Avenue remained unsurfaced during the Second World War and was one of the first private roads adopted in peacetime by the corporation. The mission church of St Peter, a small white building with a belfry turret, was built for the Abbey parish to the design of Sir Charles Nicholson, and opened in 1939, as the first part of an intended larger development over a one-and-a-half-acre plot. The neo-Georgian *Monkmoor* Hotel, which retains its bowling green, bears the date 1929, and was intended to serve the 500 houses that had been built nearby since the First World War.[59]

The eastern side of Monkmoor Road is occupied by the Whitehall estate, and by houses built privately on plots laid out by the council on the Racecourse estate, for which Alfred Mansell & Co. offered help with finance in 1926.[60] A curious selection of buildings lines the road between Abbots Road and Clive Road. The post office occupies a stylish detached house, and there are two buildings in a faintly Art Deco style, one a tool depot, the other a Chinese takeaway. The Co-operative Funeral Service occupies the corner site of an earlier Co-op grocery shop.

A large house and a cottage at Judith Butts in the mid-19th century comprised a suburban dairy, where the beasts in 1851 were attended by a Welsh cowkeeper. The house accommodated William Bowen, a retired housepainter and property owner. The council bought the property in 1931 and built 100 houses by the summer of 1932. Most of the houses are in semi-detached pairs. The lintels are made up from roof tiles, as are the arches over the central access tunnels of the three blocks of four. The council built 135 houses on an adjacent plot between 1957 and 1960, prior to the extension of Woodcote Way into Telford Way crossing the new bridge over the Severn opened in 1964.[61]

The Airfield

The landscape beyond the Monkmoor Road traffic island was shaped by an airfield established by the Royal Flying Corps (subsequently the RAF) early in 1918, at first an acceptance park for new aircraft, and then a school of reconnaissance and aerial photography. The buildings were incomplete at the time of the Armistice, and 450 yards of light railway track used in construction were sold in June 1919. The site was offered for sale in 1922. Two hangars were removed, but two Belfast hangars remained, one of which was adapted in the 1920s as a sports centre, with indoor tennis courts, and a licence for music and dancing.[62] The runway lay on the opposite side of Monkmoor Road from the hangars, in the area now crossed by Woodcote Way.

41 Houses that appear once to have been military barrack blocks of the First World War, in Glenburn Gardens.

The pioneering pilot Winifred Spooner, whose family lived at Woodfield, landed at Monkmoor in 1927. Berkshire Aviation tours staged an air circus there in 1931, and a three-seater monoplane crashed on take-off without loss of life in 1932. Grass track races were held on the airfield in the late 1930s.[63] The hangars had a dilapidated appearance by 1936 but reverted to military use in the Second World War, when they were occupied by an RAF salvage unit, and subsequently reverted to industrial use. From the summer of 1949 they accommodated Hartley's Electomotives, a company established in 1940, which after the Second World War manufactured wiring harnesses for Airey houses and milking machines of Swedish design.[64]

Most of the domestic buildings of the base, opposite the second remaining hangar, the officers' and sergeants' messes and quarters, the barrack huts and the institute, were offered for sale in 1922. By 1927 some had been adapted as houses forming Glenburn Gardens. Most have been altered and the cul-de-sac has been extended, but Nos 9 and 10 are brick, single-storey buildings, which appear to be barrack blocks. The women's hostel, offered for sale early in 1920, was adapted as an isolation hospital opened on 22 November 1923, jointly administered by the borough and Atcham R.D.C., and succeeding that in Monkmoor Hall. An 'open air' ward was added in 1928. After the Second World War the hospital was used for children until 1957, then for geriatric patients until its closure in 1991.[65] The site is occupied by Corsten Drive.

Sixteen nearby huts built by the RAF during the Second World War were occupied by squatters in August 1948, in defiance of the local authority which had intended to use them as a temporary junior school. The squatters remained, although there was no running water and the nearest lavatories were 50 yards away. In 1951 the council adapted seven more huts as dwellings in order to accommodate squatters from Harlescott, and 20 families remained there in 1954.[66]

The peninsula enclosed by the River Severn beyond Monkmoor Farm is occupied by the sewage treatment works, whose construction is commemorated on Nos 297-9 Monkmoor Road by the borough crest and the inscription 'Richard Scoltock Hughes, Mayor, 1900'. Beyond the entrance to the plant is the site of Monkmoor Hall, a 13-bedroom mansion, built about 1840 and demolished in 1961, the home in the 1850s and '60s of William Butler Lloyd. After being sold in 1883, the mansion had various occupants until in 1909 it was opened as a sanatorium for scarlet fever patients. Ten private patients were accommodated in the building, while those who were publicly-funded had beds in a wooden hut in the grounds.[67] Monkmoor Farm was the home in the early 19th century of Isaac Taylor, who combined farming with the stage coaching business at the *Lion Hotel*, which he sustained with skill as railways opened in the 1840s and '50s. He held annual sales of Leicester and Southdown sheep, Hereford and Alderney cattle and Monkmoor-bred pigs.[68] The farm buildings are now industrial units. The track beyond, cut off by the Shrewsbury by-pass of the 1990s, is unenticing, but to Wilfred Owen and his brothers it was a road of enchantment to the ferry boat and watermill at Uffington. The area is 'enshrined in Owen mythology'.[69]

The Whitehall Estate

Whitehall, one of the most distinguished dwellings in Shrewsbury's suburbs, was built between 1578 and 1582 by Richard Prynce, a London lawyer, whose shoemaker father had acquired land in Abbey Foregate. Stone from demolished monastic buildings encloses a timber frame, and sandstone walls protected the property on three sides. The estate passed to Prynce's descendants, the Earls of Tankerville, who leased it in the late 18th century to the Wingfield family. The Earl sold the house with 28 acres in 1835 to Dr Samuel Butler, then headmaster of Shrewsbury School, who died in 1839 and never moved into residence, although his widow lived there from 1840. The Revd Thomas Bucknall Lloyd, grandson of the headmaster, bought the property in 1856, when he was vicar of St Mary's, and regarded it as his Shrewsbury home when he was rector of Edgmond and Archdeacon of Salop, although it was sometimes let to tenants.[70] It was occupied by the Army Pay Corps during the First World War, before being sold to two men who opened it as a hotel on 1 May 1920. A charity ball took place there in January 1921 and in June 1922 the hotel hosted an open-air performance of *As You Like It*, but the venture was unprofitable. The furnishings were sold in 1923 and in 1931 there were attempts to place it with the National Trust. In 1935 it was advertised as a holiday residence, for hunting or golf, and the Society for the Protection of Ancient Buildings was credited with saving it from demolition. The Pays Corps returned during the Second World War and remained until they departed for Preston in 1947, after which it was used for government offices.[71]

The Revd T.B. Lloyd bought only the mansion, and the remainder of the estate passed to the headmaster's grandson, also Samuel Butler, subject to his surviving his aunt and his father, whose death in 1887 allowed him to develop the property. Roads were laid out, which he named Bishop Street after his grandfather, Canon Street after his father, Clifford Street after Clifford's Inn, his London home, and Alfred Street after his clerk. The dates 1889 on No 82 Bishop Street and 1890 on Nos 9 and 81 indicate the start of building. By the spring of 1891 there were six houses in Canon Street, 14 in Bishop Street, and several on the plots fronting Monkmoor Road. By 1901 there were 93 houses with four building in Canon Street, 87 in Bishop Street, three, including a grocer's shop kept by a retired policeman in Clifford Street, and five, with a shop under construction, in Alfred Street. In 1903 the council took responsibility for Alfred Street, part of Clifford Street and the newly laid-out King Street, south of the mansion.[72] The houses on the estate are characteristic of those built for lower middle-class occupation in many towns in the 1890s. Most follow the tunnel-back plan, and have fiery red brick fronts, with duller bricks of local origin in the side and rear elevations. Stained glass and decorative tiles adorn some porches. Many houses were built by James Reynolds, a deacon of Claremont Baptist Church, who lived at No 16 King Street, where the profusion of outbuildings suggests that he had his base. Henry Hudson, author of *Wild Humphrey Kynaston*, lived at Charnwood House, Canon Street, and Joseph Livesey, grandson of the temperance reformer, and head of a Shrewsbury printing business, at No 17 Bishop Street. The estate was completed in the 1920s when the builder George Edwards used concrete blocks to construct Elizabethan Gardens, the houses at the western end of King Street and on adjacent plots on Monkmoor Road. A hedge that prevented access from the eastern part of King Street was removed in 1928.[73]

The Racecourse

Shrewsbury's racecourse was re-located to Monkmoor in 1832 when the 5th Earl of Tankerville granted permission for meetings to be held on his estate where a course of a mile and 185 yards was laid out, and the first meeting took place on 18-20 September 1832. Tankerville leased the 56-acre course in 1834 to a committee, headed by Richard Taylor, the maltster, who subsequently bought it for £10,000. The grandstand, designed by Thomas Carline, was built in 1839 and incorporated a public house that was let to the former landlord of the *Angel* in Abbey Foregate.[74] The first of many spectacular happenings on the course was a balloon ascent by Mrs Margaret Graham during the autumn meeting in September 1838. In 1845 the Royal Show was staged there, but the attendance was disappointing, supposedly because Shrewsbury lacked a railway. The racecourse was used for cricket matches by 1846, and a national archery meeting took place there in 1854.[75]

By the 1850s a race meeting was held in May and another in November, but by 1869 it was acknowledged that, while the autumn event was one of the best of the year, the spring meeting was unattractive. The races were managed from 1843 by John Frail, the Conservative Party agent, and acquired an unsavoury reputation. Pickpockets were arrested and tried in 1856. During the spring meeting of 1857 police arrested the organisers of evening cockfights, held in a public house on Wyle Cop. In 1878 a flight of bookmakers caused a riot.[76]

Frail's death in 1879, and the expiry of his company's lease in 1883, threatened the future of the course. In 1885 the Revd. Charles Wightman and J. W. Woodall alleged that racing brought to Shrewsbury 'some of the greatest blackguards in existence'. The last meeting under Jockey Club rules was held in November 1885. A National Hunt meeting took place on 18-19 October 1887, after which the company was wound up and the land offered for sale. In 1888 Alfred Attfield, a corn merchant, bought the course for £12,000 as an investment, anticipating that some land would be sold for building but that racing would continue. Other courses closed at this time. That at Northampton became a public park in 1882, while the Lichfield races on Whittington Heath ceased in 1895.[77]

There was a football pitch on the course by 1876, where a match floodlit with arc lamps, powered by a Siemens generator driven by a portable steam engine, took place two years later. The Royal Show took place there in 1884 when huge areas of shedding were erected. In 1886 more than 3,000 attended an athletics meeting, with entertainment by a Volunteer band. A tradesmen's garden party, part of the Jubilee

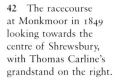

42 The racecourse at Monkmoor in 1849 looking towards the centre of Shrewsbury, with Thomas Carline's grandstand on the right.

43 Nos 31/33 Abbots Road, built on the Racecourse estate in 1928 as a result of collaboration between Shrewsbury Borough Council and the British Legion, whose crest they bear.

celebrations in July 1887, featured dancing, roundabouts, a shooting gallery and a Punch and Judy show, as well as a cricket match, a lawn tennis tournament and music from an Artillery band. The Shropshire Yeomanry Cavalry staged occasional horse races as parts of military reviews.[78]

In 1912, as the prospect dawned of hosting the Royal Show of 1914, the grandstand, the weighing room, the telegraph offices and the turnstiles were sold, ending hopes of reviving racing, and it was proposed to lay out 60 lots for a garden suburb after the event. The show left a pair of Garden City-style houses on the north side of Crowmere Road (Nos 28-30) that supposedly accommodated the show foremen, and a concrete model farmstead off the present Clive Road, demolished to make way for housing in 1945.[79] The outbreak of the First World War prevented progress with the garden suburb. The wartime airfield did not incorporate the racecourse, but improvements to Monkmoor Road facilitated peacetime suburban development. Six months after the Armistice the 56-acre site was offered for sale, but found no buyers. It remained unsold until 1925 when the council bought it for £8,500, intending to use 18 acres for 204 council houses, three acres for a school, eight acres along Monkmoor Road for private building, and the remainder as open space.[80]

Contracts for building council houses were let in small lots in accordance with variations in government funding. Racecourse Crescent, Racecourse Avenue and Crowmere Green were named in 1926, and Abbots Road in the spring of 1928. By the autumn of 1928 the council had built 180 houses on the estate and had laid out several football pitches. The council purchased two acres on Crowmere Road for the erection of 28 houses, built, in partnership with the Shrewsbury Housing Trust, in two stages in 1929 and 1932, and named Gwyn Close after the former owner. They were intended for people from 'the worst sunless and airless courts' being demolished during slum clearance schemes. Another partner was the British Legion, whose crest remains on Nos 31/33 Abbots Road, built in 1928. A third was the builder, William Higley, who constructed 12 houses for the council that were sold for private occupation.[81] Eight hard tennis courts were laid down, with a pavilion that remains. The council took pride in the 'open air' senior school designed by the Derby architect Bernard Widdows. Its foundation stone was laid in July 1929 by Alderman W.M. How, and it was opened a year later by his cousin, William Ralph Inge, the celebrity Dean of St Paul's. An adjacent infants school, designed by the borough engineer A.W. Ward, followed in 1934-5. By 1937 the council had built 300 houses on the Racecourse, and about 100 more were constructed by private enterprise. A further 27 acres of land at Crowmoor was purchased for houses and another junior school but building was delayed by the Second World War.[82]

Crowmoor

Crowmoor Farm was part of a 290-acre estate offered for sale by the Earl of Tankerville in 1842. The railway to Wellington enclosed a narrow field south of the road to the farm, that during the 1870s was filled with 30 cottages, all of two storeys except for a three-storey building housing a grocer's shop. The first 13, that realised a gross rental of £170 p.a. in 1914, were called Springfield Terrace, and the next five comprised Mayfield Place. The four plain cottages called Haughmond View (Nos 73-9) bear the date 1880. Most of the houses on the northern side of Crowmere Road form part of the Racecourse estate, but Nos 28 and 30 are legacies from the Royal Show of 1914, and Nos 30A and 26A, of more recent date, were built in their gardens.[83] In 1912-3 Salop County Council acquired 128 acres of Crowmoor Farm, and built farmsteads for six smallholdings along the approach from Monkmoor Road.[84] Four of the farmsteads (Nos 54, 64, 66 and 89 Clive Road) remain, surrounded by post-Second World War housing.

In 1939 the only houses on Crowmere Road beyond Bell Lane were in Gwyn Close, but the corporation owned land in the area, and acquired more in 1943 for its post-war housing programme.[85] Towards the end of the war 38 pre-fabricated bungalows were built for the Air Ministry on Crowmere Road opposite the present primary school, and were occupied by VE day. They had been vacated in January 1958, when the council offered the materials for sale, but were quickly vandalised. They had timber frames clad in asbestos panels, which suggests that they were Uni-Seco 'prefabs'.[86] Sixty German prisoners of war were laying sewers at Crowmoor in 1945, but the first houses were not completed until more than a year after VE Day. Erection in Abbots Green, Upton Lane, Clive Road and Crowmere Road of 100 aluminium prefabs began in April 1946, after which three were delivered daily. The first tenant, an ex-RAF regular, moved in to No 15 Crowmere Road on 31 May 1946.[87]

Kent & Sussex Contractors Ltd began building the first 100 permanent houses in May 1946 but shortages of bricks and timber caused delays and the first four were not complete until June 1947. Only 48 were finished by April 1948, and only 63 by September. Progress on a contract for 32 houses by a consortium of local builders was almost as slow.[88] Late in 1946 the Ministry of Health sanctioned the erection at Crowmoor of 100 prefabricated BISF (British Iron & Steel Federation) houses. Once begun, construction proceded rapidly, and in a few weeks at the end of 1948 frames were erected for 40 houses. By September 96 of the 100 were complete in the lanes and cul-de-sacs around Ragleth Gardens. By the autumn of 1951, about 300 permanent brick houses were complete on and around Abbots Road and Clive Road, some of the chalet type, some in terraces of six with porthole windows in the end bays. The primary school on Crowmere Road opened in 1951-2, and the Roman Catholic church of St Winefride in December 1955. The first service was held at the Baptist church at the corner of Bell Lane on 12 October 1958.[89] Crowmere Road was extended to give access to private developments, and the council built additional houses, particularly for old people. The aluminium prefabs have been replaced, but the BISF houses remain.

The Column

The 133ft (40m) high Column, designed by the Chester architect Thomas Harrison, commemorates the role in the Napoleonic Wars of Rowland, 1st Viscount Hill, victor of the battles of Bayonne in 1813 and Toulouse in 1814 and a corps commander at Waterloo. The foundation stone was laid on 27 December 1814, and the structure was completed on 18 June 1816, the first anniversary of Waterloo. The statue was put in place in 1818. The iron staircase was the gift of the civil engineer John Straphen, who carried out contracts on the Holyhead Road, on which the Column, with that commemorating the 1st Marquess of Anglesey at Llanfair PG, was a notable ornament. A nearby cottage housed the keepers of the monument, the first of whom, George Cooper Oakley, fought with the Blues at Waterloo, and died on the 31st anniversary of the battle.[90]

44 The Column, 133 ft high, built to the design of Thomas Harrison of Chester in 1814-6. The statue of Lord Hill was put on the top in 1818.

The construction of the Shirehall, completed in 1966, and the opening of Haycock Way in 1970, radically changed the landscape around the Column. It overlooks the junction of the roads to Wellington and London, and to Wenlock and Worcester, turnpiked respectively in 1725 and 1752. An 18th-century stone shows distances to various towns, and a drinking trough for cattle was placed nearby in 1915.[91] A cast-iron milestone from the Wenlock Road trust remains on the south side of Abbey Foregate, and one from the London Road trust near Bell Lane on the north side. The trusts' tollhouses at Emstrey and Weeping Cross were too distant to affect suburban development.

About 1850 the solicitor and banker William Wybergh How built an Italianate villa north of the Column that he named Nearwell. The son of a clergyman, he was born at Whitehaven, and moved to Shrewsbury as a young man. He was the father of William Walsham How, hymn-writer and bishop, and Thomas Maynard How, who followed his professions, as did his grandson William Maynard How. In 1855 T.M. How married Mary, daughter of the Revd Charles Inge, whose nephew, William Ralph Inge, Professor of Divinity at Cambridge and Dean of St Paul's, often visited Shrewsbury. After the death of W.M. How's spinster sister in 1943, Nearwell became a student hostel, but the county council had already chosen the site for its headquarters. A protester complained that the effect of a shirehall at the Column would be 'worse than the atom bomb'. Nearwell remained until 1963, and the Shirehall opened three years later.[92]

Nearwell has gone but Woodlands, its near-contemporary, a red sandstone villa on the opposite side of Abbey Foregate, remains. It was built in 1864 by John Hazledine, son of William Hazledine the ironfounder, who moved there from Moreton Villa. His son, William St John Hazledine, was an invalid and a bachelor, and after his death in 1910 it was offered to let. The 12 acres of grounds encircled several small houses and extended to the boundary of Brooklands. The houses in Woodlands Park, within the grounds, were built in 1939-40. Woodlands was used as a boys' home by the Salop Police Court Mission in the 1930s, and was occupied, briefly, as a youth hostel in 1939 before serving as military billets during the Second World War. The Youth Hostels Association returned in 1945 and remained until the 1990s.[93]

Belvidere

Belvidere Road was laid out about 1840, and linked Abbey Foregate to three suburban mansions.[94] From a junction west of the Column, it ran along the eastern boundary of Nearwell, past Column Villas, now demolished, and St Giles's Vicarage, now part of the Shirehall. It continued past houses of the 1930s on the present Belvidere Road (Nos 10-28), through the fields of Portland Nursery, crossed the railway, and then followed the present Belvidere Lane. The link to Crowmere Road was established in the late 1940s.

Portland House was built by 1851 when it was the home of a railway agent, but by 1861 it was occupied by the nurseryman Henry John Olroyd, who transferred his business to the site. It was taken over by Edwin Murrell from 1885 but Murrell lived in a house among greenhouses, while Olroyd remained at Portland House until he died. Murrell was a nationally-known grower of roses, whose family continued his business until they moved it in 1961 to the by-pass. His specialism is commemorated by the names of the roads of the 1960s built over the nursery grounds.[95]

Belvidere Paddocks, previously Belvidere Place, a *cottage ornée* in the Swiss style, in four acres of pleasure grounds, was built by 1840, and in 1851 was the home of the solicitor John Hawley Edwards. The house has been demolished and its grounds used for housing and playing fields, but its approach lined with Wellingtonias remains, together with a lodge with Tudor chimneys and rustic bargeboards.[96]

The Elms was built, probably in the 1840s, for Thomas Girdler Gwyn, a London-born landowner. It stood in a plot that in the 1820s consisted of two long narrow fields, and was approached by a circuitous tree-lined drive more than quarter of a mile

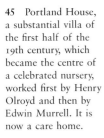

45 Portland House, a substantial villa of the first half of the 19th century, which became the centre of a celebrated nursery, worked first by Henry Olroyd and then by Edwin Murrell. It is now a care home.

FOR THE MOST RELIABLE

Garden Seeds

SEND TO

Edwin Murrell,

Seed Merchant,

SHREWSBURY.

CATALOGUES GRATIS
AND POST FREE.

46 An advertisement of the 1920s for Edwin Murrell's Portland Nurseries. While the advertisement is for seeds, Murrell's specialism is revealed by the illustration.

long. The Elms is now in the hands of the county council who use it, with buildings in the grounds, as a care home.

The Belvidere Gardens estate, comprising Belvidere Walk, Belvidere Avenue and Elmfield Road, was developed by A.G. Roberts, of Elmfield, Preston Street, whose company diverted a footpath to facilitate building in 1927. Most of the houses were built in the late 1930s when the view of the rose gardens was a selling point for semi-detached dwellings that cost £660.[97]

Beyond the Column

Among the few buildings that stood beyond the Column in 1816 was the church of St Giles, the chapel of a 12th-century leper hospital, but part of the parish of Holy Cross. Its churchyard was the burial ground for the parish, and only funeral services were performed there in the early 19th century, apart from afternoon worship during the Eel Pie Wake in July and the Cherry Pie Wake in August. Restoration began in 1827, regular services commenced in 1836, and St Giles became a parish in its own right from 29 December 1856.[98] Memorials in the church to the families who occupied Nearwell, Highfields and the Hollies reflect the history of the surrounding suburb.

In about 1794 Charles Bigg established his 'Botanic Gardens' between the London and Wenlock roads, supplying suburban gardeners with requirements ranging from hyacinth bulbs to spruce trees. Bigg was succeeded in 1842 by his son-in-law William Potts, whose two assistants took over the business in 1849. One of them, Henry John Olroyd, was soon running the nursery, and employed 12 people in 1861. When the site was offered for sale in 1851-2, it included a conservatory measuring 46 ft x 18 ft 6 in (14 x 5.6m) with iron columns supporting its roof, five greenhouses and a propagating house. Apparently it did not attract a buyer. In 1862 Olroyd announced that the lease was expiring, and that he was moving to Portland Nursery. Building land was again advertised in 1867 but most of the area was not built-up until after the First World War.[99] The nursery's shop at No 14 Pride Hill is ornamented with flowers, fruits and figures of Ceres and Pan cast at Coalbrookdale.[100]

The *White Horse* tavern was trading by 1780, and in 1832 had a skittle alley, a quoits grounds and stabling that the landlord hoped would attract custom from the racecourse.[101] Beyond it, the Armoury, a two-acre military depot, was designed by James Wyatt and built in 1806 costing £10,000. Critics alleged that it was intended to create patronage, that it was scarcely used, and that it was prone to seizure by marauding colliers from Ketley. It consisted of a two-storey building, 135 x 39 ft (41 x 12 m) flanked by cottages and two fireproof magazines. It was sold in 1827 to William, 3rd Lord Berwick, who proposed to make it an assembly room for people taking the waters of Sutton Spa. It was purchased by quarter sessions in 1854 for a military depot. The cottages were subsequently occupied by NCOs, with children whose birthplaces reflected the obligations of the British Army, in Canada, the Caribbean and India. After Copthorne Barracks opened, the Armoury was sold in 1881 to Thomas Howells of Highfields. It then served for dances, bazaars and flower shows, and even as an opera house where 'The Repentance of Ethelred the Unready' was performed in 1887. During the First World War it was a social centre for Belgian refugees accommodated at Prestfelde.[102] The principal building was demolished and rebuilt near the Welsh Bridge in the 1920s, but the cottages remain. Their dispersed layout and the high boundary wall testify to their military origins.

47 A view from the top of the Column, probably in the 1940s, showing London Road to the left and Wenlock Road to the right. The *White Horse*, with a Standard Vanguard on its car park, extends from one road to the other. The buildings in the foreground were demolished in the 1970s when Haycock Way was constructed, and included the second Column House, later the *Column Hotel*. The plot beyond the *White Horse* was occupied by a garage, beyond which is the St Giles's Gardens development of the early 1920s, with houses on both main roads and on the short St Giles Road that connects them.

48 Highfields Dairy, a model dairy on the Highfields estate, built by Henry Treasure for Thomas Howells in 1879.

Preston Street

Preston Street, named in 1883, otherwise Brick Kiln Lane, leads to a ferry at Preston Boats that was established by the 14th century and to a coal mine on the far bank of the Severn. Field names show that brickmaking once flourished in the area, but it had probably ceased by the 1840s. At the junction with Abbey Foregate stands St Giles School, a polychrome brick building of 1874 in the Gothic style, which remained an all-girls establishment until the present school of that name opened in 1968. Beyond a two-storey terrace (Nos 4-18) of brick cottages, whose doorcases incorporate pediments and scrolls, and a semi-detached pair (Nos 20-2) of similar style are two pairs of villas (Nos 24-30) in brick with stone dressings, drip moulds, bay windows and rustic bargeboards, inscribed with the date 1880 and the initials of Thomas Middleton Howells of Highfields. Allotments extended round the corner of Preston Street from the Column Lodge until the building of the Belvidere Gardens estate in the 1930s. The Highfields estate, including houses on the north side of Preston Street, was developed by George Wimpey & Co. from 1959 when detached houses cost £3,200. Hidden amongst Wimpey's houses is the delightful Highfields Dairy, built in 1879 for Thomas Howells, of brown Broseley bricks, clad in mock timber-framing, with dark strawberry tiles on its roof.[103]

London Road

When the Column was built there were no notable houses beyond it, but from about 1820 detached villas were constructed along the main roads, and on the lane to Sutton, interspersed with small cottages accommodating gardeners, grooms, coachmen and butlers.

The most influential of the mansions was Highfields, built in the 1840s for Thomas Howells, a retired farmer, father, in middle age, of Thomas Middleton Howells, a Cambridge graduate, who between 1882 and 1902 landscaped the gardens around the house and extended his estates. Highfields became part of Prestfelde School in about 1946.[104] Column House was built in the 1850s for Christopher Hicks, a solicitor. For a spell it was a girls school, then the residence of Alfred Mansell, the land agent. It was adapted during the Second World War as offices that were extended into huts in the grounds, and was occupied by the county architect's department from 1947 until 1966, and then by the county library. One hut became the headquarters of Shrewsbury's Air Training Corps in 1951.[105] The Cedars, a two-storey brick villa in an Italianate style, was built in the 1850s for Richard Davies, a printer and bookseller.

Prestfelde was built in the 1860s, apparently for the solicitor Edmund Cresswell Peele, who moved to Kingsland in the late 1880s. It was then the home of Major General William Herbert, son of the 3rd Earl of Powis, who retired to Winsley Hall, Westbury, in 1904. The house accommodated Belgian refugees in the early part of the First World War, and from March 1917 until March 1919 served as a hospital. In 1929 the Revd G. Kendal Dovey opened a preparatory school which prospered and passed to the Woodard Foundation in December 1948, when the site extended over 23 acres.[106] Beckbury, a three-bay brick dwelling, formerly Beckbury Villa, built in the 1850s, was the home until the 1880s of William Powell, who hired out traction engines, and of his widow who owned properties in Castlefields, and was sold in 1929 by the executors of T.M. Howell.[107]

Mayfield Drive and Sunfield Gardens, laid out soon after the Second World War, preserve the names of two villas of the 1860s that were adapted as offices, and demolished in the late 20th century. Mayfield, originally Clifton House, appears to have been built for Elizabeth Phillips, a wealthy widow. In the late 1870s it was re-named, and occupied by Laurence Burd, estate agent. Sunfield was then the home of Thomas Bodenham, landowner and botanist, who owned more than a thousand books.[108] Beyond Mayfield Drive is Beckbury House, another villa of the 1850s, whose first occupant was John Leake, a bookseller. After the death of his widow it passed to the solicitor Henry Wade. In 1851 there was a market garden in the area that in 1872 was tenanted by the Olroyds of Portland Nurseries, who left in 1880. A soaring Cedar of Lebanon and a spectacular Wellingtonia are evidence of their presence.[109]

Amongst the villas along London Road are smaller two-storey dwellings. The six cottages in Beckbury Terrace have pediments over their doors, and date from before 1851, and the three stuccoed houses in Peel Place were built in the 1860s. Nos 73-83 London Road are substantially-built semi-detached pairs of the 1930s, with integral porches.

Shrewsbury College of Arts and Technology was formally opened in May 1961. The adjacent crematorium was built in 1958, and beyond it are survivors of the 21 smallholding farmsteads built by the county council on 472 acres purchased in 1919. The fields at Emstrey have been used for many sporting purposes including, in 1934, grass track motor cycle racing.[110]

On the south side of London Road, the St Giles Gardens development (Nos 4-14) dates from 1922-5 and includes similar houses in St Giles Road and Wenlock Road. No 18 is a three-storey Edwardian villa, in

49 Column House, built for a solicitor in the 1850s, a building that exemplifies the varied uses to which the larger houses in Shrewsbury's suburbs have been put. It was for a time a school, then reverted to residential use, became offices in the Second World War, and then the headquarters of the county library. It awaits a new use in 2006. Yew trees, supplied by one of Shrewsbury's nurserymen, adorn its grounds.

red brick with hanging tiles. Maple Lodge, Maple Cottage, and Maple Terrace (Nos 24-34) date from the 1860s, and are in red brick, with polychrome string courses. Beyond St Giles Churchyard is a semi-detached pair of the 1850s (Nos 36-8), originally called Hortulan Villas, in the Gothic style, with high gables, drip moulds, blue ornamental ridge tiles and arched chimney stacks. The area extending to the Armoury remained open until Nos 40-48 were built along a service road, with turret windows, overhanging eaves and other features of the late 1930s.

In 1899 the surveyor John Withers, acting for the landowner H.R.H. Southam, announced the availability of building plots on the Armoury Fields, that until 1882 were used as a militia drill ground, those on London Road 'suitable for residential purposes' and those fronting Wenlock Road appropriate for villas. The London Road plots of the Armoury Fields estate (Nos 64-94) were developed gradually from 1900, most of the houses being built between 1920 and 1939, although Athlone (No 68), a three-bay house with elaborate stone dressings, dates from 1903. Ebnal Lodge (No 96), previously Woodville, is an eight-bedroom brick house, with grounds including a croquet lawn, tennis court and paddock that extended to Wenlock Road. It dates from the 1890s, and was probably built by Sidney Jones, a Dulwich-born architect.[111] There were 15 houses by 1925 at the London Road end of Armoury Gardens, then a cul-de-sac. Its extension to Wenlock Road was completed in 1932-3, and there were 32 houses in the road by 1939, mostly semi-detached pairs. Nos 12/14 are built of concrete blocks, and Nos 8, 10 and 16 occupy plots that once ran through from London Road.[112]

Wenlock Road

Several buildings in the fork between the London and Wenlock roads were destroyed when Haycock Way was built in the 1970s, among them a second Column House, that was the home of Wilson Marshall, from 1880 manager of the Midland Railway Carriage and Wagon Works, an engineer who, as a teenager, while working for Fox Henderson & Co., supervised the erection of the water towers of the Crystal Palace at Sydenham.[113] The house later became a hotel. Nos 11a-27 are part of the St Giles Gardens development, and beyond are the almshouses, on the edge of St Giles' churchyard. Houses of various dates from the 1920s line a service road extending to the Armoury boundary. There were no houses beyond on Wenlock Road before the laying out of the Armoury Fields estate in 1899, except for Hafod and Ebnal Lodge (then Woodville). The first houses on the estate were Nos 67-93, known before the Second World War as Springfield Gardens. The first three were described as newly-erected, when, already tenanted, they were offered for sale in 1906.[114] The houses beyond are mostly of the 1920s and '30s. Hafod, now No 111, the Tower Nursery, is a three-storey building in Ruabon brick, with a tower supporting a water tank and a not-very-spacious belvidere.

50 'No-fines' houses on Sutton Way on the Springfield estate, built in the early 1950s.

51   Chalet-type houses, of a kind built on several council estates in Shrewsbury, on Pool Rise on the Springfield estate, framed by Swedish whitebeams.

Ebnal Road and the adjacent service roads were laid out in a 7.4-acre field in 1938, and semi-detached houses were offered at £625 on the eve of the Second World War. The roads remained swampy hollows during the war, and were amongst the first to be surfaced by the corporation in 1949. Beyond was a property called The Lodge, built after 1902, and replaced in 1957 by the *Springfield Hotel*, the first new licensed premises in the town after the Second World War.[115] The hotel stood in spacious grounds between the two main roads, and was replaced by Huxley Close in the 1990s. The north side of Wenlock Road beyond was lined by ribbon development by 1938.

The area around the junction of Sutton Road was called Islington in 1830 and for some decades afterwards. Three dwellings (No 1 Sutton Road and Nos 34/36 Wenlock Road) occupying a single building, were sometimes known by that name, and the inn called the *Peacock* by 1841 was once the *Islington*. People walked from the town to play on its bowling green, laid out by 1854. The *Peacock*'s bowls team was still called the Islington Bowling Club in the 1920s. Nos 34/6 were built by A.G.Roberts in 1909. Armoury Terrace (Nos 58-76), 10 two-storey red brick cottages with a yellow brick string course between the floors, was built by Thomas Southam of the Hollies in the 1860s.[116] A provision shop occupied No 1, probably from the time it was built. Oreton Cottage (No 84), previously Oak Cottage, was for many years a post office. Islington Terrace (Nos 86-98), seven two-storey brick cottages with pilasters and pediments round the front doors, was built by 1842 and accommodated servants of the nearby villas, including a groom, a gentleman's servant and three gardeners in 1861. No houses apart from Springfield lay beyond Islington Terrace until the 1930s. The houses beyond No 100 were built in the 1930s in the same development as Sutton Grove, in a huge field extending between the Sutton and Wenlock roads. Those on the service road beyond No 136 were part of the Springfield estate built in the 1950s.

Springfield House, a modest-sized mansion, had been built by 1832, when it was offered to let with 30 acres, stables, a coach house and piggeries. It was probably enlarged in 1851, when a tenant left, and the census shows only a bricklayer, an employer of nine men, lodging on the premises. The house was then a dairy farmstead, but it became the favoured residence of William Noel Hill, 6th Baron Berwick of Attingham, who was living there by 1861 when he succeeded his brother to the title. In ill-health, he spent most of his latter years there. It was subsequently let to tenants, and was sold by the Hill family in 1922. It was a riding school in the 1930s and in the post-war years.[117]

52 Holy Cross School on the Springfield estate, built to the design of the county architect, A.G. Chant, in 1951-2.

The council began negotiations for the purchase of the 46-acre Springfield estate late in 1948, intending to use the house as a community centre. It was converted into apartments and stood until the 1970s. More than 300 houses were constructed on the estate between 1949 and 1955, 150 of them 'no fines' concrete houses, built by George Wimpey & Son. The remaining family homes were of conventional brick and tile construction, bordering sinuous roads lined with prunus, cherry and Swedish whitebeam. Bungalows for old people were built from 1954. The county council built houses for policemen and firemen on Wenlock Road, and plots on Sutton Road were sold to private builders. The council brought into recreational use the area beyond the estate including the mere. Holy Cross School, in the Dutch Modernist style, with a rectangular chimney and glass brick walls, was opened in September 1952.[118]

Into Sutton Road

Nine half-acre plots in Pikes Head Furlong on the southern side of Wenlock Road and along Sutton Road were advertised in 1831 as building plots 'not beyond the purchase of a retiring tradesmen or the gentleman of small fortune'. The location was extravagantly lauded:

> On the verdant banks of the Rea Brook it commands at once views of the most cheering and pleasing, encircled by scenery the most extensive, delightful and varied, without an object around to annoy or prove unpleasant, and possessing in itself everything that could tend to promote the health and longevity of those who may live upon it; being on a fine, rich, dry, gravely loam. Its geographical situation is such as at once renders it desirable, being elevated above the plain of Salop, and having all the healthy freshness of a clean, country air, while its proximity to the town affords every opportunity of enjoying those conveniences peculiar to a town residence … the majestic Wrekin, with all the undulated hills and mountainous scenery of Worcestershire and North Wales are seen in beautiful panoramic views.

Some plots were sold quickly, others were still advertised in 1839, and some were not built-up until the 1860s, including Brooklands, the Italianate villa that was the home of the solicitor, Henry Wace.[119] Lorne House (No 2 Sutton Road), a rambling brick house with Tudor chimneys and rustic bargeboards, formerly called The Lynn, and St Giles Cottage, was built by 1840. It was the home of Edward Blakeway Tipton, sub-distributor of legal stamps for an area that extended to the Welsh coast and secretary of the Salop Fire Office, and subsequently of his spinster daughter. Reabrook Lodge (No 8) was also built by 1842, and when offered for sale in 1893 was said to be 'in the most popular residential locality of Shrewsbury'.[120]

Oadby Lodge, previously The Wainhams, had been built by 1851 when the census recorded only a gardener in residence. When it was let at £80 p.a. in 1883 it had six bedrooms, a butler's pantry, a coach house, a stable, and more than three acres of pleasure grounds on which a tennis lawn had been laid out by 1887. The house was adapted in 1911 as an office for Post Office engineers, which was extended during the First World War into two adjacent houses.[121] The house was probably renamed when it reverted to residential use in the 1920s. Stonehurst, formerly Abbotsmead, was used as a school until the 1950s, after which it was adapted as flats, and a cul-de-sac was laid out in its grounds. The Cottage (No 30), in the Regency style, probably occupies the last of the nine lots offered for sale in 1831 that was taken up immediately by the attorney Thomas Bowdler.[122] Laundry Lane leads to the Burnt Mill on the Rea Brook, which had two waterwheels and four sets of stones in 1856, and stood in a 40-acre holding. It fell out of use after Richard Owen, the miller, retired in 1886, and in 1888 was converted to a laundry which operated until 1996.[123]

Oaklands, a stone house with Tudor chimneys, windows in the Gothic style, and numerous outbuildings, was the home from the 1860s of George Burr of the Kingsland lead works and his descendants. Abbotsfield, whose first occupant was a retired farmer, was adapted as government offices in the mid-20th century before being demolished to make way for a cul-de-sac. The adjacent Ravenscroft was built by the tailor John Woodall after he retired from his shop on Mardol Head in 1861. He succeeded his father in business at the age of 15, and was in turn followed by his son, John Whitridge Woodall. Woodall was a member of the Abbey Foregate Congregational church, but was best-known as superintendent of the Coleham Mission, and his son was an equally active dissenter and temperance advocate.[124] Millmead, a purpose-built boarding school, was adapted as flats in the mid-1960s when 62 houses were built in its 11 acres of grounds. It was designed in 1899 by A.E. Lloyd Oswell for Wyndham Deedes, from the Limes school in Belle Vue. There were 29 boarders and seven domestic servants in 1901. After the Second World War the school was the setting for Conservative Party fêtes visited by Lord Woolton and Robert Boothby and actors from 'Mrs Dale's Diary' and 'The Archers'.[125]

Millmead was the last building on the west side of Sutton Road until the 1960s. Beyond it lay the boundary between the

53 Brooklands, the Italianate villa built in the 1860s on one of the plots near the Column originally offered for sale in 1831, and occupied for many years by a bachelor solicitor.

54 Millmead, not a converted villa but a purpose-built preparatory school designed by A.E. Lloyd Oswell in 1899 for the headmaster Wyndham Deedes. It remained a school until the 1960s.

parishes of St Giles and St John, Sutton, where only 60 people were living in 1931. Sutton Road was the route to the saline spring of Sutton Spa, that remained a popular destination for Bank Holiday strollers well into the 20th century. The waters 'to which one does not get accustomed without the exercise of a little effort' were said to have been 'imbibed by a goodly number of persons' on Easter Monday 1894, and in 1936 the couple who lived in Spa Cottage regularly sold Sutton water to visitors but did not drink it themselves.[126] The ruins of the cottage remain off Hexham Way.

The development of the north side of Sutton Road beyond the *Peacock* was due to the wine merchant Thomas Southam who probably bought seven one-acre plots suitable for 'genteel villas' offered for sale in 1857, and built The Hollies in a flamboyant Baroque style before 1861. Southam, son of a land agent from Stottesdon, was four times mayor, a guardian, magistrate and county councillor, and proprietor of the brewery in Chester Street. He owned the three villas on the town side of The Hollies (Nos 11a-17). All have distinctive yellow chimney pots and Nos 11a and 15 retain elaborate cast-iron ornamentation. Southam owned land on the opposite side of the road and between the London and Wenlock roads that was developed after his death. The Hollies had ten bedrooms and stood in 3½ acres of pleasure grounds that included two tennis courts. The Church of England Waifs and Strays Society adapted the house in 1929 as the St Saviour's Home, marking its opening by a procession from St Giles church. In 1950 the county council converted it to an old people's home, and it now serves as a training centre.[127] Most of the houses beyond, as far as Sutton Grove, date from the 1920s or '30s, and those beyond No 49 were built by private owners or developers on sites sold by the borough council in the 1950s. The building of Sutton Grove, whose houses have many of the characteristic details of speculator-built dwellings of the late 1930s, was interrupted by the Second World War, when semi-detached houses were being offered at £625. It remained unadopted, and by 1949 was 'a swampy thoroughfare [...] typical of many of Shrewsbury's orphan roads'.[128]

Sutton did not really become part of Shrewsbury's suburbs until after 1960, but the by-pass of 1933 cut through the parish and the houses on its southern side show that, without the intervention of the Second World War, it would probably have been completely built-up. Three farms – Sutton Hall, Sutton House and Sutton Grange – remain in the parish, and the church of St John was restored by a Greek Orthodox congregation in the 1990s.[129]

CHAPTER VI

Coleham and Belle Vue

The suburbs along the roads to Longden and Meole Brace grew up haphazardly. Thomas Southam observed in 1875 that:

> In Belle Vue they have one of the finest sites to be found anywhere for building purposes, almost utterly spoiled by the way in which the buildings have been put up. Every man has done according to the light of his own eye, and has put his back door in front of his neighbour's dining room.[1]

The bridge foot settlement on Coleham Island and the burgage plots along Longden Coleham originated in the Middle Ages. Longden Coleham was transformed by industrialisation in the three decades after 1790, when the ironfounder William Hazledine became a substantial property owner in the area. In the next generation, railways shaped the area's topography and employed many people. The area had a high concentration of public houses.

The *Swan* next to the Congregational premises, de-licensed and demolished in 1928, had stabling for 30 horses, piggeries, and facilities for billiards and bagatelle. In the 1870s its landlord George Darlington hired out flags, banners, triumphal arches and cannon for fêtes and banquets. After Coleham Bridge was damaged in the flood of February 1795, Carline and Tilley completed its replacement on 1 November of that year.[2] The three-storey houses, Nos 5-9 Coleham Head and Nos 1-4 Reabrook Place, have classical detailing and were built before 1832. 'Back houses' behind them have been demolished. The alleyway by the *Globe* led to a boatyard, operated in the late 19th century by Richard Ellis, that was probably the launching place in 1858 of the paddle boat *Christiana*, which hauled barges of materials for the construction of the Severn Valley Railway. The Revd James Colley, vicar of Holy Trinity, used the approach to the railway overbridge

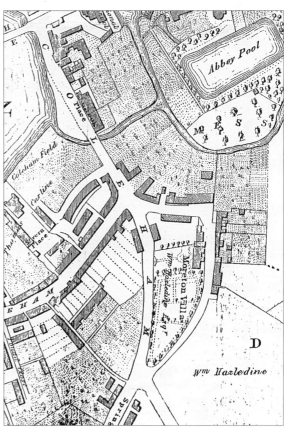

55   Moreton Villa and its ornamental grounds, as depicted on John Wood's map of Shrewsbury, published in 1838.

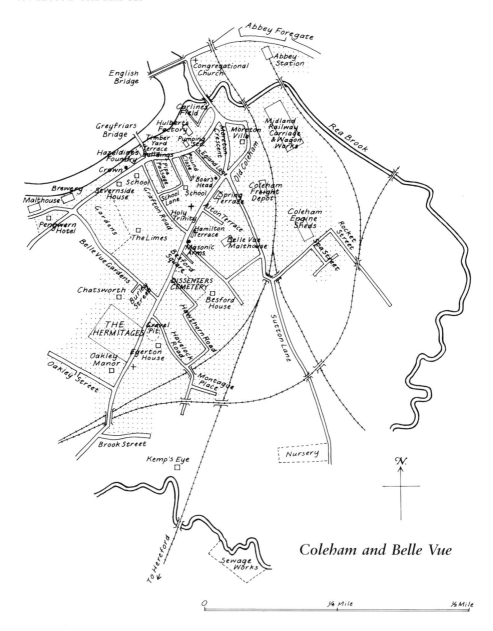

Coleham and Belle Vue

for religious meetings in the 1860s, and commotion broke out in 1884 when the Blue Ribbon Army, a militant temperance body, assembled there to hear a sermon by J. W. Woodall of the Coleham Mission.[3]

The roads to Meole Brace and Longden separated outside the *Seven Stars*. The former followed the course of Old Coleham until 1826 when the turnpike trustees built a straighter line, Moreton Crescent. About forty small cottages lined Old Coleham in the 1830s, and there were more than fifty by the 1860s, but all have gone. The landmark that makes sense of a much-changed landscape is the *Castle* public house, previously the *Windsor Castle* and the *Bull and Pump*, which faces the old road. The inn adjoined a mansion, once called Gibraltar, that was rebuilt and named Moreton Villa by William Hazledine, about the time the new road was built. Its grounds occupied the whole southern end of the 'island' between the old and new roads. Hazledine's family lived at Moreton Villa until 1864, after which it was the home of two surgeons, J.N. Heathcote, who was there until 1882, and H.N. Edwards, who moved to Chaddeslode soon after 1902, when the mansion was demolished and replaced by a brick terrace called Peace Cottages (Nos 1-18).[4]

There were scarcely any houses on Moreton Crescent for 50 years after it was laid out. In 1882, probably when the tenancy of Moreton Villa changed, J.R.W. Hazledine sold 25 building plots. Moreton Terrace and Menai Terrace, on the west side, bear the date 1882, and Wolseley Terrace, an early work of W. Scott Deakin, was built by 1888.[5] The two-storey houses on the east side (Nos 23-39) were probably built after the demolition of Moreton Villa.

Longden Coleham

Longden Coleham was a medieval suburb. Speed's map of 1610 shows houses on either side of the road extending almost as far as Kingsland Road. The pattern of plots on the south side, although distorted by Moreton Crescent, suggests medieval planning. The timber-framing visible in the two-and-a-half-storey building, No 50, and the density of public houses – the *Plough & Harrow* (No 26), the *Cross Foxes* (No 27), the *Hen & Chickens* (No 37) and the *Three Tuns* (No 42) – are further evidence of early settlement. Coleham was an artisan suburb in the Middle Ages, but 18th-century evidence suggests gentrification with substantial houses and ornamental gardens.[6]

The apartments of the 1970s, which line the south side of Longden Coleham, replace two-storey terraces, with classical detailing on their door cases, most of which had been erected by 1832. The corner house was occupied by a fish-and-chip shop in the 20th century, and for many years in the 19th century was a grocer's shop that included a post office. From 1878 it accommodated a temperance Cocoa House, intended to serve men going to work. 'Nothing could be better for the English workman [...] than to begin the day well with a good substantial breakfast of tea, coffee or cocoa in preference to strong drink', proclaimed its promoters. The former church hall was built in 1905 as the missioning headquarters for a Church Army captain attached to Holy Trinity parish.[7] Egland Lane gives access to two short terraces Moreton Cottages and Egland Cottages which appear to date from the 1830s, and to have been built by William Hazledine, who probably manufactured their cast-iron chimney pots. The *Plough & Harrow* adjoining Egland Lane had stables that in 1873 could accommodate 15 horses. A brewhouse was equipped in 1857 with a 200-gallon copper and a 20-strike oval mashing tub. Temperance reformers objected to the renewal of its licence in 1899 because its side entrance was accessible to children. The next entry was Bakehouse Yard, where there were 11 houses in 1861. The entry to Pound Close adjoined the *Hen & Chickens*, a terraced house until the present building was erected in the 1930s.[8] Pound Close, location of the parish pound, was filled in the 1860s by about 30 houses, of which the five in Stant's Row were doubtless erected by Joseph Stant. School Lane, between Nos 40 and 41 Longden Coleham, led to Trinity School, and provided access to more than 30 houses, most of which were replaced in the 1960s. Thomas Salter, the builder from whom Salter's Lane takes its name, lived at Lorne House. Three Tuns Passage, that joined Longden Coleham next to the public house of that name, was a smaller entry, lined by four houses.

The Taylor family, pipemakers in Broseley in the early 18th century and subsequently in Birmingham and Gloucester, made clay tobacco pipes from about 1830 in Pipe Passage, sometimes Pipe Shut, which joined Longden Coleham between Nos 51 and 52. In the late 19th century there were more than 30 houses in the passage which *The Builder* described in 1861 as a double row of houses with no yards at the back nor even any back windows. Pigs occupied the spaces in front of the houses, water came from one shared pump, and there were few privies. About the time pipe-manufacture ceased in 1894, the passage was re-named Fairford Place. Francis Taylor, the last pipemaker, began work in 1871 tramping across rural Shropshire selling the family's wares to innkeepers.[9]

The building occupied since 1920 by the Salvation Army and inscribed 'Gospel Mission Room 1873' was designed by Bidlake & Fleming of Wolverhampton and opened in October 1873. It was intended to appeal to 'those who never normally attend church or chapel', accommodating a congregation that previously met in Hulbert's mill. In 1881 a minister called it 'an oasis in the desert'. The chairman in the late 1880s was Thomas Pidduck, a doctor and Congregationalist. The superintendent for many years, and provider of teas at anniversaries, was J.W. Woodall, the clothier. In the 1880s the temperance-orientated Blue Ribbon Army was associated with the mission. Brakes took 200 people to Haughmond Hill on the annual outing in 1889.[10]

Coleham School, designed by A.B. and W. Scott Deakin, was built in 1909 on a site occupied in 1832 by four cottages, and subsequently by the corporation's stables. A cul-de-sac was laid out in the late 1870s at the Belle Vue end of what became Greyfriars Road, and authority to build the link to Longden Coleham was obtained in 1908. Construction began early in 1914, and the road was almost complete by the autumn.[11]

The Industrial Zone

Little is known about the right bank of the Severn above its confluence with the Rea Brook before 1790, but in the subsequent 30 years it became the most heavily industrialised part of Shrewsbury. Factories were adapted to new uses, and some new terraces were built in the late 19th century. Many industrial buildings were demolished in the 20th century, but the area retains evidence of its manufacturing past.

The river bank upstream from the confluence, occupied by Carline Crescent, served in 1768-74 as the yard where stones were shaped for the English Bridge. The area was later owned by the Carline family, builders and architects who, before 1830, built a V-shaped range of cottages, that by 1841 totalled 23 dwellings, and came to be called Carline Fields. Ten more, called Carline Terrace, were added in the 1870s. The houses remained occupied until about 1960.

Hulbert's Mill

The next site, whose principal building is now the Barnabas Centre, was sold by John Carline in 1789 to Powis & Hodges who built a woollen mill with two five-storey buildings, one 93 ft x 33 ft (33.9m x 12m), the other 86 ft x 33 ft (31.3m x 12m), and a four-storey block, 86 ft x 33 ft (13.8m x 12m), in which power for carding engines, spinning jennies and fulling stocks was obtained from a steam engine and a water wheel. The venture did not prosper, and in 1799 demolition was impending. The buildings survived, to be leased in 1803 by a Mancunian, Charles Hulbert, who, with partners, intended to weave calicoes from yarn spun at Llangollen, and send them to

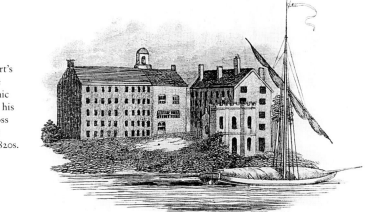

56 Charles Hulbert's cotton mill and the cottage in the Gothic style that he called his 'castle' viewed across the navigable River Severn about the 1820s.

Morda for printing, but the government leased three floors of the largest building for a military store. Hulbert built a Gothic villa, his 'castle', near the river. The mill opened with 97 workers and soon employed as many as 200, but Hulbert lacked capital, lost skilled workers to mills in Lancashire and Cheshire, and was threatened with violence when he contemplated introducing power looms. In 1814 he turned to retailing, and moved to the centre of Shrewsbury. He sold the mill in 1825, and in 1831 it passed to Thomas Carline. For the rest of his long life Hulbert made his living as an auctioneer, publisher and writer of antiquarian books.[12]

Two storeys of the 86 ft x 33 ft mill had been converted to ten dwellings by 1795, and Hulbert continued to adapt the buildings when, in 1809, he made the ground floor of the front block into houses (subsequently Nos 108-14). Buildings in the courtyard were also converted into dwellings, known as Factory Yard, Severn Square and Severn Court, where 35 houses were recorded in the census of 1841. Hulbert observed in 1837 that there were nearly 50 'neat dwellings' in the factory, but neatness was not the attribute normally associated with the area after an influx of Irish migrants following the famine of the late 1840s. The 1851 census records eight lodging houses run by Irish people, some set up by and all accommodating railway navvies, with a total of over 100 inhabitants, a mean of 12.9 per house. In 1861 there were 42 dwellings in Factory Yard whose occupants included 25 Irish-born agricultural labourers, ten of them householders, and nine Irish-born hawkers. There was a disturbance in 1860 amongst the 'denizens of that locality which forms a "little Ireland" in Coleham', and fighting in 1861 involved Patrick Digley, 'one of the colony of Irishmen who have localised themselves in Coleham Factory Yard'. The 1871 census recorded 31 dwellings in Factory Yard, five of them in Hulbert's now-tenemented 'castle', 14 in Severn Square and 13 in Severn Court. Twenty-four of the heads of the 27 households were Irish, mostly from Co. Mayo. The sanitary inspector found in 1871 that there were three empty and 28 occupied dwellings in Factory Yard, accommodating 154 people. Most of the dwellings were single rooms used for both living and sleeping. Drinking water was obtained from the River Severn, and the inhabitants shared the use of 18 filthy privies. The mayor visited the yard, 'found the place very offensive indeed', and agreed to use his influence with the owner's sister to effect improvements. By 1875 the 'notorious Factory Yard' had been cleared but its occupants had crowded into Pipe Passage and Terrace Buildings.[13]

WILLIAM EDWARDS,

BUILDER,

Public Works Contractor,

SCULPTOR and MASON.

OFFICE and WORKS—

The Factory, Coleham, Shrewsbury.

Tel. 449.

Highest Testimonials for Church Restoration and Decoration from
Sir Chas. Nicholson, Bart., F.R.I.B.A., and Mr. H. C. Corlette,
F.R.I.B.A., Architects, Lincoln's Inn, London, W.C.

57 An advertisement of the 1920s for the last business to use Charles Hulbert's mill premises, the builder William Edwards. By this time the building was very dilapidated.

Thomas Palmer acquired the factory in 1851, but sold it in 1876 to William Morgan, who bisected it. Having demolished one of the mill blocks and the 'castle', he sold the rear part in 1878 for the erection of a drill hall, opened in May 1881. Artillery pieces were moved from the Quarry and volunteers first paraded there late in June. The hall was a venue for civilian events, including a meeting protesting against the Home Rule for Ireland bill in 1893 and an industrial and art exhibition in 1896. The government built a riding school in 1913 on adjacent land purchased in 1911. During the First World War, the drill hall accommodated the depot company of the 4th battalion KSLI, whose main body was in the Far East, while the riding school housed the Shropshire Royal Horse Artillery. The military acquired the rest of the factory site just before the Second World War, after the dwellings in the former mill were condemned on 4 April 1939, and kept it until 1995-6 when it was sold to the Barnabas Church.[14]

The upper floor of the mill building fronting Longden Coleham was adapted from 1872 as a velvet factory by Samuel Hughes of Salford, who had installed nine weaving frames by March of that year, while the ground floor remained in residential use (Nos 108-114), as did four dwellings to the rear still known as Factory Yard, although only one was occupied in 1881, two in 1901 and none in 1891. The religious group that had used those rooms moved in 1873 to the Mission Room in School Lane. Hughes's velvet manufactory closed, and the rooms he occupied passed in 1891 to Hudson Davies, who had been making brushes in Mardol since 1818. In 1890 the empty rooms were used for the meeting that launched the political career of Thomas Deakin. Davies made brushes from the bristles of many animals, employing about 50 people, who travelled in horse-drawn brakes to the Wrekin on an outing in 1892. In 1909 Mrs M.J. Harley owned the business, but by 1922 she had moved it to Abbey Foregate 'loop' road. The building was used as a builder's store, prior to its demolition.[15]

The first religious services in the factory were conducted soon after 1802 by Hulbert himself, a fervent Evangelical, who knew Mary Fletcher of Madeley. The Revd James Colley, vicar of Holy Trinity, conducted worship in the yard in the 1850s. A ragged school with 80 children met in the buildings from 1859, and more than 100 teachers and friends sat down to a New Year tea in 1864. The non-denominational congregation meeting there in 1873 moved to the Coleham Mission Room.[16]

Coleham Pumping Station

The Coleham Pumping Station was part of a sewage disposal scheme drawn up for the corporation from 1894 that ended the practice of treating the River Severn as a sewer. The site was purchased for £675. Work on the system began in August 1896, and the foundation stone of the pumping station was laid on 21 October 1898. Construction was delayed by the lack of working drawings, by a strike of bricklayers, by a crack in an engine casting caused while it was en route by rail from W.R. Renshaw & Co at Stoke-on-Trent, and by problems with the 30 ft (10m) deep sewer through Longden Coleham. The engines were first steamed in November 1900, and the engine house was formally opened on New Year's Day 1901. Renshaw's engines were meticulously maintained and pumped sewage until the installation of electric pumps in 1970, shortly after they had been recorded on a 45 r.p.m. record.[17]

West of the factory was a timber yard with a steam-powered sawmill, established by 1817 when it was occupied by William Hazledine. It was taken over by William Blockley, who lived nearby, employed more than 20 men in the 1850s, and was succeeded by his son John. The site remained in commercial use until the 1990s.[18]

The three-storey, eight-bay block called Terrace Building has a 51 ft 6 in (15.7m) frontage to Longden Coleham. The shallow depth of the building lends credence to the traditions that it was part of a tannery, probably a drying shed with louvred openings between the piers, that one Hugh Sylvester intended to convert to a brewery. After being crippled by a fall, he adapted it as tenements and emigrated to Pittsburg. The conversion had taken place by 1829 when 15 tenements in the building were sold.[19] Some of the ground-floor tenements were adapted as shops.

The most celebrated manufactory in Coleham, the foundry of William Hazledine, was established about 1796. By 1840 it extended from Terrace Buildings to the *Crown Inn*, a distance of some 258 ft (93m), with a clock tower bearing the date 1805, the year when Hazledine completed his contract to supply the ironwork of the Pontcysyllte Aqueduct. A steam engine blew the cupola furnaces and powered machine tools, and at its peak the foundry employed 400 workers. After Hazledine's death in 1840 it passed to his foreman, William Stuttle I, whose name appears on the bridges at Eaton and Craigellachie. Some buildings were disused by 1856 and Stuttle's son's executors sold the stock in 1872. Arthur Lowcock, who manufactured economisers for steam engine boilers, leased the foundry in 1878, but occupied only two-thirds of the premises, the

58 The building that comprises Nos 117-22 Longden Coleham which is the only surviving part of the foundry established by William Hazledine in the 1790s, that was subsequently managed by William Stuttle and Arthur Lowcock.

remainder, east of the entry to Greyfriars Bridge, being adapted to other uses. After Locock's business closed in the 1920s the shops and houses in Riverside Close replaced most of the foundry buildings, the only survivor of which is a three-storey, ten-bay structure (Nos 117-22) that was probably the fitting shop.[20]

A ferry linking Coleham with St Julian Friars was established by 1869, when an old man threw water over the ferryman, who prevented him collecting drinking water from the ferry steps. In 1878 Thomas Trouncer, the brewer, bought some of the foundry land and proposed to build a toll bridge but the corporation resolved to built a free bridge, and a Pratt truss, by the Cochrane Engineering Co of Dudley, opened on New Year's Day 1880. The ferry gave its name to Boathouse Yard, a group of five houses, one of which survived until the 1950s. The shops north of the bridge approach were built in 1960.[21]

The appearance of the *Crown Inn* (No 115), suggests that it dates from the late 17th or early 18th century. The property extends to the riverbank, and in the late 19th century it was a venue for rowers. There are 23 two-storey cottages (Nos 88-112) between the *Crown* property and the former brewery. Crescent View (Nos 88-90) has classical details, suggesting a mid-19th-century date, but the remainder are later, and may have replaced more prestigious buildings, including Severn Cottage, once the residence of Samuel Pountney Smith.

Trouncer's brewery was established in 1807, and in 1828 brewed 120 barrels daily from eight vats. William Hazledine's executors sold the site to Thomas and Thomas William Trouncer in 1845. Under three generations of the family, the firm acquired many licensed houses. The business became a limited company in 1894, and passed to the control of the head brewer, George Burbage.[22] Brewing ceased in 1955 and, after being used for packing eggs and storing greengrocery, the buildings were converted into apartments in the 1990s. The adjacent flats occupy the site of a malthouse.

59 A view of Longden Coleham from the opposite side of the River Severn showing the remaining building of Hazledine's foundry, the houses of the 1930s built on much of the foundry site, the *Crown Inn*, and, in the distance, Severnside House, designed by Samuel Pountney Smith and for a time his home.

The last of the factories that lined the Severn occupied the site on Kingsland Road, downstream from Rad Brook that is now a recreation area. Here in 1816-7 Charles Bage built a single-storey shed to accommodate looms for weaving linen cloth, a remarkable building, 90 ft (27.45m) long, with a brick vaulted roof spanning 30 ft (9.14m). It accommodated 30 hand looms and 24 power looms, worked by a steam engine. He employed 70 people, but the business did not prosper, and after his death in 1822 his widow closed the factory in 1826. Thomas Burr, a London plumber who moved to Shrewsbury about 1812, and made lead pipes in Beeches Lane, bought the site in 1829, and it was developed after 1836 by his sons, Thomas and William Burr. They purchased land on either side of Bage's premises, and by 1847 the complex included two steam engines, a rolling mill, a melting furnace and casting bed, a hydraulic pipemaking machine, and ovens for producing white lead and red lead. A 150 ft (46m) high shot tower was constructed in 1853. The

60   Tiles and stained glass ornamenting one of the houses facing Longden Road on the Lime Street estate, built in 1906-7.

works caused pollution across the centre of Shrewsbury. It closed early in 1894 and was soon demolished, the shot tower collapsing on 3 May 1894.[23]

The Lime Streets

Lime Street, formally named in 1913, and adjacent houses in Longden Road (Nos 67a-75) were built on a site formerly occupied by about 30 allotments. From about 1903 Thomas Pace widened the main road, and constructed houses that were among the last in Shrewsbury intended for sale to private landlords. Those on Longden Road, built in 1906-7, display the characteristic decorative features of the period, fiery red Ruabon bricks, with string courses of pressed bricks, mock timber-framing in the gables, tiled roofs, stained glass, and decorative tiles in the steps. The houses on the side roads are less ornate, and ten (Nos 2-20) have frontages of concrete blocks.[24]

The Way to Sutton

The old and new lines of the road to Meole Brace meet by the *Boar's Head* inn, where they are joined by the lane to Sutton, called Betton Street since the 1880s. Nine houses including Rose Villa and Rosehill (Nos 11/12) had been built on the western side by 1832. The Shrewsbury & Hereford Railway built a freight depot on the eastern side in the 1850s. Flats now occupy the site of the nine houses in Binnall Terrace, built in 1871. Sutton Lodge, a two-storey house in the Italianate style with a three-storey tower, was the home by 1881 of William Jones, a Welsh-speaking native of Llanbrynmair, who returned after migrating to Pennsylvania in the 1860s, settled in Shrewsbury, and in 1869 founded a malt business.[25] In 1888 he constructed the Belle Vue maltings on an adjacent plot. The maltings worked for a century, and have been adapted as offices.

Bynner Street, linking Sutton Lane with Trinity Street, was laid out by 1871. Its nucleus was the *Prince of Wales* public house, the present No 34, a double-fronted villa with classical detailing, dating from before 1861, and not the present *Prince of Wales* (No 30). The Belle Vue Maltings appear to have been built in the pleasure grounds of the original inn. In 1881 the only other houses were the detached villas (Nos 36-40), on the north side, but Hope Cottages (Nos 13-9) were built in that year, and there were 35 terraced cottages in the street in 1891.[26]

61 William Jones, the Welsh-speaking maltster from Llanbrynmair, who became a successful entrepreneur in Shrewsbury in the second half of the 19th century.

Sutton Lane resumes its original name beyond the bridge across the Shrewsbury & Hereford Railway and is lined with houses of the 1970s. In the 19th century it provided access to a nursery that by 1833 was worked by the Instone family. The Sutton Dale tennis club was established there in the 1920s, with 19 grass courts, a putting green and a pavilion big enough for dances, but after a dispute over Sunday play the courts fell into disuse before 1939.[27]

The Joint railways concentrated locomotive running shed activities in Shrewsbury at Coleham in the 1880s, and the grid of streets laid out in a single field south of the depot, described in 1927 as 'a suburb of about 100 working class houses chiefly occupied by railway men', has long been called the 'back of the sheds'.[28] The corner where Scott Street turns into Rocke Street follows the line of an ancient lane to Burnt Mill. By 1881 there were four houses in Sutton Terrace (Nos 1-4 Spa Street) and eight in Rocke Terrace (Nos 1-8 Rocke Street). There were 87 on the estate ten years later. Scott Street and Rocke Street were formally named in 1883 and Rea Street and Spa Street were taken over by the corporation in 1888. In 1888, 53 of the 82 heads of households worked on the railway. More than 40 houses were built by J. Parson Smith to designs by A.B. Deakin,

62 Railway workers' houses in the Gothic style: Hawarden Cottages in Rea Street, which bear the date 1883.

including Nos 1-23 Rocke Street, Hawarden Cottages (Nos 37-44 Rea Street) and Nos 1-11 Rea Street, all of 1883. Deakin was also responsible for Nos 28-31 Rea Street built in 1884, and for Nos 12-27 of 1885. Some but not all of the houses are of tunnel-back plan. Many are ornamented with yellow brick string courses, and Hawarden Cottages have Gothic doorways with trefoils in the spandrels. Cowper Cottages (Nos 29-30 Rea Street), dating from 1889, have an attic storey, Gothic doorways and drip moulds over leaded light windows. A mission of Holy Trinity parish, an Italianate building in Spa Street, was consecrated in 1886 'for the large colony that has recently sprung up in this neighbourhood chiefly composed of men engaged in the railway works'. Designed by Oswell and Smith, it was built of Lilleshall Co. bricks, roofed with Parson Smith's tiles, and decorated externally with terracotta by Cooper of Maidenhead, and internally with tiles from Craven Dunnill.[29]

Scott Street was described in 1927 as a morass, made worse by a nearby waste tip, and by traffic generated by 16 houses recently built beyond the railway bridge in Reabrook Avenue, where the council installed sewers in 1928. The area was regarded in 1935 as 'Shrewsbury's most modest suburb [...] one of those places one hears about but rarely', and in 1945 as a 'rather odd backwater'. There were about 30 houses in the avenue in 1939, and building resumed in 1959 when the Alverley Property Co. built 94 houses on the Grove estate.[30]

Belle Vue Road

Belle Vue Road was previously known as Meole Coleham. Building beyond the Sutton turning began in the early 19th century. No 23, with a Regency-style roof has a single-storey shop front added, in the manner of countless shops that line the radial routes out of London. Spring Terrace (Nos 25-9) built before 1832, is enclosed by a wall of large sandstone blocks, and was fashionable enough in the 1880s to attract J.L.Della Porta, the Italian founder of a Shrewsbury department store. Albafont House (No 31) is an imposing detached villa. The protruding bricks at the end of the adjacent three-storey terrace (Nos 33-9) suggest that its builder intended to extend it. This was probably Kempster's Terrace, built by 1831, which took its name from the landowner Charles Kempster.[31] The eight two-storey houses comprising Alton Terrace lie at right angles to the road, along a track that gave access to brickworks. Beyond them are Wilmington House and Rodwell, a semi-detached pair in the Italianate style,

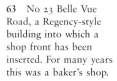

63 No 23 Belle Vue Road, a Regency-style building into which a shop front has been inserted. For many years this was a baker's shop.

and St Osburg's, a three-storey villa with adjacent workshops, that appear to be for coachmaking. Brick workings were also reached along the drive past a two-storey house (No 45) that was standing in 1832 and was for several generations the home of the Lea family, cab proprietors.

The west side of Belle Vue Road was built up between 1830 and 1880, with little regard for building lines. The timber-framed *Boar's Head* dates from the mid-17th century, and included a brewhouse, a malthouse and a skittle alley in the 1850s. There were four houses in its yard and eight, called June Cottages, along the adjacent Egland Lane. No 20 Belle Vue Road was licensed as a beerhouse, the *Engine & Tender*, from the 1850s, and in the 1890s was the headquarters of Shrewsbury Homing Club.[32] The six cottages in Child's Row, at right angles to the road, on the site of the modern bungalow (No 30), were built by 1861 and named after Charles Child who lived at No 32, a classically-proportioned villa. The adjacent house with Italianate detailing (No 34) was once Grosvenor Villa, while the pair adjacent to Holy Trinity church were called Milton Place.

Holy Trinity Church

Holy Trinity church, in St Julian's parish, was planned from 1835, and consecrated on 25 August 1837. On census Sunday in 1851, 550 people attended its evening service. A chancel designed by Samuel Pountney Smith was added in 1861, and a new nave, the work of A.E. Lloyd Oswell, in 1887, when it was reckoned that the population of the area had doubled in 50 years.[33] The adjacent vicarage dates from 1857. Trinity School was opened on Coronation Day 1838, and new buildings were added in 1866.[34]

Greyfriars Road was not laid out until 1914.[35] The four three-bay houses on an elevated bank beyond it were called Longner Terrace in the 1870s. Three groups of two-storey cottages extend to Belle Vue Gardens. Laurel Place (Nos 60/2) have classical detailing, as do those beyond, that include a shop bearing an ancient blue enamel *News of the World* sign. The corner house (No 76) was known as Belle Vue Villa or Shelfield. Beyond Belle Vue Gardens are Belle Vue Place (Nos 78-84), a three-storey terrace of four houses, and Bank Terrace (Nos 86-90), a two-storey range of three houses with Italianate detailing. Laurel Cottage (No 92) is a double-fronted two-storey villa, while the two-storey terrace, once called Rose Cottages (Nos 94-8), bears the date 1836.

64 Belle Vue Place, Nos 78-84 Belle Vue Road, probably built in the 1850s, and one of the more imposing groups of houses in the scattered ribbon development along the road.

65 Rose Cottages, Nos 94-8 Belle Vue Road, which bear the date 1836, and were some of the first houses to be built during the spasmodic development along this part of the main road.

Trinity Street and the Besford Estate

Trinity Street was built on the estate surrounding Besford Cottage (Besford House), which was built before 1832. The first phase of development was principally due to William Hotchkiss, who lived in the house in 1851 and farmed the adjoining 22 acres, and Daniel Climie, a Scots civil engineer involved with the Shrewsbury & Hereford Railway, who built the stations on the line to Crewe. Climie lived in Spring Terrace in 1851 and augmented his living by operating a nearby brickworks that employed 17 men. Building plots on land occupied by Hotchkiss, served by a new road, went on the market in 1853.[36] Climie built an estate with the same colour coding that he applied on the railway to Crewe, where he used blue brick for first-class stations, and red brick for second-class. The pivot of his development was the polychrome brick *Masonic Arms*. Flanking it on Belle Vue Road were four lofty blue-brick houses forming Honiton Terrace (Nos 47-53), named after his wife's birthplace. The Climies lived at

66 Honiton Terrace, the upmarket part of Daniel Climie's development in Belle Vue. The Climie family lived in the end house on the right.

67 Trinity Place, Nos 85-90 Trinity Street, the plebeian portion of Daniel Climie's estate.

No 53. At right angles were the 15 red-brick cottages of Trinity Place (Nos 85-90). Climie left Shrewsbury for Scarborough in September 1865, and his houses, yard and unused building land were offered for sale. The adjacent terrace, Nos 69-75 Trinity Street, dates from 1878, and the large houses with classical detailing at the end of the street (Nos 55-60) from the 1850s.[37] Among their inhabitants in 1861 were George Valducci, a stone carver, who had moved from London in 1856 to set up business at the General Cemetery, and William Stuttle II, the ironfounder.

William Hotchkiss, 'proprietor of houses', lived in 1861 in one of 17 houses that had been completed in 'Hotchkiss Buildings', now Besford Square, at the Belle Vue end of Trinity Street. His building materials were offered for sale in 1866, together with the property that comprised the 12 houses on the southern side of the square, five on the eastern side including the shop on the corner, and ten partially-completed houses backing onto Trinity Street, which were occupied by 1871. By 1871 Hotchkiss was working as a bricklayer and had moved to Drawwell Street.[38] Thomas Cadwallader occupied the shop (No 57) by 1866 and his family were grocers there until the early 20th century. The matching house (No 59), rising to four storeys, with the attic floor lit by a Diocletian window, was occupied for many years by Thomas Colley, a dairyman.

Richard Maddox moved to Besford House in the late 1850s. Shrewsbury-born, he regarded himself in 1861 as a 'retired draper' but in 1862 he established a business in High Street that became a department store employing 300 people. In 1882-3 he laid out a drive, with a lodge cottage that accommodated his Welsh coachman, enabling him to access Besford House without passing along Trinity Street. A.B.Deakin rebuilt Besford House in 1891. Maddox came to own Trinity Place and most of Besford Square. He died childless, after which his partner, William James Scott, husband of his wife's niece, moved to Besford House. Scott died in 1907 and his wife in 1909, and the estate was sold to Henry Evason, of Rose Hill, Betton Street, like Maddox and Scott, a member of the Abbey Foregate Congregationalist church. He sold the house to the Atcham Board of Guardians who converted it to a children's home in 1911. Evason made land available for widening Trinity Street, and in 1914-5 built the two terraces on its southern side, Nos 20-29 and Nos 32-41, whose original name, Besford Avenue, remains on a faded signboard. He laid out five building plots for his family, called Linden Gardens, at the end of the street.[39]

Richard Maddox also owned the cemetery alongside the drive to Besford House, which passed to Evason in 1910. The cemetery opened in 1852 and was intended for the Dissenters, but after 1856 many Nonconformists used the General Cemetery. The burial chapel in the Early English style, completed in 1857, was occupied as a dwelling in the early 1920s, but in 1929 was taken over by the Apostolic Mission, that had previously met in Frankwell. The first interment for many years, and probably the last, took place in 1930. The church was destroyed by fire in 1943, and in 1948 was rebuilt, nearer to Belle Vue Road, using materials from a disused chapel owned by the same denomination at Minsterley.[40]

Brougham Square, an enclave of unpretentious two-storey cottages approached from Trinity Street, was laid out during the 1860s, before the building of the adjacent Belle Vue Maltings, and was probably named after Henry, Baron Brougham & Vaux, the great lawyer, who died in 1868. Nos 1-7 Brougham 'Place' were built by 1871, and most of the other 20 houses were erected during the following decade. Nos 15/16 in the eastern corner display elements of timber construction, and may have been adapted from an earlier, non-domestic building.

The Limes Estate

Opposite the drive to Besford House is the estate, extending to Longden Coleman, centred on The Limes, a villa built by 1832. It was developed by the architect and builder Samuel Pountney Smith, who by 1851 was living at Severn Cottage, Coleham. He sold Severn Cottage in 1852, probably because he had built Severnside House, the three-storey, Mansard-roofed dwelling on the opposite side of the road. In 1861 he appears to have been building the adjacent terrace, in which a wagon arch gave access to his yard and brickworks. The present Coleham Row occupies the site of cottages, built by 1832, which formed part of his property. By the late 19th century there were 24 cottages on the estate, Nos 63-6 and 82-3 Longden Coleham, and Nos 1-9 Coleham Row.[41]

About 1862 Smith moved to the Limes itself, but put it on the market in 1869. In 1871 it was occupied by Thomas Barry, an Irish clergyman and schoolmaster who accommodated 11 boarder pupils, but Smith returned soon afterwards. In 1876 his daughter's marriage to a clergyman attracted much attention. Detonators were set off on the railway, and the wedding presents included one from Smith's cottager tenants. Smith took to the Limes oak panelling from the Old Mansion in the Square, from St Mary's church, and from country mansions that he refurbished.[42] In 1891 it was the home of Capt. George C.P.Freeman, chief constable of the county force from 1890, who in 1900 led his men in a ceremonial bicycle ride to Wellington. From 1892 Wyndham Deedes established there a boarding school that he transferred to Millmead, and between 1899 and 1914 it was occupied by William Drew, headmaster of the school that became Kingsland Grange. The next occupant was Mrs F.M.K. Bulkeley-Owen, widow of the founder of All Saints, Castlefields. The estate was offered for sale in 1914. By 1925 The Limes was a nursing home, and still served that purpose in 1955, but was subsequently adapted as government offices.[43]

By 1871 Smith had built two remarkable pairs of semi-detached houses, Myndton, Morfe, Kinnersley and Wilderhope, in a French Renaissance style, with Mansard roofs, polychrome slatework, and re-used ancient panelling within. They were let to clergy, army officers and widows and spinsters living on investments. The Revd Thomas Butler, canon of Lincoln, and father of the author of *Erewhon*, lived at Wilderhope

House in the mid-1880s, and his daughter, founder of St Saviour's Home, remained there until her death in 1916.[44] The Royal Army Pay Corps then occupied the other three houses, and all four remained in military use during the following decades.

Belle Vue Gardens

The property south of the Limes evolved as a residential street, Belle Vue Gardens, in the late 19th century. In the 1830s the track that became the road gave access to 11 allotments to the south, to a field on the northern side in which was a kettle hole, and to six allotments, abutting those on the site of Lime Street. The adjacent houses on Belle Vue Road (Nos 54-98) were built by 1875 and by 1871 the track was called Belle Vue Gardens and was lined by nine houses. The first was Bank House, home of a retired farmer John Parker, beyond which was the drive to Chatsworth, a three-storey mansion, occupied by George Mitchell, an outfitter whose shop was on Pride Hill.[45] A nursery now occupies its grounds. Six double-fronted, two-storey houses with classical detailing (Nos 51-61) were also built by 1871. The next houses, erected between 1875 and 1881, comprise one of Shrewsbury's suburban curiosities, a pair of lofty three-storey dwellings (Nos 28/30), each with a tower with a louvred upper storey, having Mansard roofs, with polychrome slating and first-floor balconies. The garden of No 28 is adorned by the stone tracery of a church window in the Decorated style.[46] The pair were probably built for the printer and antiquarian, Henry Adnitt, who was living there in 1881 when they were known as Montague Villas. The pair were called Montreux in 1891, and ten years later, when Adnitt had departed, No 30 was Thornlea and No 28 Montreux. Edward Burley of Tankerville Street built Burley Street, originally Carlton Terrace, eight brick cottages, between Bank House and the drive to Chatsworth, in the mid-1880s.[47] In 1901 they were occupied by a cross-section of Shrewsbury's working class – a brewer, a coachman, a police constable, an upholster, a joiner, a railway carriage painter, a bricklayer and a carpenter.

68   One of the two houses (No 28 Belle Vue Gardens), making up the pair once called Montreux, built in the late 1870s. The purpose of the tower with the louvred upper storey is not evident.

The cul-de-sac was extended to the limit of the property in 1888, the road beyond the present Nos 41 and 30 being wider than the original. The first buildings on the extension were Wrekin View (Nos 18/20) of 1891, The Ferneries (Nos 22/24) of 1892, and St Saviour's Home (No 29), designed by Lloyd Oswell, and dedicated on 31 March 1890. The charity was founded in 1882 by Miss Butler of Wilderhope House, and was made over in 1896 to the Waifs and Strays Society, who ran the home, with a matron and sub-matron and about 15 inmates, until it moved to Sutton Road in 1929. The extended cul-de-sac was taken over by the town council in 1891, and in 1893 negotiations commenced with landowners concerning its extension to Longden Road, on which work began in May 1896.[48] The first building on the extension was a three-storey detached house (No

69 A stone window in the Decorated style, doubtless removed from one of Shropshire's larger medieval churches during restoration in the 19th century, that is displayed in the garden of No 28 Belle Vue Gardens. The printer and antiquarian Henry Adnitt may have been responsible for its presence there.

25) with Baroque detailing combined with mock timber-framing, and copious displays of stained glass. In 1901 there were 13 houses and a pair under construction in Belle Vue Gardens, excluding Burley Street. There were 18 in 1901, 24 in 1903, and 45 in 1938. Ruabon bricks give the road an Edwardian appearance.

During the First World War the corporation discussed with Lord Barnard's agents the prospects for roads and building plots between Belle Vue Gardens and Longden Road. They gave priority to the latter, and expansion south from Belle Vue Gardens did not begin until the 1930s. Belle Vue Gardens was linked to extensions of South Hermitage and Oakley Street by Raby Crescent, named after the peer's home in Co. Durham. The streets were formally named in 1935, but few houses had been built by 1939 and building plots were cultivated as allotments during the Second World War. In 1958 the county council resolved to build a care home, Briarfields, on the eastern side of Raby Crescent. Uppington Avenue, named after the centre of Lord Barnard's Shropshire estates, joins Belle Vue Gardens at the end of the 1888 cul-de-sac, and was laid out in 1937.[49]

The Hermitages

The name Hermitage may derive from the settlement of a medieval ascetic in the area, but its modern uses come from the house called The Hermitage (No 81 Belle Vue Road), which with its neighbour, Belle Vue House (No 83), is a complex brick structure of three-and-a-half storeys, ornamented with timber framing and stained glass. In the early 19th century the house, or its predecessor, was used as a lunatic asylum by James Johnson, son-in-law of a Mr Proud of Bilston, a celebrated carer of the mentally disturbed. In the mid-19th century the Hermitage was occupied by George Edward Leake, whose properties in the Belle Vue area were sold in 1889 after his death. The streets named after the Hermitage lie on

70 Ingardine, named after a hamlet in Farlow, on the Clee Hills, a substantial semi-detached house built on West Hermitage between 1896 and 1901.

the opposite side of the main road, on a six-acre site that in 1832 consisted of 52 allotments. By the summer of 1896 roads were laid out and sewers, gas and water pipes installed. An auction of 32 building sites attracted fervent interest but no more than eight were sold.[50] By 1900, 14 plots on North Hermitage, South Hermitage and West Hermitage had been used for semi-detached pairs, and three were occupied by detached dwellings, including the very large, three-storey Twyford on the main road, built in 1897. The only houses bearing a date are Mona Villas, a two-storey semi-detached pair of 1899.

The Oakley Cottages Estate

Oakley Street derives its name from John Oakley, a grocer who bought a plot called Banky Piece in 1801 and erected two substantial houses called Oakley Cottages, both now demolished, that stood in the present Oakley Street on either side of the junction with Oak Street. By the early 19th century there was a terrace of about 14 small cottages, later Nos 102-128 Belle Vue Road, on the site of the flats of the 1960s at the north end of Drawwell Street. In 1859 the Oakley Cottages estate was sold to the Shrewsbury Freehold Land Society, probably because construction of the railway to Welshpool was imminent. A straight road, at first Junction Road, but by 1881 Oakley Street, replaced the circuitous drive to the existing villas and was lined with plots suitable for similar dwellings. Two other streets were laid out, Oak Street which joined Oakley Street between the two existing villas, and Cemetery Road, later Drawwell Street, facing the railway. Members balloted for 44 plots on 3 April 1860.[51]

The society laid out small plots on Cemetery Road where there were 20 houses by 1871. Fieldwork suggests that they represent 13 different builds, the most substantial being the four houses (Nos 18-21) once called Myrtle Cottages. Between 1910 and 1941 the principal connection between the Shropshire & Montgomeryshire Railway and other railways was on the wide section of track facing the road.[52]

The most prestigious plot on the estate was on the main road where a mansion, called Oakley Manor, was built in the 1860s to the design of Samuel Pountney Smith. The first occupants were women living on investments. In 1895 it was bought by Henry Exell Rogers, partner in Richard Maddox's department store. Rogers died in 1913 and between the autumn of 1914 and 1917 the house served as the St John's Auxiliary Military Hospital. Between the wars it was the home of Joseph Della Porta, the department store owner, and Vincent Greenhous, the motor dealer. It was requisitioned by government in 1939, occupied by the British Aluminium Co. until 1943, then as an army officers' mess, and from 1962 until 2004 as local government offices.[53]

Oakley Street proved attractive to retired tradesmen and to people living on investments, and grew from eight houses in 1871 to 13 in 1891. Holly Lodge, in an extravagant Italianate style in red and yellow brick with a stone port-cochère, framed by a magnificent cedar of Lebanon, was built before 1871 for John Calcott, a retired shoemaker, and was later occupied by John Blockley, the timber merchant. Cleveland House and Derwent House, a semi-detached pair in polychrome brick, were designed by A.B.Deakin in 1877. The plots in Oak Street were smaller and were occupied more quickly. There were 12 houses in 1871 and 25 in 1881. As was usual on a freehold land society estate, they were built in small groups and display varied architectural styles: Gothic on Nos 11, 15 and 28, and classical on Nos 7, 9, 14 and 16, with much polychrome brickwork. The garden walls of the original Oakley Cottages remain. Oakley Street was extended in the 1930s to join South Hermitage.

71 Drawwell Street, originally Cemetery Road, part of the Freehold Land Society's Oakley Cottages estate, laid out in 1860. The 20 varied houses appear to represent 13 different builds. The street was the least prestigious of the three that comprised the estate, which is doubtless why it faced the railway to Welshpool, opened in 1861. To the left of the line were the tracks of the Shropshire & Montgomeryshire Railway line to Welshpool, and between 1910 and 1941 this was the principal interchange between the light railway and the main line system.

Belle Vue Road, South

South of the dissenters' cemetery are two, two-storey terraces with classical detailing, May Place (Nos 61-5 and Nos 67-73). No 77 is a Regency-style villa with a hipped roof, at right angles to the road, next to The Hermitage (Nos 81/3).[54] The adjacent semi-detached pairs (Nos 85-91), once Ormonde Place, were built about 1850 by the Bourlay family. Guillaume Bourlay, who taught dancing at the court of Louis XVI, fled from the French Revolution and by 1803 had settled in St John's Hill, where he taught dancing, and his wife made overcoats and stays. His descendants still taught dancing and lived in Belle Vue in 1960. Belle Vue Cottages (Nos 93-103) have scarcely any land at the rear because a gravel pit lay immediately behind. The six were sold in 1896 for £715. The ten houses in Glendower Terrace (Nos 2-20 Havelock Road), were built in 1911-2 on the southern rim of the pit. They were sold as part of the portfolio of Mrs E. Pugh in 1916 when the gross rental was £182 p.a.[55]

In the 1830s Hawthorn Road and Havelock Road were lanes linking scattered houses amongst the fields. The former provides access to the Regency-style Oak Lodge, and after three right-angle bends joins the latter near a former cobbler's workshop. There were seven houses in Hawthorn Road in the mid-1880s and 16 by 1903. It was taken over by the council in 1905.[56]

Havelock Road was called Berwick Road in 1871. South of the gravel pit Thomas Groves built two imposing yellow brick semi-detached pairs, called Brampton, Darton, Vectis and Egerton, in 1881. The latter was the home in old age of Thomas Deakin. Nelson Place (Nos 32-42) bears the date 1910. Randlay bricks are visible in the garden wall of No 32. Most of houses on the eastern side were built by 1850. Those in Berwick Place (Nos 7/9a) are three-storey houses in the classical style, with a verandah, and the plate of 'F. Bourlay, Dancing Master' alongside the front door of No 7. Edwardian wings obscure the early 19th-century core of Strathlyne (Nos 11/3). The

72 Darton House, one of four semi-detached houses built in 1881 near the gravel pit in Havelock Road by Thomas Groves. The similar Egerton House was the home in his latter years of Thomas Deakin.

six two-storey houses with herringbone lintels and classical doorcases adjoining the junction with Hawthorn Road were once called Belle Vue Place.

A bridge over the railway to Welshpool gives access to Montague Place, on a triangular 'island' surrounded by railways after the completion of the P.S.N.W.R. in 1866. In 1878 Henry Treasure planned a road that continued the old lane to a bridge over the railway to Hereford. Its dominant feature is a terrace of 16 houses (Nos 5-20) built in 1879 in red brick, with sandstone drip moulds, a string course of pressed bricks with relief diamond patterns, and lofty stacks in a Tudor style, topped by yellow octagonal chimney pots, and carved bargeboards on the end gables. Among the houses opposite, No 42 is distinguished by string course of terracotta plaques and decorative tiles in its porch. Bridgend, bearing the date 2001, is a well-observed pastiche of the 1879 terrace. The varied houses in the western part of Montague Place include Olive Cottages (Nos 48-9) of 1901.[57]

The *Belle Vue Tavern* on the main road, parts of which are in the Arts and Crafts style, was known as the *Plough* for more than a century from the 1860s but has reverted to its original name. The semi-detached pair Glynne Villa and Weston Lodge (Nos 125/7) were built in 1880, while the detached Strathearn was an exercise in the Queen Anne style by A.B. Deakin completed in 1888. Lexden Gardens, the adjacent terrace of four substantial houses of the 1880s, remains separately numbered. No 1 was the home of T.H. Burd whose books, lustre ware and oriental antiques were auctioned in 1905, while No 4 was at first a girls' school.

73 Berwick Place, the terrace built before 1832 on the lane that was later named Havelock Road. No 7 on the left bears a plaque indicating that it was the home of 'F.Bourlay, dancing master'.

74 The principal terrace in Montague Place, Nos 5-20, built in 1879 by Henry Treasure, on the 'island' in Belle Vue, surrounded by railways.

Belle Vue was missioned by the Primitive Methodist minister John Quarmby, who served in Shrewsbury from 1876-80, and the foundation stone of a chapel, with a red brick Gothic front and polychrome ornamentation, designed by John Wills of Derby, was laid in March 1879, and opened the following June. A school room was added in 1883. At the chapel's jubilee in 1929, a celebratory address by the revered American divine, Samuel Parkes Cadman, drew such crowds that it had to be delivered in the Abbey Foregate Congregational church.[58]

The land east of the Belle Vue Road, that slopes towards the Rea Brook, was a source of gravel in the 19th century, and remnants of quarries are visible from the modern Summers Gardens. The first cottages beyond (Nos 129-37) were called Hollywell Terrace in the 1880s. The *Grove* public house dates from 1866 and from the beginning made its own malt and brewed its own beer. Beyond is Grove Terrace, ten two-storey cottages (Nos 149-67) built by 1871.[59] Shrewsbury West station on the S.&.M.R., opened in 1911, stood close to the bridge.

Two roads give access to houses east of the main road within the old borough boundary. The properties on Brook Street are defined by the course of the old P.S.N.W.R., which suggests that it was laid out between 1866 and 1875 when it appeared on Tisdale's map. The approach to Brook Street is framed by Willow Cottages, 12 polychrome brick houses built by 1875. There were 24 houses on the north side of Brook Street by 1881, including three in Garden Cottages. Walter Deakin the architect, then a 26-year-old bachelor, was living in 1891 at No 1, which is inscribed 1877. Most of the houses are modest two-storey brick terraces, but Clyde Villa (No 21) is a double-fronted detached villa, the home of a retired army captain in 1881. Sussex House, a three-bay Italianate villa, is approached by a footpath from Sussex Drive, a post-Second World War development off Brook Street, and from Montague Place. It was called 'Mr Smith's new house' in 1881 and was the home of John Smith, a native of Camberwell, who made his living as a 'keeper of tolls'. Kemp's Eye in the mid-19th century was the home of a clergyman and then of a solicitor's clerk. In 1881 it was the centre of a 17-acre dairy holding that was sold in 1928 to make way for Kemp's Eye Avenue and Links Road, where there were 41 houses by 1938, mostly semi-detached pairs.[60]

Longden Road

Until the 1920s Longden Road was a lane between tall hedges, lined by half a dozen scattered cottages between Kingsland Road and the Cemetery. In 1916 the borough surveyor agreed with the representatives of Lord Barnard a strategy for the development of land between Belle Vue Gardens and Longden Road, including the widening of the latter, a task completed in the early 1920s.[61]

In 1832 there were about 50 allotments between Longden Road and Kingsland Road, in the centre of which stood Luciefelde, sometimes Leightonvilla, a Regency-style two-storey villa, in red brick with herringbone lintels and overhanging eaves, built in 1825 by William Leighton, who had prospered through his coaching business at the *Talbot Hotel*. His son, the Revd William Allport Leighton, served as a curate at St Giles and Holy Trinity, but after 1848 performed only occasional ecclesiastical duties. He built a tiny chapel in the garden where he held services with his fellow clergy. He was a botanist and antiquarian, and the chapel was floored with tiles from Wroxeter. By 1850 another villa, also called Luciefelde, had been built in the angle between Kingsland Road and Longden Road, and was occupied by Thomas Trouncer, the brewer. Building on the allotments began in the 1890s with the construction of the imposing three-storey pair (Nos 8/10), in brick, with stone dressing, mock timber-framing, hanging tiles and stained glass. No 10 was the home of Henry William Adnitt, stationer, archaeologist and joint secretary of the Horticultural Society, and was called Coney Green, after ancient field names. The Leighton family moved from Luciefelde in 1936 and the garden chapel was demolished in 1937, but the villa remains amongst the houses built on the allotments. The home of the Trouncers was adapted in 1938 as the *Pengwerne Hotel*, a 'charming country hotel in the town', but was demolished in 1997.[62] The entrance to Luciefelde Road from Longden Road is framed by two semi-detached pairs, each with a single gable filled with rustic weatherboarding, a feature repeated elsewhere along the road.

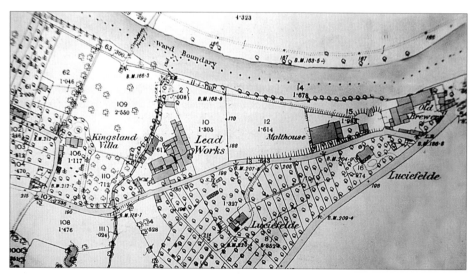

75   The 25 inch to the mile Ordnance Survey map of 1882, showing the junction of Kingsland Road and Longden Road, with Trouncer's Brewery, the adjacent maltings, Burr's lead works on the banks of the Rad Brook, and the two houses called Luciefelde, with their surrounding allotments, and the tiny chapel in the garden of the older house.

76 The house on the corner of Longden Road and Luciefelde Road, built in the late 1930s, with overlapping rustic weatherboards in its gable, a common feature of the more expensive houses built on the south side of Shrewsbury in that period.

77 While the Midland Red had a monopoly of suburban bus services in Shrewsbury, private operators ran buses to villages in the surrounding countryside, and one of them, J. Williamson, worked from a depot on Longden Road, as shown in this advertisement of 1947.

In 1920 three fields extended from the north-west side of Longden Road to the Rad Brook, between the allotments around Luciefelde and the hamlet of Red Barn. The first was occupied from the mid-1920s by Vane Road. A lane through the next field approached a pair of old cottages that have been replaced by later buildings (Nos 38/40 Longden Road). Four houses in the next field, including No 86, inscribed 'Eden Lacy 1926', had been built by 1928, and building of individual houses and small groups continued into the 1930s. A commentator in 1937 described the development of Longden Road as 'a steady filling up of gaps'.[63] Houses were interspersed with shops, and the building next to No 62 was for many years a bus depot.

The retaining wall alongside the south-west side of Longden Road beyond its junction with Belle Vue Gardens is evidence of the scale of widening and re-grading in the early 1920s. The houses in the two fields between Belle Vue Gardens and the Longden Green estate were built after 1928. They vary in size from No 11a, a very large detached dwelling with walls rendered and hung with tiles, to No 25, a tiny bungalow, and in style, from the Arts and Crafts in No 17 to the International Modern in No 11. The pairs framing the entrance to Arbourne Gardens are built of concrete blocks, as are three houses in the cul-de-sac itself.

Longden Green

The 164 houses on the Longden Green estate are 'homes fit for heroes to live in' built by the corporation immediately after the First World War, under Christopher Addison's Housing Act of 1919. The estate occupies the site of Wynne's Cottage, an 18-acre dairy farm, occupied from 1852 by Humphrey James, cow keeper, and subsequently by his son and grandchildren. One of its four fields, accessible from Oakley Street, was the venue in the 1880s for the shows of the Holy Trinity and Meole Cottage Garden Society.[64]

The borough council acquired the property in December 1918, and two months later revealed plans to build houses, interspersed with playgrounds and open spaces. The farmhouse was demolished and Alderman Thomas Deakin turned the first sod on Thursday 24 April 1919. High tenders caused delays, and the final decision to build was not taken until December 1919 after the proportion of cheaper houses had been increased. Construction was delayed by the bureaucracies controlling the distribution of materials, and by shortages of bricklayers and plasterers, but eight houses were occupied by the end of September 1920, and 51 by May 1921.[65] A year later 148 were finished, and the remaining 16 almost ready. A planned village institute overlooking the green was never built and its site was filled with old people's bungalows after the Second World War. The first tenants included men who complained about shell shortages on the Western Front when a parliamentary candidate spoke on the central green in 1922. The cost of each house, including land, exceeded a thousand pounds, and there were complaints that the designs, based on Raymond Unwin's pattern book, were too lavish.[66]

CHAPTER VII

The Parish of Meole Brace

The settlement centred on Meole Brace parish church has an unmistakable village quality, but the parish was bound up with Shrewsbury long before 1760. It included common land within the borough on Kingsland, and the ancient wayside hamlets of Porthill and Red Barn. The parish belonged to the diocese of Lichfield, but was transferred to Hereford in 1929. There were measures of independence, including a 'very smelly and inefficient' parish sewage works, built before 1901 that still operated in 1945. Its muddy remnants lie near Sutton Grange.[1]

The first houses in Meole Brace west of the borough boundary on the road to Hereford are Croft Cottages. The substantial houses beyond extending into Upper Road are of early 20th-century date, one of them (No 30) bearing the date 1909. Outside No 40 is a stone, conserved in 1930, inscribed 'From The Gates in Shrewsbury 1 mile, 1750'.[2] Opposite is Mile End Cottage (No 31), a Regency-style house near the site of the tollhouse that controlled the road to Hereford.[3] A second gate beyond the bridge controlled access to the turnpike road from the lane to Sutton. Most of the houses on the eastern side are of 20th-century date. The Shrubbery, a large semi-detached pair, was occupied in 1871 by an engine driver and, less surprisingly, a property-owning widow. Most of the terraced houses between Upper Road and Hereford Road, and on the eastern side of the latter, were built in the 1860s. By 1881 they included nine houses in The Terrace, seven in Rea Place, nine in Eaves's Cottages, 13 in Sutton View, nine in Poplar Cottages and seven in Laurel Cottages. Rose Cottages (Nos 107-21 Hereford Road) are inscribed 1873. Four pairs – Ivy Cottages, Darwin Cottages, Banbury Cottages and Lyle Cottages – were built in the 1880s, and four called Laburnum Cottages were under construction in 1891. A professional phrenologist, the son of a bricklayer, was living at No 2 The Terrace in 1901. Occupants of Poplar Cottages in 1881 included two engine drivers, two widow annuitants, a spinster dressmaker, a coal merchant and a clerk to a coal merchant.

The community around the crossroads where the road to Hereford was joined by Mill Road and the lane from Sutton was destroyed by the building of the by-pass in 1933. The new road crossed the Rea Brook on a concrete bridge, caused the demolition of the village inn and smithy, and then making its passage through two narrow fields bisected Upper Road and crossed the railways before running along the perimeter of the General Cemetery to its junction with the road to Longden. The landscape was further changed by the widening of Hereford Road in 1965, the construction of Hazledine Way in 1978, and the impact of the retail park and the A5/A49 by-pass in 1992.

In 1851 Meole Brace was a suburb, 'a continuation of pleasing villas and good residences, occupied by gentlemen and tradesmen, who have by the exertions of honest industry, acquired a tolerable share of the conveniences and comforts of this life'.[4] The community was centred on two public houses on the main road, near to which were a smithy, the village post office, a butcher's shop, and Evans's almshouses built in the

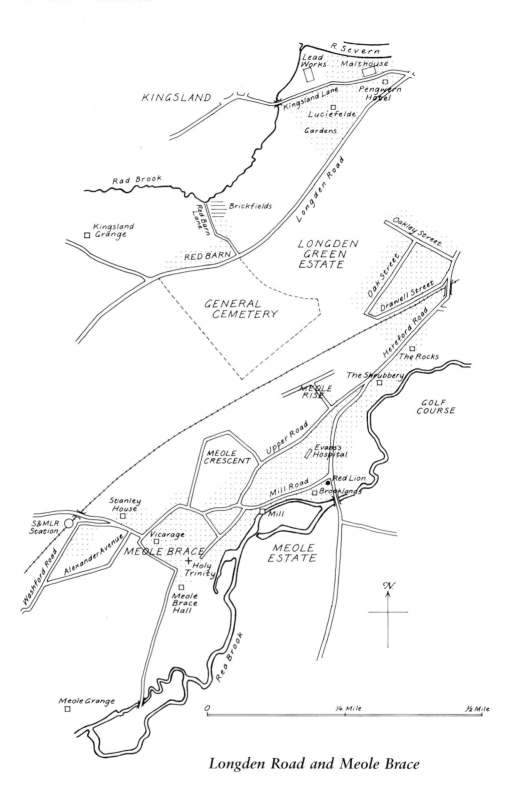

Longden Road and Meole Brace

1840s. An annual venison feast took place in the 1790s, and a quoits club flourished a century later. The *Bowling Green* inn was rebuilt about 1850 when its landlord was Richard Vickers, once driver of the mail coach to Holyhead. The green, 'this pleasant suburban place of recreation […] the scene of much harmless amusement', had existed 'longer than the oldest inhabitant can even pretend to remember'. The inn had alleys for skittles and ninepins and boxes for pigeons, and held an annual tea party in July. When it became a private residence in 1860, a newspaper commented 'as with coaches and coachmen so with the suburban bowling green, it is numbered with the things that were'.[5] The *Red Lion* was the venue for the annual wake, celebrated for the 125th time in 1863 with a supper in November. When the *Red Lion* was demolished to make way for the by-pass a licence was granted to *Brooklands*, a private house, apparently built in the 1870s by William Hughes of Meole Brace mill as his retirement home. The landlord in the late 1930s hired out Rolls Royces, while in 1937 a garage was built alongside the by-pass, close to the Meole Brace Fish Bar and Café which had 'a pretty tea garden'.[6] The golf course, established in 1891, was extended in 1903 and 1921, and a new club house was built in 1934. The club moved to Condover after the building of Hazledine Way in 1978 reduced the size of the course.[7]

The village of Meole Brace, isolated by the by-pass, retains its rural atmosphere. The medieval parish church was replaced in 1799 by a brick building that was succeeded in 1869 by the church of the Holy Trinity, by Edward Haycock II, in Redhill and Shelvock stone, with tiles by Maw & Co in the porch, and glass by Morris & Co., designed by Ford Madox Brown, Sir Edward Burne-Jones and William Morris himself. Much of the cost was born by Richard Juson, later of Monklands, who grew up in Meole Brace and made a fortune in Canada.[8] The Bather family, lords of the manor and owners of over 100 acres in the township in the 19th century, enjoyed the temporalities of the parish church. Family members were incumbents for 110 of the 125 years after 1778. Archdeacon Edward Bather established a National School on Vicarage Road which moved in 1861 to a purpose-built school that had a life of almost a century before it was replaced in January 1960.[9]

Meole Mill, powered by 'the Rea Brook which meanders through the rich meadows covered with fruitfulness and studded with plantations', was worked in 1851 by William Hughes, who had four employees in 1871. Ten years later he had moved to The Brooklands, and his son Henry Arthur Hughes worked the mill which was converted to roller mill operation, and was reckoned a considerable business when it was offered for sale in 1908. In 1912 it was adapted by the Shrewsbury Ice Factory & Cold Storage Co. to supply ice to butchers but closed during the Second World War.[10]

The village was inhabited largely by people living on invested incomes or working directly or indirectly in agriculture. It includes several very old houses, including the much-altered 'Ye Olde House' on Mill Lane, a pair inscribed 'MBP 1735' on Vicarage Road, and the tiny cottages in Church Row, occupied in 1881 by two labourers, a gardener, a sewing mistress, a police constable and a shoemaker. More houses were constructed in the second half of the 19th century for people living on investments. Stanley House was built by 1875 and Nos 6 and 7 Mill Lane date from 1893. Those living in the village in 1881 included Robert Hyde, a woollen manufacturer from Stalybridge, at the Sycamores, Robert Muckleton, a retired Shrewsbury mercer, at Melville House, and, at Stanley House, Anna Maria Atkinson, a 49-year-old widow, whose two daughters had been born in India. Some smaller houses were occupied by those who ministered to the needs of the wealthy: gardeners, grooms, coachmen, butlers and laundresses.

Church Road leads south from Holy Trinity past Meole Brace Hall, home of the Bather family in the 19th century, and of the botanist J. Cosmo Melvill from 1904. Fieldhouse Drive was an early post-Second World War venture of Fletcher Estates, whose managing director, Roy Fletcher, lived at nearby Meole Grange.[11] Maesbrook, a large house of 1912, now a nursing home, overlooks the dried-up leets of Pulley Mill. It replaced the home of the novelist Mary Webb, who lived there from about 1901 until her marriage to Henry Webb at Holy Trinity church on 12 June 1912. For a decade she was a familiar figure riding in a trap through Meole Brace, where her father George Meredith was a churchwarden. She only began writing novels after she moved with her husband to Weston-super-Mare.[12]

On the northern edge of the village the part of Upper Road west of the by-pass, was built up from the 1880s. Shane's Cottage and Oriel Cottages (Nos 27-31) bear the inscription 1888. The six houses in Fairfield View (Nos 7-17) were occupied in 1891 by a solicitor's clerk, an independent spinster, a farm labourer, a warehouseman at Burr's lead works, an insurance agent and a music seller's assistant. The houses on the west side were built after 1901.

The streets alongside the railway west of Stanley Lane were also built from the 1880s. The Red House, on New Road, now Washford Road (No 1), a three-bay polychrome house with some stained glass, dates from 1882. There were six houses on the road in 1891 including Holly Cottages (Nos 9/11) which bear the date 1888. Victoria Road was laid out but apparently not named by 1885 when Eaton View (Nos 12/14), a semi-detached pair ornamented with terracotta plaques, was built. There were 30 houses on the two roads in 1901, and four under construction. Building on Alexandra Avenue had begun by 1916, but most of its semi-detached pairs and detached bungalows were built after the First World War.[13] Evenwood (No 45) dating from 1938 is an unusual chapel-like building. Meole Brace station, by the railway bridge, opened in 1911 by the S.&.M.R., offered occasional trains to Abbey station.[14]

78   A five-storey block of flats in Moneybrook Way, Meole Brace, built for Shrewsbury Borough Council by George Wimpey & Co. in 1954, using a poured concrete construction system.

During the 1920s and '30s Icke & Rowson built three estates totalling over 230 houses that initially were the cheapest in Shrewsbury. In Meole Crescent, linking Upper Road with Vicarage Road, are almost 100 houses in sixes, fours and pairs, mostly in smooth-cast decorated with brick diamonds and mock timber-framing. They were said to be 'suitable to the needs of the average working man', and cost as little as £475. Meole Walk, north of Vicarage Road, developed in 1936-7, is a cul-de-sac, where semi-detached houses with roofs of asbestos tiles cost £495 or £550. Meole Rise, on the site of allotments, west of Upper Road and north of the by-pass, was constructed from 1937, and consists of 96 houses, mostly semi-detached pairs.[15]

The principal development in Meole Brace between 1945 and 1960 was the construction of the council's Meole (or

Moneybrook) estate, on a 50-acre site between Hereford Road and the Rea Brook. It was built at speed, the first contract for 196 houses being let to Bryants, the Birmingham contractors, in June 1954. Its most notable feature is a series of blocks of flats, five of five storeys, one of four storeys and two of three storeys, built by George Wimpey & Co., using a system involving pouring liquid concrete into shuttering that was erected to the full height of the blocks. Salop County Council opened the secondary school, while the estate was being built, in September 1956.[16]

Red Barn

Red Barn, an ancient wayside hamlet on Longden Road, consisted in the 19th century of about a dozen cottages, two public houses, the *New Inn* and the *Red Barn*, and a brickyard in the valley of the Rad Brook was worked in 1826 by the cartographer, Americus Hitchcock. In 1851 several brickmakers lived amongst neighbours who were mostly farm labourers, but brickmaking ceased by 1871. In 1891 most householders found employment in Coleham, as railwaymen, foundrymen, brewers and lead workers. One terrace of tiny cottages (Nos 130-6) remains, and several old cottages, two with Gothic doorways, stand in Red Barn Lane. The *Red Barn* public house was rebuilt in 1935-6.[17]

The General Cemetery, established in Meole Brace parish after Ranger's report on the sanitary condition of Shrewsbury had drawn attention to the dangers caused by overcrowded burial grounds, was consecrated on 25 November 1856, when some burials had already taken place. The chapel was designed by Samuel Pountney Smith. The cemetery was enlarged in 1899, and again in the 20th century, and remains a rich source for Shrewsbury's history, with memorials to leading figures in public life, enlightening inscriptions to less-well-known people, and simple, evocative stones commemorating the dead of the Second World War of many nationalities.[18]

Roman Road

On the corner of the 1933 by-pass and Longden Road are two houses (Nos 63/5) with stylish Art Deco features. The by-pass follows an earlier lane, now Roman Road, whose original course provides access to Kingsland Grange, a substantial house with mock timber-framing constructed in 1884 by Henry Treasure, the builder. In about 1904 he went to live on the Welsh border, and in 1910 W.B.C.Drew moved there with the boarding school he had founded at The Limes 11 years earlier. Kingsland Grange is now wholly a day school.[19]

On the western side of the by-pass is The Ferns, a large house now a nursing home, that probably pre-dates the Second World War, and the Priory School, built as the Priory School for Girls, designed by A.G. Chant, and opened in 1939. The land opposite, where Priory Ridge was built from the 1950s, was previously the playing field of the Priory Boys' School.[20]

In 1930 the houses along Roman Road, included Clonard and Tregwyn, approached up a common drive, York Cottage, Canonvale and Canonvale Cottages. Tregwyn was the home of Herbert Francis Harries, saddler, and borough councillor who acted as honorary Chief Constable in the borough between 1916 and 1918. Plots were developed by James Kent Morris and W. A. Sherratt, and in 1937 it was observed that 'nearly all frontages on by-pass to Porthill Road have been taken up by a good class of detached and semi-detached houses'.[21] Ridgebourne Road linking Roman

Road with Radbrook Road, was lined by 1938 with 20 houses in a comfortable style derived from Arts-and-Crafts, most of them set amongst rhododendrons, copper beeches, cedars and wild garlic. Frank Shaylor designed No 21 in the International Modern style.

The estate that includes Grange Road, Grangefields Road and Grangefields, part of Bank Farm Road, and houses on a service road on Longden Road, was built on the land of the 141-acre Bank Farm, offered for sale in 1920. At the end of the summer building season of 1937 a housing estate was 'springing up' near the projected school for girls. In 1939 W.A. Sherratt offered semi-detached houses, claimed to be 'the prettiest in Shrewsbury', at between £700 and £800.[22] The rough- and smooth-cast pre-war houses have hanging tiles, mock timber-framing, rustic bargeboards, capacious bay windows and low-sloping tiled roofs. The estate was completed after 1945 and the plainer post-war houses can readily be recognised.

Kingsland[23]

In the Middle Ages Kingsland was part of the common pastures of the borough. Some land was enclosed by the mid-18th century, when recreational facilities were probably more important to townspeople than grazing rights.[24] Race meetings were held there until the Bicton course was laid out in 1729, after which the corporation enclosed an area where the subscribers could take the air, on foot, horseback or in carriages.[25] The Kingsland coffee house, a white building, kept by Abraham Johnson in the late 18th century, became a tea garden after 1800, with facilities for bathing, quoits, and bowls, and arbours with seats. From 1838 this became a private asylum 'offering to the higher classes of society the seclusion so desirable for their rank in life'. The building was replaced in the late 19th century by a pair of semi-detached villas (Nos 16-18 Canonbury). The tradition of resorting to Kingsland for leisure pursuits of all levels of respectability continued into the mid-19th century. In 1868 the ferry boats were overcrowded when hundreds flocked to see a fight between two females for a prize of five shillings.[26]

Kingsland was the venue every Trinity Monday for Shrewsbury Show, a procession of the trade guilds to their arbours, around which were enclosures for drinking and dancing. There was a maze by the shoemakers' arbour that remained until 1796 when a windmill that stood until 1861 was built on the site.[27] In the 19th century the show was attended by travelling showmen, whose attractions were open on the Sundays before and Tuesdays after the procession. The event declined during the Napoleonic Wars and in 1810 was said to be 'hastening to its oblivion', but leading townsmen revived it in the 1820s. The guilds lost their legal status under the Municipal Corporations Act of 1835, and a sparsely-attended show in 1836 provoked pessimistic predictions, but there was a further revival in the mid-1840s, followed by previously unimaginable growth after the opening of railways.[28]

The contingents in the procession, whose routes to Kingsland varied year by year, were headed by burlesque figures. Crispin and Crispianus led the shoemakers, the god Vulcan the smiths, and Peter Paul Rubens the house painters. King Henry I took part because he granted the town's first charter, but it is less clear why the tailors were led by Cupid and the Stag, the builders by Henry VIII, the cabinet makers by the Black Prince, or the flax dressers by Catherine of Aragon.[29]

The railways transformed the show into a regional event. In 1850 the arrival of more than 15,000 excursionists made the show the best for several years. In 1853, 42

79 A mid-19th-century view of the trades guilds' arbours on the common land at Kingsland.

special trains, besides regular passenger services, brought in 32,000 people. Increased attendances and growing intolerance of rowdy behaviour amplified condemnation of the show, particularly from evangelical clergymen. It was also criticised for being out of tune with popular culture, something that organisers countered by introducing new burlesque figures, such as Jenny Jones and Edward Morgan, characters in a popular song about the Vale of Llangollen composed by Charles James Matthews. By 1875 the annual show of the Shropshire Horticultural Society provided an impeccably respectable alternative.[30]

Kingsland was colonised first by institutions and then by villas. Thomas Farnolls Pritchard designed the Foundling Hospital that from 1760 accommodated orphans sent by the Thomas Coram Foundation in London, who were set to work manufacturing woollen cloth. The project was unsuccessful, and the hospital in London ceased to despatch children from December 1772. After several short-term uses, the building was acquired in 1786 for the six united Shrewsbury parishes who adapted it as a workhouse, of which the windmill was a part.[31] The parishes obtained a licence in 1821 enabling the establishment of a lunatic asylum in the east wing of the workhouse, which from 1835 was managed privately by the governor. There were 93 inmates in 1841, but it was found unsatisfactory by government inspectors in 1850, and had closed by 1853.[32] The six parishes became a union under the Poor Law Amendment Act of 1835, and a boy who grew up in the 1850s remembered seeing old men from the workhouse dressed in white smocks taking walks over Kingsland and sitting on riverside seats. Such indulgences were not permitted to paupers held by the Atcham union, but from 1871 the two unions were amalgamated, and the inmates from Kingsland transferred to Cross Houses.[33]

Villas, like the hospital, were constructed on enclosed land around the common. Kingsland House was built in the early 1790s for the lawyer Joseph Loxdale, on land leased from the corporation, that he eventually purchased in 1834. The house may have been designed by Thomas Telford. It was let after Loxdale's death, but in 1856 two-thirds of the building was taken down and rebuilt, and it became the home of John Loxdale, for 38 years clerk to Quarter Sessions, three times mayor, and the owner when he died of 200 dozen bottles of wine and five carriages. The 17-bedroom residence was sold in 1891 to the tanner, James Cock, who offered to let or sell it as a hunting box in 1909, but it remained in the ownership of his family until Shrewsbury School bought it in 1931.[34]

Kingsland Bank (No 6 Canonbury) was built for the Drapers' Company by Thomas Farnolls Pritchard, and by 1851 was the home of Charles Burr the lead merchant, who carried out radical alterations. His sister Jane still lived there in 1891. Severn Hill was probably built soon after Kingsland House, probably by William Rowton, a banker, who insured it in 1804. It was the home from 1821 of the dissenting minister the Revd James Craig, whose second marriage in 1832, when he was aged 65, was to the 20-year-old niece of William Hazledine's wife, who lived there as a widow until the 1880s. The governors of Shrewsbury School bought the house in 1891, but sold it almost immediately, while retaining some of its grounds, only to re-purchase it in 1924. Ridgemount, the other substantial villa in the area, previously 'Kingsland', 'Kingsland Castle' or 'Kingsland House', appears to have been built by the banker Peter Beck who insured it in 1802. It stood in a 16-acre property that he consolidated from several small plots. Ridgemount was bought and sold by Shrewsbury School in 1891, and re-purchased in 1921.[35]

In the 1850s, a master brickmaker James Jones, employing six men, a tobaconnist, a miller and an iron moulder, lived in houses around the guilds' arbours. The *Beehive* inn, for a period the *Severn House*, earned most of its revenue in Show week. Some new and substantial villas were constructed in the area. Rosemount (No 9 Canonbury), built before 1833 for the draper, John Woodall, was soon occupied by a private school that remained until the house was sold in 1898. Francis Ferrington, the headmaster, had 16 boarder pupils in 1871. In 1860 the gunmaker Samuel Ebrall built the Gothic Canonbury House where his widow remained in 1901.[36]

Kingsland was transformed by three interlinked events in the late 1870s and early '80s. First, the Home Secretary, using powers under the Fairs Act of 1871, consented on 6 March 1878 to a request from the corporation to abolish Shrewsbury Show. On Trinity Monday only a few straggling supporters followed the Black Prince and Peter Paul Rubens to Kingsland, and thereafter enthusiasts attempted, unconvincingly, to keep the Show alive in Abbey Foregate.[37] Secondly, Kingsland became accessible through the construction of a long-advocated bridge. The Kingsland Bridge Company was established in 1872, and obtained an Act of Parliament in 1873, but delays meant that another act had to be sought in 1880. The two-hinged arched bridge of 212 ft (64.6m) span was designed by Henry Robertson, the borough MP, and built by the Cleveland Bridge & Engineering Co. It was opened to toll-paying traffic on 30 July 1882, and remains a toll bridge.[38]

80 The *Beehive*, Kennedy Road, which, long before the road was laid out, was the hub of drinking activities at Shrewsbury Show. It was de-licensed about 1895, more than a decade after the Show ceased, and became a post office in 1913.

These developments were subsidiary to a complex series of events concerning Shrewsbury School and its relationship to the town. The school, esteemed in the reign of Elizabeth I, had declined in the 18th century, but was revived from 1798 by Samuel Butler, later bishop of Lichfield. His successor Benjamin Hall Kennedy, ensured that Shewsbury was included in the Public Schools Act of 1868, which created a new governing body that met for the first time in 1871. The headmaster from 1866 was the ambitious Henry Whitehead Moss, who was only 25 at the time of his appointment, and made the re-location of the school from the town centre the principal item on the governors' agenda.[39]

Friction between the governing body, the headmaster and the corporation was caused by the classical curriculum and by the obligation on the school to provide a free education to the sons of burgesses (although no new burgesses were created after municipal reform in 1834), but above all by proposals for re-location. The corporation favoured a site near Belle Vue Gardens, which Moss regarded as a vicious neighbourhood. He and the governors wished to move to Coton Hill, where buildings were to be designed by Samuel Pountney Smith. Their position was weakened when Moss administered 88 birch strokes to the son of John Loxdale in July 1874. A compromise was reached whereby the school would move to Kingsland, in spite of Moss's abhorrence of locating a public school in a workhouse, and the council would achieve its long-held ambition of developing the common land. The workhouse was sold to the governors for £8,000 in 1875, and the school acquired a further 10 acres from the corporation. The agreement drew criticism, one newspaper deploring 'the meddling and muddling and wholesale blundering which marked every movement of the secret committee system in the sale of the Kingsland property'. The school moved to Kingsland in April 1882, and the still-unfinished buildings were formally opened, in July, when old Salopians who attended were accommodated in spare bedrooms all over the town.[40]

The same week the council advertised 80 leasehold building plots on the former common. Within two years 27 lots had been let and 14 houses were completed or building.[41] Covenants ensured that no house worth less than £60 p.a. was built on the larger plots, while only houses worth £40 p.a. or more could be erected on the smaller ones. St Milburga's (No 29 Kennedy Road) was one of several houses built on double plots. The estate was called Kingsland Upper Road and Kingsland Lower Road until 1936 when the former area was named Ashton, Butler and Greville roads, and the latter Kennedy Road.

Kingsland gained impetus from the enterprise of the school's housemasters, who built and operated their houses as profitable businesses. It was remarked in 1884 that 'the School builders and master's houses formed a nucleus around which a large number of residences of the better class have arisen with surprising rapidity'.[42] While Sir Arthur Blomfield was adapting Pritchard's Foundling Hospital and designing School House (No 2 Ashton Road) in the Queen Anne style, and the college chapel in ecclesiastical Gothic, two housemasters, John Rigg and Charles Churchill, built boarding houses in what is now Ashton Road in 1882, and E.B. Moser added a third in 1886, all three designed by the London architect William White. In 1884 Moser invested in two houses for letting that were designed by Lloyd Oswell (Nos 3/15 Ashton Road). Over the next 50 years the school acquired more property and by the 1930s had a compact ring-fenced campus with room for development.[43] The school persuaded the council in 1895 to ensure that the *Beehive* would cease to be a public house, and the building became a post office in 1913.[44]

81 Ridgebourne House, No 33 Kennedy Road (now the Junior High School), built in 1885 by the younger James Cock, the tanner, using labour from the tannery and the design of an architect from Burnley.

Many substantial citizens built houses on Kingsland. One of the first was the solicitor E.G.S. Corser who moved to Lauruiston (No 5 Ashton Road), designed by A.B. Deakin in the Queen Anne style, with terracotta ornamentation. Abbotsford (No 11 Kennedy Road) was designed in 1889 for the printer W.W. Naunton by A.E. Lloyd Oswell, who shared responsibility with Samuel Pountney Smith for Ebor House (No 31 Kennedy Road), in the half-timbered style with encaustic tiles in its hall, the home of the gunmaker, Samuel Ebrall, and subsequently of two of Shropshire's chief constables. Ridgebourne House (No 33 Kennedy Road) was built in 1885 for the young James Cock, the tanner, designed by an architect from Burnley, and built by workers from the tannery, using bricks from J.C. Edwards of Ruabon, and tiles made by Parson Smith. The grandest of these grand houses was Cyngfeld (No 39 Kennedy Road), designed by Thomas Lockwood for the solicitor, banker and 'Lord High Everything Else' in county affairs, E. Cresswell Peele, and built in 1884, with fine brickwork, much half timbering, leaded light windows, and Peele's initials set in the abundant stained glass.[45] The building was sold in 1913, used during the First World War as a hospital, and served military purposes in the Second World War, before becoming a nurses' home in 1947.[46] Common bricks were taken to Kingsland from kilns at Copthorne along a tramway, built by Treasures in 1879, but more exotic materials were also used, roofing tiles by Parson Smith, bricks from the Lilleshall Co., terracotta from Ruabon, decorative tiles by Maw & Co. and fireplaces from Coalbrookdale. While it provided contracts for Shrewsbury's leading architects, some houses were designed by men from London, Liverpool and Chester. The roads were lined with beeches. Kingsland was described in 1936 as a suburb of 'magnificent houses in which live some of Shrewsbury's best known inhabitants'.[47] While the School has colonised some houses, there has been no significant office development, and Kingsland remains one of England's best-preserved High Victorian suburbs.

CHAPTER VIII

Frankwell and the Roads to the West

Frankwell is the most paradoxical of Shrewsbury's suburbs. It has the strongest identity, reflected in communal celebrations and mutual self-help in times of flooding, and the most distinguished legacy of domestic buildings from the distant past. In the 19th century it was the most densely populated of the inner suburbs, and yet was one of the slowest to expand.

Frankwell is a bridge-foot settlement, comparable with those of other European cities, with Sachsenhausen across the Main from Frankfurt for example. Water Lane leads to a ford over the Severn that was probably a crossing point in the early Middle Ages. The bridge of St George was built by the mid-12th century, and 100 years later was known as the Welsh Bridge. Celia Fiennes observed in 1698 that it was inhabited as well as fortified. J.M.W. Turner memorably recorded it in 1795 when John Carline and John Tilley were building its replacement further downstream.[1] Land arches of the medieval bridge remain near the Welsh Calvinistic Methodist chapel, designed by Thomas Tisdale, that opened in 1865.[2] The main roads beyond the Welsh Bridge were managed by a turnpike trust between 1758 and 1877. Frankwell's many inns catered for travellers from Shrewsbury's hinterland in mid-Wales. Frankwell accommodated noisy and polluting trades, and varied cargoes were handled in the warehouses on its quay.[3] Frankwell was in St Chad's parish, but had its own places of worship in the Middle Ages, the chapels of St George and St Cadogan.

82   Frankwell was a bridge-foot settlement, on the far side of the Welsh Bridge, painted by the Revd Edward Williams in 1787, less than a decade before its demolition.

Frankwell traditionally asserted a degree of independence from Shrewsbury as 'the little borough', and had institutions of its own in the 19th century. The Millington Club in the 1870s dined together, arranged musical entertainments, played football, and organised an excursion to Llangollen.⁴ The Woodfield Club was patronised by the Gould family who lived in the mansion of that name on Porthill.⁵ The Working Men's Club occupied the former *Prince of Wales* inn, providing tea and coffee, a reading room, a skittle alley, a billiard room and a bagatelle board, as well as arranging concerts and spelling bees, and a visit to Henry Robertson's house at Palé, Merioneth.⁶

Frankwell's outstanding feature is the range of timber-framed buildings that lines the main road. Evidence of the suburb's status in the Middle Ages is provided by the surviving half of a two-bay cruck-framed hall house (No 92), and by a semi-detached pair of early 15th-century houses (Nos 111-12), each with two-bay frontages with cusped up-and-down bracing and a side passage. Three 15th-century shops with jettied chambers above (Nos 22-25) were demolished in 1982.⁷ Architectural evidence abounds of Frankwell's prosperity during the reigns of Elizabeth I and James I. The building of 1576 that stood on the corner of New Street, until it was removed to Avoncroft Museum in 1970, was the *String of Horses* inn (Nos 26-7), although it housed a Co-operative shop in its latter years.⁸ The fellmonger's house (Nos 4-7) dates

83 A surviving land arch of the old Welsh Bridge, adjacent to the tyre depot that occupies the former Welsh Calvinistic Methodist chapel at Frankwell.

84 Evidence of medieval settlement in Frankwell: Nos 111-12, a pair of early 15th-century houses.

85 The architectural splendour of 16th- and 17th-century Frankwell: Nos 113-14, built around 1620.

from about 1590 and was built with first- and second-floor workshops about 70 ft (21m) long, above ground-floor shops. The square building with a jettied gable on the approach to the bridge (No 165) has been dated by dendrochronology to 1603, while No 127, of three bays and three storeyed, jettied at two levels, and with a magnificent first-floor great chamber, dates from 1610. One of the most imposing buildings in the suburb (Nos 113-14), built about 1620, was divided into residential accommodation to the north, with plastered walls, and business premises to the south.[9] A fine range of late 17th- or early 18th-century buildings lined the corner at the approach to the old Welsh Bridge, of which the *Anchor* inn remains.[10]

Frankwell's legacy of timber-framed buildings was less influential after 1760 than its inheritance of medieval burgage plots, laid out to a module of about two perches (33 ft, 10m), and approached from the street through passages. In the mid-19th century 12 plots were lined with sufficient houses to be numbered as courts. Many of the court houses were built after 1760, and building continued at least until the 1840s. Almost all were demolished in the 20th century.

Courts in Frankwell in the 19th century

Number	Name(s)	Location: between Nos	Maximum number of buildings
1	Up Court	13 and 14	3 houses, 1 malthouse.
2	Frankwell Court	16 and 17 (*Wheatsheaf*)	9 back-to-back houses
3	The Rookery, Rookery Shut, Healing's Passage	21A and 22	11 houses
4	Swan Yard	84 and 85 (*Swan*)	5 houses
5	Plimmer's Passage	90 and 91	4 houses
6	Cawthron's Passage	95 and 96	5 houses
7	Gittins's Passage	110 & 111	14 houses
8	Bell Passage	Behind 111 (*Old Bell*)	3 houses plus workshops
9	-	125 and 126	3 houses, 1 lodging house
10	Bakehouse Passage	Next to 129	16 houses
11	Balcony Passage, Plough Passage, Plough Court	131 and 132 (*Plough*)	14 houses, 1 malthouse
12	Anchor Passage	136 and 137 (*Anchor*)	4 houses
-	White Horse Passage	Behind *White Horse*	20 houses

86 The entry to Plimmer's Passage between Nos 90 and 91 Frankwell.

Four houses in Court No 6 were built in 1841 by William Cawthron, a London cabinet maker who settled in Frankwell, and retired to Devon in 1851, leaving the business to his son, whose descendants were angered by the compulsory clearance in the 1930s of roomy, three-bedroom cottages, 'whose only fault was that they were up a passage in Frankwell'.[12]

When the council gained powers to demolish slums, the clearance of court houses in Frankwell was a priority. Three houses in White Horse Passage were condemned as unfit for human habitation as early as 1913, and piecemeal clearance followed in the 1930s. In 1938, 29 houses remained occupied in Courts 1, 2, 4, 6, 7, and 8. Most of the remaining courts were demolished by the end of 1958.[13]

The construction of small houses on narrow plots created the unhealthy living conditions for which Frankwell was notorious. George Godwin wrote in *The Builder* in 1861:

Over the Welsh Bridge there is a picturesque district of ancient gabled houses called Farnkwell, where the ground behind the houses is higher than the floors; the inhabitants for generations having thrown all their refuse here, whence it has never been carted away. It is a quarter occupied principally by the working classes [...] The passages leading out of the main road are in a terrible condition; in one a dog was licking a puddle of blood, in another a chimney sweep had invested the entrance with sable coatings too sooty to penetrate [...] rag and bone premises maintain the foetid characteristics. The architecture of this district deserves a more appreciating treatment.[14]

87 A surviving sign indicating that Plimmer's Passage was once Court No 5 in Frankwell.

88   The entry to Gittins Passage, Frankwell, in the late 19th century.

The area had scarcely changed 50 years later when a national newspaper reporter wrote:

> ... the most soul-depressing area of all is what is locally known as the little borough of Frankwell across the Welsh Bridge [...] Very few Salopians have ever penetrated to the extremities of the many tortuous passages, shiny with the grease of generations, that lead to the holes there where men and women live and little children are dragged up in this dark quarter. Indeed the ordinary townsman knows scarcely anything of such matters. The courts and alleys lead nowhere; their entrances are difficult to find; their inhabitants are uninviting; the odours an abomination.[15]

Those who lived in the courts had few places of recreation other than the pavements. Respectable Shrewsbury found the suburb intimidating, and considered it a source of crime and vice. The borough's recorder pronounced in 1836:

> Frankwell and Coleham have usually been the main haunt and resort of the profligate gangs of juvenile offenders, and their still more wicked abettors, who infest the town, pilfering from the honest and heedless tradesman – the hole-and-corner boroughs, if I may so express it, to which these noxious vermin run for refuge when pursued. I need not tell you that in Frankwell, particularly, are whole rows of houses tenanted by shameless and wretched females to which thieves and robbers have frequently been traced.[16]

Criminals and prostitutes certainly frequented Frankwell in the 18th and 19th centuries, but their presence should not obscure its role as an industrious working-class suburb. The industries of Frankwell were the traditional manufactures of market towns.[17] Pre-eminent among them was malting. Twelve malting businesses were listed in Frankwell in 1786. Malthouses are recorded at the *Anchor* in 1841, the *Compasses* in 1847, the *Royal Oak* in 1848, adjacent to the fellmonger's building in 1861, at the

Plough in 1868, the *Crown* in 1871, in Bakehouse Passage in 1873, in White Horse Passage in 1922.[18] The largest complex was The Glen, a range of three-storey buildings, probably built by John Gittens in 1829, capable of wetting 240 bushels of barley every four days. The buildings remain, unmistakably maltings, with low ceilings and small windows that were barred rather than glazed.[19]

Brewing was also practised in Frankwell, principally at inns, including the *Anchor*, the *Old Bell*, the *Cross Guns*, the *Crown* and the *Royal Oak*. The Frankwell Brewery of the late 19th century adjoined the *Old Bell* and, with plant provided by a well-known brewing engineer, could produce up to 200 barrels of beer weekly in the 1880s.[20]

Pastoral as well as arable farming provided raw materials for the manufactures of Frankwell. The Fellmongers' building (Nos 4-7) in the early 19th century included workshops for skinners and a warehouse for wool, and in 1871 Henry Hudson, a skinner employing five men, was trading there. Wool was extensively traded in Frankwell. Richard Drinkwater, a prominent property owner, was in business at warehouses in Frankwell by 1803, and wool sorters lived in the suburb throughout the 19th century. The trade attracted people from northern England. Bernard Dyson, a wool merchant born in Colne, Lancs, was living in 1871 at No 1 Providence Terrace, where his neighbour at Nursery Cottage was Isaac Clough, a woolstapler from Bradford. The Irishman Isaac Eakin, who in 1871 had 15 employees in his wool, malt and seed business, was the principal merchant in Frankwell in the late 19th century, and his Mansard-roofed warehouse, occupied by Halls in 2006, was designed by A.B. Deakin in 1888.[21] Previously there was a tannery on the site, worked in 1851 by John Evans, a native of Llanfyllin, and in the 1860s by James Cock, who in May 1868 was charged with polluting the Severn with lime water. Later that year Cock appears to have moved to the tanyard in St Austin Friars.[22]

There were a few nailers in most market towns in the 19th century, but a surprisingly large number made their livings in Frankwell in the 1830s and '40s. Thirteen lived in the Rookery in 1841, nine of them members of the family of John Clarke, males and females, aged between thirteen and thirty. Seven nailers worked in Frankwell in 1851, and two remained 30 years later. There were two small engineering works on the riverside in the 20th century, the Frankwell Forge, and the Atlas Foundry, best-known for restoring the locomotives of the Talyllyn Railway in the 1940s.[23]

Many of Frankwell's working class were individual craftsmen, shoemakers, tailors, cabinet makers, some of whom worked from home for masters based in the town centre. James Phillips who lived in New Street in 1851, but had a shop in High Street, employed 50 tailors. Makers of pewter, bend ware and maltmills traded in Frankwell in 1803. The area attracted some polluting trades. A soap boiler was working there in 1796, and cork cutters at No 105 in 1891 and No 152 in 1901. In 1869 James Kent Morris established a candle factory in Water Lane, and in 1881 when he lived at No 70 New Street employed seven men and two boys.[24]

Public houses were scattered densely in the maze of Frankwell's buildings – 15 were recorded in the 1881 census. Two maltsters, a tinsmith and a timber merchant were amongst the innkeepers following other occupations in 1881. On census night in 1861 there were 12 overnight guests at the *Seven Stars*, four at the *White Horse*, six at the *String of Horses*, eight at the *Bell*, and nine at the *Harp* beerhouse. Some pubs provided sporting facilities such as the Russian bagatelle board and the fancy wood card table available at the *Anchor* in 1850. Some had extensive stabling, not all of it necessarily on the same site. The *String of Horses* could cater for 11 horses, the *Crown & Anchor* for ten, the *Cross Guns* for 30, and the *Bell*, supposedly, for eighty.[25]

Lodging Houses

89   The Sweep's Lodging House by the Welsh Bridge. No 3 Frankwell, photographed not long before its demolition in the early 1970s.

Travellers were also accommodated at Frankwell's lodging houses, clustered around the foot of the Welsh Bridge. Common lodging houses were institutions in every English market town in the 19th century. Inmates usually slept in mixed dormitories, and prepared their own food and drink in communal kitchens. Most were transient, skilled tradesmen 'on the tramp', hawkers and peddlars, itinerant entertainers, collectors of rags and old iron, military recruiting parties, but some stayed over long periods, gangs of farm labourers, and people with just sufficient resources to avoid the workhouse. The most notorious establishment in Shrewsbury was at No 3 Frankwell, 'the Sweep's lodging house over the Welsh Bridge', a three-storey, three-bay brick house, with a wagon arch giving access to a yard at the rear. In 1841 it was kept by Joseph Evans, a 42-year-old Oswestry-born chimney sweep, employing four young sweeps who lived in. He and his wife had an eight-month-old baby, and accommodated three other relations and 15 lodgers. Fifteen were again recorded in 1851, but there were 29 in 1861, and 20 in 1871. By then Evans was widowed, but still working as a sweep, and the lodging house was run by his daughter, the wife of Edward Williams, a grocery assistant. Joseph Evans had died by 1881, when there were 17 lodgers, but there were only five in 1891, and ten years later the Williamses had moved and a washerwoman occupied the house.[26]

The inmates of No 3 Frankwell were characteristic of those of common lodging houses throughout England. In 1841 they included a cotton spinner and an iron moulder, and two Irish fruit sellers. In 1851 there were three railway navvies and two besom makers. Five German musicians, a bird catcher and two drovers were there ten years later, and a Bavarian sextet and a Liverpool-born sailor in 1871. A German quintet in 1881 kept company with an Irish fish hawker, a shipwright born in Sunderland and an Italian musician.

A lodging house at No 138 Frankwell close to the *Anchor* is first recorded in 1861, when it was kept by Alexander Williams, an Oswestry-born labourer, and his wife Esther, born in West Bromwich, who had 21 inmates, including a showman born in Sligo, and his 14-year-old 'show woman' daughter, two cattle drovers and a rag gatherer. There were 16 lodgers in 1871 and 18 in 1881 including a labourer born in Parma. Esther Williams, by then a widow, was managing the house in 1891. Seven of the 14 inmates were German musicians. By 1901 No 138 Frankwell has passed into the keeping of John Groom, born at Ford, who had 18 lodgers including three Italian musicians. His near neighbour William Pugh, in White Horse Passage, kept a lodging house, with 16 inmates. A sign advertising 'model lodging houses with well-aired beds' was painted on the imposing range of buildings in that corner of Frankwell.[27]

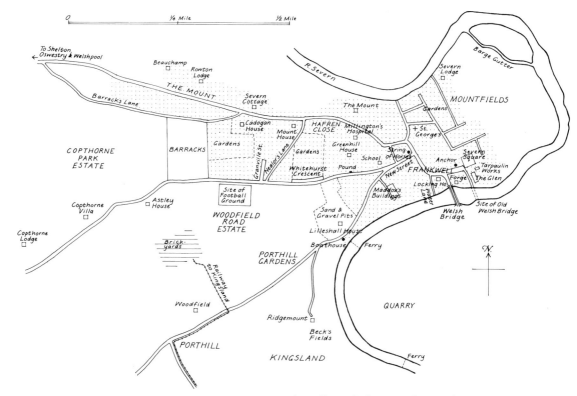

Frankwell and the roads to the west

The Frankwell lodging houses were the most notorious in Shrewsbury. They show that this inner suburb continued into the 20th century to cater for travellers, and analysis of the inmates illuminates the links between Victorian Shrewsbury and the wider world.

New Street

The western end of Frankwell was transformed from the 1960s. Road widening began in 1903 when a building on the corner of New Street was demolished, but in the late 1960s the whole of the 'island' bounded by New Street, Chapel Street and the main road towards The Mount was demolished. It included two courts with entrances in Chapel Street, four former inns, the *Cross Guns*, the *Malt Shovel*, the *Golden Lion* and the *String of Horses*, and had been the home of 289 people in 1881. St George's School, established by Dr Robert Darwin in a room in Chapel Street in 1834, moved in 1879-80 to a building west of the island, designed by A.B. Deakin, which was used until the school moved to Woodfield in 1982. The turnpike trust undertook to widen and ease the gradient of a 70 yard (64 m) stretch of New Street in 1827, which probably accounts for the additional storey that appears to have been added below the ground floors of the houses in Providence Terrace (Nos 66-9).[28]

Wesleyan meetings began in New Street in 1840, in a room hired by Thomas Brocas, of Copthorne House. After Brocas's widow died money was raised by the congregation at St John's Hill for a new chapel that was opened on 23 October 1870. The adjacent premises on the town side in the late 19th century were the yard and steam saw mill of the builder John Gethin.[29] The flats constructed in the 1960s, with walls covered with hanging tiles, succeeded Quarry View (or Maddox's) Buildings, two blocks incorporating more than 50 two-bedroom dwellings built by John Maddox, a maltster, probably in the 1830s, and demolished in 1959 under the borough's slum clearance programme.[30] The borough bowling green and recreation ground at Silk Meadow were opened in 1914.[31]

New Street is lined by houses varying from tiny mid-19th-century terraced cottages through modest semi-detached pairs of the early 20th century to Severn Villa, offered for sale in 1903 with eight bedrooms, a landing stage and stabling for four horses.[32] The *Boathouse* inn was associated with the Harwood family who built and worked vessels on the River Severn. Lead and timber were handled there in the 18th and early 19th centuries. Landlords also provided cruises on the Severn, rowing boats, a bowling green, an American Bowling Saloon, and a refreshment kiosk.[33] The adjacent suspension bridge replaced an ancient ferry in 1923, and stimulated housing developments at Porthill.[34] Lilleshall House was the home of the builder Richard Lloyd Jones who operated the sandpit on the site of Sandringham Court.[35] Park Avenue, four semi-detached rendered pairs, with central gables and porthole windows, was built on another part of the sandpit in the 1920s.

The nursery garden in New Street that has been used by the corporation since 1947 was established by 1803, and in 1832 the premises extended from New Street to Copthorne Road. In 1857 the 'far-famed Frankwell Nursery' passed from Thomas Edwards to William Pritchard who had 16 employees in 1881. His family reduced the size of their holding in 1898, when their stock included 175 poplars and more than 300 apple, pear and plum trees.[36]

James Kent Morris, who developed the oil blending enterprise of Morris & Co., bought land on Porthill about 1905, on which 18 houses, laid out on Garden City lines, had been built by 1910, and about 40 before the outbreak of the First World War. He himself lived at No 1 Porthill Gardens.[37] Walter Vickery, an outfitter from Somerset with a shop in High Street, also developed housing in the area, and lived at Worlebury.[38] Woodbank Drive occupies the site of Woodfield, a mansion with stabling, a coach house and pleasure gardens, probably built in the 1850s by George Burr of the lead works, and later the home of Philip Gould, a London-born merchant.[39]

Before the road to Minsterley reaches the 1933 by-pass it passes through Porthill, an ancient wayside hamlet similar to Red Barn. A tollgate was situated there until 1801-2 when it was removed to Edgebold. In 1840 the tollhouse was being used as a weaver's shop, alongside which was a public house, the *Travellers' Inn*, by repute the house at right angles to the road (No 57). The landlord offered stabling for eight horses, sold clay and sand from nearby pits, and had a dairy business.[40]

The Road to Copthorne

On the north side of Copthorne Road, beyond Millington's Hospital and the St Chad's parish pound, is the Greenhill estate, centred around a rambling brick house, with rustic bargeboarding on its gables, built before 1841 for Thomas Woodward, a magistrate. The estate was sold for building in 1913, and Greenhill Avenue was built on the western part of the ground before 1927. On the opposite side of the main road the 14 houses in Providence View (Nos 11-37) and the 11 in Copthorne Rise were built before 1882, and are characteristic two-storey brick cottages of the third quarter of the century, with semi-circular brick arches over their front doors. The six houses beyond (Nos 39-49) had been erected on the site of sandpits by 1902, but the identical terrace (Nos 51-61) does not appear on the Ordnance map of that year. Two other terraces, Lessar Avenue and Breidden View, were built in the early 20th century on the edge of the sandpits. In 1832 the only houses on the north side of Copthorne Road were the 26 in the two terraces (Nos 26-48 and 50-74), once known as Whitehurst Crescent, but as Copthorne Terrace by the 1870s. The terraces are a rare survival of early 19th-century working-class dwellings. Their occupants in 1861 included two nailers, three tailors, a staff sergeant in the militia, a laundress, a blacksmith, a wood turner, a brushmaker, a tin plate worker and a cow keeper. The *Bricklayer's Arms* public house was transferred in the 1930s from the present tool depot (No 48) to the neo-Georgian building at the end of Hafren Road by Alexander Pugh, a carpenter, who succeeded his parents as landlord.[41]

In 1921-23 the council used government money for relieving unemployment to lay out Pengwern Road from Porthill to Copthorne Road, and Hafren Road continuing to The Mount, and sold lots on both to private developers.[42] Eight houses were built on Pengwern Road by 1927, including The Cottage (No 1), the home of Thomas Pace. Pengwern Road opened up the Woodfield estate, which was planned by Shayler & Drake. Woodfield Road was laid out by 1927, and about 80 houses were built by 1931, when work was progressing on Woodfield Avenue. This is an archetypal inter-war development of detached and semi-detached houses, with hanging tiles, mock timber-framing, integral porches, stained glass and porthole windows. Frank Shaylor designed Nos 103/05 Woodfield Road, overlooking the by-pass, in a Georgian style, with rendered walls, tiled hipped roofs, and subtle fenestration. The Woodfield Tennis Club was established in 1931 amongst the waste tips of Treasure's brickyards.[43]

Hafren Road cut through land that had been allotments. Building plots were offered for sale in 1923 and were was quickly filled, mostly with semi-detached pairs. The 24 houses in Hafren Close were built by the council in 1934 for families displaced by slum clearance in Barker Street.[44]

The houses on the south side of Copthorne Road beyond its junction with Pengwern Road include five built in concrete blocks (Nos 91, 101-7) of which one has the date 1911 cast on a gate post, and the house designed by Frank Shaylor for his mother-in-law (No 97), which is rendered and has three tiny windows above the tiled roof of its porch. The houses beyond (Nos 109-35), and those in Copthorne Drive were built on the former Shrewsbury Town Football ground, 'the scene of many triumphs and disappointments', on which building sites were offered for sale in the summer of 1910.[45] Beyond the junction with Copthorne Drive are seven brick-and-render semi-detached pairs (Nos 129-55) followed by a terrace inscribed 'Greystones 1909', with gabled pavilions at each end, built of concrete blocks, which were cast on site.[46] The adjacent terrace is similar but its pavilions have higher and steeper gables. Beyond the junction with Porthill Drive are more concrete houses (Nos 185-95), in stepped pairs forming a terrace, and inscribed 'Copthorne Gardens 1911' in the balustrade that forms the garden wall. Seven semi-detached pairs built of concrete blocks line the northern side of Copthorne Road beyond the barracks. Apart from some isolated villas, these marked the limit of building before the First World War.

Building commenced in Copthorne Drive before the First World War, and two rather ponderous semi-detached pairs (Nos 11-14) bear the date 1915, contrasting with two other pairs (Nos 15-18) in red brick with tiled roofs that resemble houses in Bournville. The town council took responsibility for the older part of the street in 1928. Bricks and concrete blocks, possibly abandoned when building ceased after 1914, are mixed in several houses on the arm of the drive that links with Porthill Drive (Nos 57/8, 62-4, 67-73), and concrete blocks are used as quoins and in string courses in houses at the northern end Porthill Drive, taken over by the council in 1935.[47]

The construction of barracks caused controversy in 19th-century towns. Margaret Oliphant in *Miss Marjoribanks*, published in 1866, describes attempts to influence a general visiting the fictional Carlingford to assess its fitness as the location of a barracks. The attractions of 'dashing' young officers, and the threat posed by the rough soldiery, were evenly balanced.[48] There were similar debates in Shrewsbury in 1872 when the implications of Edward Cardwell's military reforms became evident. Alderman Southam, the brewer, welcomed the stimulus that a barracks might give to

90 Houses on Woodfield Avenue built in 1931, characteristic of those on the Woodfield estate, and of other middle-range private development in Shrewsbury of the inter-war years, with bow windows, rendered walls on the upper storey, tiled roofs, and some stained glass.

91 Houses that are not typical of the Woodfield estate – Nos 103-5 Woodfield Road, close to the 1933 by-pass, designed by Frank Shaylor.

trade, but Alderman How, the solicitor, regretted that it might 'cause the better class of inhabitants to refrain from coming here'.[49] Quarters for the 43rd and 53rd regiments of foot were built on fields between Copthorne Road and the old road to Shelton, that had been bought by Dr Robert Darwin in 1821, sold by his daughter, and purchased by the War Office in 1875. Further land that had once been Darwin's was acquired by the military in 1913. Henry Treasure contracted to build the barracks at a cost of £65,000 in 1876, and completed the project in the closing weeks of 1878, having used about four million common bricks made on the opposite side of Copthorne Road, together with Maws tiles in the corridors and terracotta caps by J.C. Edwards on the boundary walls.[50]

92 A post-First World War house on Copthorne Drive in which concrete blocks have been used for string courses and quoins.

Nealor's Lane, a footpath to the Mount, crossed an area that was covered with allotments until the early 1920s. The cul-de-sac Granville Street dates was laid out in the late 1870s, when Woodland Villa and Copthorne Villa were built. On the main road Cannon Villas date from 1887, and West View was built in the 1860s for William Swain, a retired ironmonger. Salop County Council intended Bromley House, an old people's home, to commemorate the Festival of Britain, but it was not opened until 29 June 1953. The houses beyond occupy plots laid out by Thomas Tisdale on the site of a nursery, put on the market by Henry Newton in 1853.[51] Gordon Villas and Gordon Place (Nos 98-108) were, as the names suggest, not built until 1885-6, but Copthorne View Terrace (Nos 110-2) has classical proportions and is built in pale local brick, in contrast to the exuberant style and fiery red brick of its neighbours.

Beyond Kelsall's Lane, the only houses on Copthorne Road before the First World War were five villas, a few rural cottages and a tollhouse. Asterley House (No 211), a vicarage-like dwelling, in red brick with stained glass, was built in 1876 for the grocer, Thomas Asterley Maddox, whose initials it bears. The Italianate villa, originally West View House, with a carriage drive and a vinery, was built about 1880

93 Netherton, Nos 102-4 Copthorne Road, a semi-detached pair of 1885-6, adorned with terracotta and stained glass.

94 Gordon Place, Nos 106-8 Copthorne Road, built in 1885, commemorating the death of General Gordon at Khartoum, and beyond them Copthorne View Terrace, in a more classical style, built in 1855, which stood in isolation for some 30 years before being reached by the tide of new building spreading from Frankwell.

95 The building of Greenacres Road was interrupted by the outbreak of the Second World War. The house on the left retains features characteristic of the road: rendered walls, windows with rounded corners, a canopy above the front door, and the curious stepped window.

for George Snook, a quarry agent, but was renamed Rosehaugh, by 1887, and is now Park House.[52]

The houses beyond were built around 1960 by the company from which Alverley Close takes its name. Greenacres Road was begun in 1937. Nine houses had been built by 1938, and more by September 1939 when work ceased. Using existing foundations, the builder W.A. Beavan erected the first house to be completed in Shrewsbury after VE-day, that was occupied by mid-January 1946.[53] Most of the houses, both detached and semi-detached, have overhanging eaves, metal-framed windows with curved corners, and stepped windows. The houses at the end of the cul-de-sac have clay tile roofs, but those nearest Copthorne Road have concrete tiles, suggesting that they were built after the war.

In January 1938 Councillor E.J.T. Perkins announced plans for an estate, with public open space in the hummocky landscape around a mere. Houses were enthusiastically marketed in the summer of 1939 but after the outbreak of war the unused plots became allotments. The building of Richmond Drive, Aysgarth Road and Leyburn Avenue had resumed by 1956. The detached Copthorne Villa was adapted as a roadhouse-style public house, the *Beacon Hotel*, which opened on 14 November 1939.[54]

Mountfields

Mountfields, the area east of Frankwell, at the western end of the peninsula enclosed by the horseshoe bend of the Severn, epitomises Shrewsbury's suburban development. There was at least one large house on its periphery in 1760, and several more by 1800. By 1830 most of the area was divided into allotments whose access tracks became its streets. Houses were built spasmodically, and by several agencies. The church of St George, designed by Edward Haycock I and consecrated on 30 January 1832, was intended for the poor from the courts of Frankwell, but may nevertheless have stimulated the building of villas for the middle class. Its proximity was one of the benefits highlighted when houses in the area were sold in 1833 and 1835, and the church was certainly popular, attracting two congregations of about 600 on census Sunday in 1851.[55]

In 1838 most of Mountfields belonged to the merchant Richard Drinkwater who lived at St George's Place (Court House, No 11), the core of which appears to date from *circa* 1700. It adjoins three one-and-a-half-storey cottages in Mount Street (Nos 17-21), which are probably even older. More than 60 garden plots extended from the close-packed houses in The Stew, by the *Anchor* public house northwards to the banks of the Severn. Building sites in two orchards in Mountfields were offered for sale in 1815, but development was slow. Mountfields House (Alma House) was the home of the printer Peter Jeffery in 1841, and Mountfields Villa and similar Regency-style houses that do not conform to later building lines were erected on the garden plots in the 1830s. There was a steady market in houses in Mountfields in the 1840s, and by 1849 at least ten had been built in the gardens, including Severn Lodge overlooking the river, the home of the surveyor Thomas Tisdale. The pace of development probably accelerated in 1848 when Richard Drinkwater offered for sale 21 gardens as building plots and eight nearby houses.[56]

There were more than 40 houses in Mountfields by 1861, some occupied by manual workers, a journeyman printer, a rope spinner and a wool sorter, but the majority by professional men, the superintendent of police, a railway goods agent, an officer of inland revenue and a solicitor's clerk, with several shopkeepers, a master jeweller, a grocer and a Scots draper. In 1865, 25 building lots were offered for sale with the promise that suitable roads were about to be laid out, and five houses and four 'very excellent sites for small residences' were sold in 1867.[57]

96 Villas in Hunter Street, some of the first houses to be built amongst the allotment gardens of Mountfields, probably built in the 1830s, long before building lines were imposed in Shrewsbury's suburbs.

One of the most interesting houses of the 1860s was Woodford House, a three-storey polychrome brick house in Longner Street, built by William Powell, who had a mercer's shop in Mardol, as the home, not only of his wife, six children and three domestic servants, but also of four male and three female shopworkers. Most traders who moved to the suburbs left their staff living above their shops in the charge of housekeepers. Woodford House was soon surrounded by terraces, and was a hostel for girls from the Priory School during the First World War.[58]

97 Woodford House, Longner Street, built in the 1860s for William Powell the mercer, who accommodated seven of his shop staff in the house in 1871, together with his wife, six children and three domestic servants.

The building of Model Cottages in St George's Street (Nos 5-8) by the Salopian Society for Improving the Condition of the Industrious Classes, occupied in 1871 by a postman, a laundress, a retired farmer and a railway signalman, encouraged the building of other working-class homes, but in 1871 Mountfields was still predominantly middle-class, its residents including John Mackay the railway contractor, the minister of St John's Hill Methodist Church, Isaac Eakin, the wool merchant and a timber merchant who employed 21 men.

A further 11 gardens were made available for building in 1883 and streets were slowly regularised. Havelock Street, an ancient trackway to the barge gutter, also the name of a thoroughfare in Belle Vue, was named Alma Street from the *White Horse* to Alma Terrace, and Hunter Street onwards to Severn Lodge. The council took responsibility for Mount Street and Darwin Street in 1888. By 1901 there were more than 150 houses in Mountfields, yet gardens were still being offered as building sites.[59] James Kent Morris bought part of the grounds of The Mount house in the early 1920s, and in the 1930s built the extension of Mountfields called Darwin Gardens. At the time of his death in 1935, Morris intended to live at No 9 into which he incorporated beams, banister rails and floorboards from Hardwick Hall, Hawkstone.[60]

Since the Second World War flats and houses have been built on vacant plots in Mountfields, but there have been few significant demolitions. The area displays a variety of suburban architectural fashions, Regency villas, Gothic model cottages, terraces in the hard blue brick that was popular in the 1860s and '70s, and houses in the Arts and Crafts style. Few areas reflect so well the forces that have shaped suburban England.

The Mount

Millington's Hospital, built in 1747-8 to accommodate 16 old people, a school master and a school mistress, was one of the first buildings to be erected beyond Shrewsbury's medieval limits, but is scarcely visible from the road through Telford's cutting.[61] Institutions were followed into the fields by villas built by professional men. Dr Robert Darwin settled in Shrewsbury in 1786, and in 1797, the year after his marriage to Susan, daughter of Josiah Wedgwood, he built the 'plain substantial family house'

98 The Mount, one of the first villas to be erected by professional men outside Shrewsbury's medieval limits. It was built for Dr Robert Darwin in 1797, and was the birthplace of Charles Darwin 12 years later.

that is called The Mount.[62] Charles Darwin was born there in 1809, and in his youth studied the flora and fauna of its extensive gardens. Robert Darwin died in 1848, and after the death of his daughter Susan in 1866 it passed to the builder's merchant Edward Lowe, and through other hands until it was purchased in 1919 by Thomas Balfour, a Market Drayton land agent. In 1922 Balfour sold part of the grounds to James Kent Morris, and the house to the Office of Works for the use of Post Office engineers. The Mount has been used as government offices ever since.[63]

The Mount in the early 19th century was Shrewsbury's most select suburb. The road to Holyhead, marked by a milestone at the end of Hafren Road, was lined by the villas of wealthy citizens. Mount Cottage (No 4) was the home of the Revd John Harding, first vicar of St George's church. The Mount House (No 6), a three-storey red brick house with Diocletian windows, belonged to the landowner John Whitehurst. Severn Cottage (later The Beeches), built by 1832, was occupied in 1851 by William Seward Wood, a Herefordshire landowner.[64] Cadogan House, a five-bay house built by 1820, was a school, kept between 1840 and 1869 by Elizabeth Nickson and her sister who usually had about ten boarder pupils.[65] Earlston Park occupies the site of Beauchamp, a large house with mock timber-framing, built by 1841, probably for Caroline Smitheman, a member of the gentry family from Buildwas. About 1870 James Cock, the tanner lived there, and in the early 20th century it was the home of Henry John Hearn, a Dorset man who took over the Circus Brewery by the Welsh Bridge in 1884, was chairman of the gas company, and mayor in 1904-5. *Beauchamp* was a hotel in the 1930s, and remained so in 1960.[66]

Cadogan Place (Nos 56-70), on the northern side of the Mount, built by 1831, is a three-storey terrace, with stretcher bricks extending from the wall, suggesting that John Whitehurst intended extend it.[67] The public house in the same style was originally the *Windsor Castle*, but was re-named the *Bull-in-the-Barn* after a tavern in the area that was notorious in the 17th century as a venue for secret marriages. In 1719 it was a small establishment, consisting only of a kitchen, brewhouse, cellar, two bed chambers and a garrett.[68] Beyond Severn Cottage are five late 19th-century houses, of which Nos 74-6 bear the date 1899. The houses of the 1930s on the Mount (Nos 102-16) and in Bryn Road were built on a 3½-acre field sold for building in 1930.[69]

Barracks Lane, which leaves The Mount by Cadogan House, is the old course of the main road, diverted by the Holyhead Road Commission in the 1820s. In 1891, 14 building plots were offered for sale, facing The Mount with access to the lane at the back.[70] Semi-detached pairs were built on some plots, but all the houses are imposing, and display Ruabon bricks, hanging tiles, some timber-framing in gables, and terracotta swags. The coach houses facing Barracks Lane are evidence of the extent to which wealthy citizens used private road transport in the late 19th century. Corunna House (No 59) is particularly large and bears the date 1899, while No 61 is rich in terracotta rosettes. Frank Shaylor designed three houses (Nos 71-5), with hanging tiles and long vertical windows, and lived in the Red House (No 73).

Richmond Drive cuts short Barracks Lane but the line of the old main road continues north of The Mount with the footpath along Shelton Lane. The caravan site to the south aroused anger amongst councillors in the 1950s. The proximity of the barracks brought military activity to The Mount during the Second World War, and as late as 1954 a gun emplacement, hastily erected in 1940, remained in the garden of No 42.[71]

The By-pass and Beyond

Land 'ripe for development' on Radbrook Road was offered for sale in 1920. By 1934, the route to Minsterley as far as the crossing of the Rad Brook was lined by detached houses in a comfortable Garden City style, many of them built by James Kent Morris.[72] No 25, with flares on its roof and on the gable in the front elevation, an arched porch and the lintels of its windows made up of roof tiles, could well have been built in Letchworth. The eroded remains of a sandstone milepost remain outside outside No 19. Maples, beeches and cedars line the south bank of the Rad Brook, while the garden on the north extends from Rad Valley Gardens.

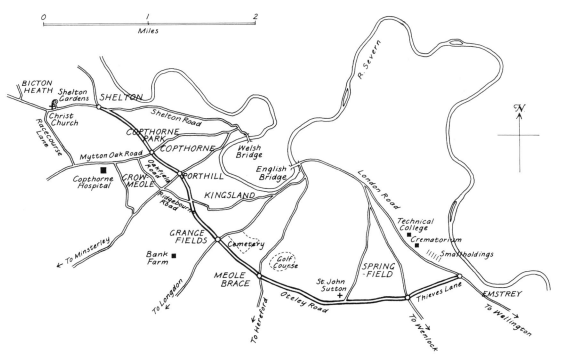

The 1933 by-pass and the southern suburbs

99 Oakfield Road was built in the early 1930s. No 33 is one of about half-a-dozen houses in the Shrewsbury suburbs in the International Modern style.

Beyond the brook, the large bungalows in Dunedin Drive were built in 1960 by a Scots architect. The *Radbrook Hall Hotel*, set amongst mature limes, beeches and oaks, originated as Radbrook Villa built before 1831, when it was the home of a clergyman. When the property was sold in 1874, the house, 'in the Italian style', with marble chimneypieces, stood in 11 acres of pleasure grounds. In the 1880s it was the home of 'Captain' Arthur Waters, the mining engineer, and from 1888 until 1905 that of Rose Beckwith, spinster daughter of a vicar of Eaton Constantine.[73] The former coach house remains on Alan Gutridge Drive. The Shropshire Technical School, or Radbrook College, was completed in 1901 and has been much extended.[74] Beyond the junction with Crowmeole Lane are five modest houses forming Radbrook Crescent, probably built before the First World War.

Oakfield Road grew up in the 1930s. The southern end was built on West Raddlebrook Field, a seven-acre enclosure that had belonged in the 19th century to the Revd J. Craig of Severn Hill, and then to John Loxdale of Kingsland House. William Deakin, who with his wife proposed to build a Tudor-style café and filling station on the by-pass, bought the land in 1927. The Madeira estate, built after the by-pass opened, included the northern end of the road, and the whole thoroughfare was taken over by the corporation in 1936, when it was lined with 44 chaotically numbered houses.[75] There were 87 in 1938. Most are semi-detached pairs, but No 33 is in the International Modern style, and others display Art Deco glass.

Most of the Kenwood estate between Oakfield Road and the by-pass was built in 1937-8.[76] The undenominational Radbrook church was opened in 1945 in the corner of Kenwood Drive, where its site can be recognised by houses (No 52-8) subsequently built on its site, that differ in style from the rest of the road.

The road to Montgomery beyond the by-pass was formally named Mytton Oak Road in 1934, when it was becoming a honeypot for developers. Mytton Oak farmhouse remains, a three-storey brick building with rustic bargeboards and Tudor-style chimneys near the corner of Crowmeole Lane. It was the home until 1915 of Robert Pool, accountant, auctioneer and secretary of the Eye, Ear and Throat Hospital, who owned many houses in Shrewsbury.[77] Other houses on the road in 1934 included the turnpike tollhouse (No 69), and the four Copthorne Cottages (Nos 42-8). Copthorne Lodge (No 4), a six-bedroom house adapted as flats, is hidden at the end of the cul-de-sac called Mytton Park. Its 3½-acre estate was developed from 1933, when Atcham R.D.C.

objected to the bungalows in Mytton Grove. By the autumn of 1933 W.A. Sherratt was developing the Madeira estate running back from the main road along Oakfield Road, and narrowly beat Fletcher Estates to the distinction of being the first builder in Shrewsbury to market his wares with a show house. Attention was drawn to the estate by the flame images in the gables of the two semi-detached pairs framing the entrance to Oakfield Road. Sherratt's exhibition house in 1933 cost £745, and in 1936 he offered five designs, with long gardens and garage spaces, that could be obtained with a deposit of up to £35 and weekly payments of 14s 7d. Well Meadow Road and Well Meadow Drive were being built in 1937.[78]

The Crowmeole estate off Oakfield Road was built on the site of a pig farm acquired with difficulty by the borough corporation in the autumn of 1947. Erection of 50 BISF houses began in February 1948, but there were delays in the finishing stages and only two were occupied by September of that year. Just over a hundred traditional houses, most of them chalet-type semi-detached pairs, were built in 1949-50, and all were occupied by the autumn of 1951, some of them initially shared by two families. The council sanctioned the building of the Oakfield shopping centre in March of that year. Children from the estate celebrated the coronation in the short-lived Radbrook church.[79]

100   The flame image in the gable of the semi-detached pair at the entrance to W.A. Sherratt's Madeira estate in Copthorne, built in the early 1930s, and matched by a similar image in the pair on the opposite corner.

101   BISF houses, designed by Sir Frederick Gibberd, on the Crow-meole estate, built in 1948-49.

The elegant Copthorne House (more recently Mytton Villa) was built in the closing years of the 18th century for John Probert, the Welsh land agent and surveyor who had interests in Shropshire lead mines. Its estate extended over more than 200 acres, on which he created pleasure grounds, houses for his staff that included a Swiss-style cottage, a grotto, a lake with a boathouse and two rustic bridges, a vinery and a walled garden.[80] In 1830-1 the estate was sold to Thomas Brocas, a lawyer and son of the gardener, china dealer, diarist, and reputed founder of Methodism in Shrewsbury. From 1831 horse-racing ceased on the estate that gave its name to Racecourse Lane. Brocas adapted a room on the west side of the house for worship conducted by ministers of the Methodist New Connexion. When the estate was sold after the death of Brocas's widow in 1868, its furnishings included paintings, supposedly by Rembrandt and Watteau, a chamber organ, a Broadwood piano, a harp and 12 dozen of 1847 port.[81] When the property was on the market in 1919 it was said to be 'capable of highly remunerative development for building purposes'. It was sold in small lots, and in 1928 Shelton Hospital bought the house and 33 acres to add to its 26-acre farm worked by patients. The house was used by health services into the 21st century. The Swiss Cottage in 1919 was the centre of a 38-acre dairy holding, on which in 1938-9 W.A. Sherratt built the 'prettiest houses in Shrewsbury' costing up to £755.[82] Building ceased during the Second World War and many plots on Swiss Farm Road remained empty in 1955. A three-bay house surrounded by later bungalows in Cruckton Close (No 5) was probably an estate staff house.

The hospital on the south side of Mytton Oak Road was built during the Second World War. Military use ended during the summer of 1946 when it was taken over by

102 Copthorne House, or Mytton Villa, the elegant late 18th-century house built for the surveyor and mines speculator John Probert, and subsequently the home of the lawyer Thomas Brocas. The house was used by various health authorities from 1928 until the early 21st century. Much private building took place on the grounds of Copthorne House in the years immediately before and after the Second World War.

Salop County Council, but remained unused until the establishment of the National Health Service under whose auspices it was re-opened on 14 June 1948. In 1958 the health authority decided to concentrate all hospital facilities in Shrewsbury at Copthorne, the Royal Shrewsbury Hospital on the north side of Mytton Oak Road was opened in 1978, and facilities have since gradually been moved away from the wartime buildings.[83]

Within a few years of the completion of the 1933 by-pass, Shelton Road, the section between the Porthill and Copthorne islands, was lined with houses, only a few of which on the northern side (Nos 12-18) have the benefit of a service road. Some are in the style of the Woodfield and Kenwood estates of which they formed parts. Two identical blocks of four houses, originally called West Grove (Nos 35-49), each have two timber-framed gables with quatrefoil panels. Nos 1-9 display Jacobean features, drip moulds, leaded windows and studded doors. Two houses are in the International Modern style: No 31 designed by Frank Shaylor, which now has pitched roofs, and No 33, Oakbarn, the home, when he died, of Alfred Barnes Deakin. Beyond the Copthorne roundabout building was in progress in 1939 but ceased with the outbreak of war. The Shorncliffe Drive area was a military camp during the Second World War, and in 1949 accommodated regiments attending the Royal Show and some Polish soldiers. In February of that year squatters attempted to take over the huts, but the officer commanding a detachment of the South Staffordshire Regiment handled the occasion with diplomatic skill and those who had gained entry agreed to move to Merrington Green. Married quarters that replaced the huts were inspected by the Minister of Defence, John Strachey, while under construction in 1950.[84]

Shelton

The junction at Shelton between the roads to Oswestry and Welshpool was changed many times; by the Holyhead Road Commission in the early 1820s, when the by-pass opened in 1933, and in the 1970s. The tollgate controlling the two roads was moved from The Mount to the junction between 1818 and 1821, but in 1829 the Commission built the tollhouse on the Oswestry road that was removed to Ironbridge in 1972, and the old tollhouse then served only the Welshpool road.[85] A milepost showing a distance of 105 miles to Holyhead stands on the town side of the intersection. A sapling planted in 1981 represents the Shelton Oak, from which, by tradition, Owen Glendower watched the Battle of Shrewsbury in 1403. Carrington Close occupies the site of the *Oak*, a roadhouse with a bowling green, opened in 1939 and demolished 60 years later.[86]

The junction marked the end of the town on the Holyhead Road, but a dispersed community of publicans, tailors, shoemakers, pig dealers, cow keepers, tailors, butchers, wheelwrights and blacksmiths extended for about a mile along the road to Welshpool across Bicton Heath. This was an ancient wayside hamlet, comparable with Red Barn, serving the needs of passing travellers, and the recreational and horticultural requirements of Salopians. Pidgeon in 1837 observed that there were at Shelton 'some neat suburban villas which unite architectural taste and rural decoration with the beauty of situation'. The Oxon estate was bought in 1832 by Edward Morris, son of a Newport lawyer, whose family owned land at Church Eaton on the Staffordshire border. It passed to his nephew, Charles John Morris, by repute one of the wealthiest men in Shropshire, who had married a daughter of Robert Burton of Longner, also an owner of land at Shelton. Morris's 364-acre estate was sold in 1930.[87]

The hospital at Shelton originated in 1845 as an asylum for pauper lunatics, the responsibility of quarter sessions and partner authorities. Overcrowding led to enlargement in the early 1880s after which the asylum accommodated up to 800 inmates. The National Health Service managed the institution from 1948. There have since been many changes to the buildings, most obviously the demolition of a crescent of staff houses at the entrance.[88]

Agitation for a chapel of ease to serve the roadside community began in 1832, but although the Methodist New Connexion opened the Bethel Chapel on the main road in 1843, which drew congregations of about 40 in 1851, Anglican opinion was that 'the evils of ignorance and irreligion' had continued.[89] On 19 May 1853 Edward Morris laid the foundation stone for a church for which he had given the land. Christ Church, Oxon, in Cardiston stone with lancet windows and a bell turret, designed by Edward Haycock II, was consecrated on 3 October 1854 by George Selwyn, bishop of New Zealand. The nearby school was built in 1860-1, and the vicarage (Oxon Priory) in 1856-7.[90]

Shelton lay outside the borough until 1934 and the 28 houses were built in Shelton Gardens bearing the initials of Atcham Rural District Council and the date 1921. Councillors were reluctant to build so near to Shrewsbury. One of them remarked, 'We shall have people coming from the town and I'm sure we don't want them'.[91]

There were blacksmiths in most ancient wayside hamlets, and by 1841 a smithy on the Welshpool road at the junction of Shepherd's Lane was in the hands of John Rowlands, who set up a foundry and began to make agricultural implements, including maltmills, threshing machines and steam engines. The Bicton Heath Foundry in 1870 included all the usual facilities of an agricultural engineering works, and two boilermakers lived nearby. It was then owned by John's sons, Thomas and Henry Rowlands, who dissolved their partnership in 1872. In the 20th century Foundry Villa became a wayside fish-and-chip shop.[92]

Bicton Heath was a venue for horse-racing from 1729 until 1831, commemorated by the name of Racecourse Lane, and the site of the kennels of the Shropshire Hunt from 1855 to 1855. The *Grapes*, now a Georgian-style roadhouse, was a venue for cockfighting in the 1790s, had a bowling green and a skittle alley in the 1850s, and was celebrated for tea and quadrille parties held annually in July from the 1850s. William Teece constructed a temporary ballroom with capacity for 200 dancers in 1868, when it was observed that 'the picnic has for years been largely attended'. The event appears to have ceased when Teece's executors sold the inn to the Lichfield Brewery in 1888.[93] A nursery at Bicton Heath was already old-established in 1804, and in 1861 its nine acres were worked by John Millman and his two employees.[94]

Shelton and Bicton Heath developed rapidly after 1960, with the building of housing estates and a business park, yet for two centuries previously the area was unmistakably a suburb, principally because of the linear settlement along the Welshpool road that originated on heathland. The landscape along the road to Oswestry that passed through enclosed fields was very different.

CHAPTER IX

Coton Hill and Greenfields

The suburbs along the roads to Baschurch and Ellesmere are the least extensive of those on the radial routes out of Shrewsbury, but they have been shaped by the same complex forces as those elsewhere. There was no planned medieval suburb in the area but there was an inheritance of ancient settlement, the timber-framed buildings of Coton Hill, site in the late Middle Ages of the mansion of the Mytton family. The timber-framed cottages, Nos 20-22 Coton Hill, were probably outbuildings of the mansion, while No 19 is a timber-framed 16th-century house.[1] In the mid-18th century only Benbow House stood between the Bagley Brook and Coton Hill.

The suburb begins where the main road crosses the Bagley Brook, draining the Old River Bed, which runs in a culvert beneath The Gateway. The education and arts centre stands on the site of a brewery established before 1820, possibly in 1792, by Thomas Hawley, owned from 1880 by Thomas Southam, and active into the 1960s. A plaque in the car park commemorates an extension in 1889.[2] The adjacent 'Old Waterworks', in Ruabon brick, functioned from 1831 until 1935.[3]

Coton Hill and Greenfields

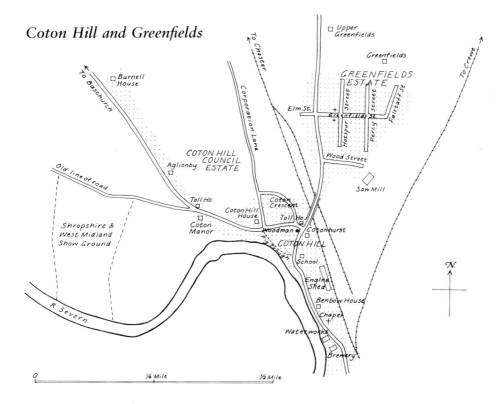

On the north side the former Congregationalist chapel, designed by A.B.Deakin, on a site donated by Thomas Pace, was opened on 11 February 1909 and closed in 1942.[2] It replaced an old house, Broome Hall, and the adjacent Royal Baths that was opened in 1831 by a surgeon, William Onions.[4] Two pairs of elegant stucco-fronted villas (Nos 73-76) were built about 1840. Three of the four were private hotels in 1938, and No 74 displays an early 20th-century Cyclists' Touring Club plaque. The gateposts caps were made at the Randlay Brickworks. Flats built in 2005 replace a garage that had its the origins in the earliest years of the motor trade in Shrewsbury, and incorporated the timber-framed Benbow House, boyhood home of Admiral John Benbow, master of the fleet in the battles of Beachy Head in 1690 and La Hogue in 1692. It was the home of the builder Henry Treasure in the 1870s, and served as St Mary's vicarage during the incumbency of the Revd Newdigate Poyntz between 1889 and 1910.[5] Within the modern development is the former engine shed of the Shrewsbury & Chester Railway, built in 1848 and closed in 1883, after which it was used for other railway purposes and latterly as part of the adjacent garage.[5]

The *Severn Apprentice* (No 60), formerly the *London Apprentice*, replaced in 1959 an inn that in the 1890s accommodated hunting horses and hunt servants. The *Bird in Hand* (No 51), meeting place of the Amalgamated Society of Engineers, Machinists, Millwrights & Smiths in the 1850s, and the former grocery shop of Morris & Co., of 1912, have mock Tudor features. Jane's Place, originally seven or eight houses, was built before 1815 by John Simpson, and named after one of his daughters. It adjoins the former school of 1874, designed by Samuel Pountney Smith, and the approach to Myrtle Cottages.[6] Alongside the railway is Cotonhurst, once occupied by Thomas Corbett, whose Perseverance Ironworks can be seen from the gardens. Cotonhurst replaced Coton Villa, the richly-furnished home in the early 19th century of Charles Nicholls, a flannel merchant, who went bankrupt in 1842.[7]

Coton Hill proper is a mixture of small cottages, ancient and modern, the oldest (Nos 12,14) of one-and-a-half storeys. They extend to the Pig Trough, the track that runs through to Berwick Road, past the polychrome Vyrnwy Cottage of 1886, and the approach to Thorneycroft and Mytton House, an imposing semi-detached pair built in the 1890s by Colonel Thomas Thorneycroft who had a boatyard nearby, and collected vessels, including the last barge on the Upper Severn to carry a commercial cargo.

103   The former engine shed of the Shrewsbury & Chester Railway, built in 1848-9, and used for other railway purposes after running shed activities were concentrated at Coleham in the mid-1880s. It is now incorporated in a housing development.

104   The view from the garden of Cotonhurst, Coton Hill, once the home of Thomas Corbett, the tower of whose Perseverance Ironworks is just to the right of the centre. In the middle distance is the railway to Crewe.

He left Shrewsbury by 1901.[8] The *Royal Oak* in the Tudor Revival style replaces a public house which had its own brewing and malting facilities in the mid-19th century, when there were six or more houses in its yard. No 25 is a substantial three-storey, three-bay house probably of 18th century date, while the terrace above, Nos 28-31, frames the entrance to Hammonds Passage, eight houses built shortly before 1881 that with Nos 28-31 Coton Hill were sold for £1430 in 1887. The *Woodman* on the corner of Berwick Road is an ancient hostelry rebuilt in 1925, whose landlord in the 1880s commended his 'fine home-brewed ales, refreshments, fine cigars and well-aired beds'. Opposite the *Woodman* is a range of three-storey early 19th-century houses (Nos 35-40) simply ornamented with wooden pilasters in the door cases, and abutting a remnant of a two-storey building of polygonal plan that may have been part of the tollhouse on the turnpike road to Ellesmere.[9]

The tollhouse for the Baschurch road was by St Mary's parish pound, opposite Coton Manor. The turnpike trust built the present main road, probably in the 1820s, leaving the old line to give access to the fields of Gravel Hill Farm that since 1897 have been the West Midlands Showground.[10]

Berwick Road is lined with substantial houses principally of the 19th century. On the western side in 1832 there were houses on five of nine plots laid out beyond the *Woodman*. Coton Hill House at the junction with Corporation Lane, a care home built by Salop County Council in the late 1950s, replaces a residence of the same name. The adjacent Quaker Meeting House occupies St Catherine's Mission Hall, a former Anglican place of worship, designed by F.M.Drake, and consecrated in October 1930.[11] The area attracted architects and civil engineers. In 1896 A.B. Deakin was living at The Poplars, Lloyd Oswell at Coton Hill Cottage and W.S. Deakin at Coton House. In 1931 the borough surveyor A.W. Ward lived at No 10a, next door to the county surveyor W.H. Butler at No 10, while the county architect A.G. Chant lived at No 8a. Coton Manor, replaced by flats in the 1960s, had terraced gardens whose scale can be appreciated from the Pig Trough. Aglionby, approached by a drive from Berwick Road, a three-bay house with a porch supported by massive pillars, was designed as his family home by the Scots railway engineer David Wyllie. Its principal rooms had marble chimneypieces. Burnell House, the last house on Berwick Road in 1900, was the home of Edward Parry, councillor, magistrate, mayor in 1870, and for 40 years manager of the Ditherington flax mill.[12]

Coton Hill House was the home of George Stanton, an Ellesmere-born property owner, magistrate, bachelor and archaeologist, whose estate included the Chapel Yard or Cricket Field between the two main roads, possibly the site of the medieval chapel of St Catherine. Thomas Pace bought the property, and during 1895 laid out 41 plots that formed Coton Crescent, and built houses on several of them. There were more than 30 houses in the crescent in 1914 when it was taken over by the corporation.[13] Many are ornamented with pressed bricks. Two pairs bear the date 1904 and one is inscribed 1909. Pace was living at Sydney House, next to his joinery works, by 1901.

Corporation Lane led to allotments where townspeople grew vegetables and flowers – there were about 90 plots in 1838 – and to nursery gardens, notably that of John Jones who employed six people on his 20 acres in 1881. There were six cottages along the lane in the late 19th century, and in the 1930s the Shrewsbury Concrete Co., which supplied precast stone for Della Porta's department store in 1933, had its plant there.[14]

The first council dwellings at Coton Hill were built by the borough corporation when government felt indebted to those who had fought in the First World War. A property of nearly 40 acres was purchased in March 1919 from the Berwick estate. Thomas Deakin cut the first sod and planted a copper beech tree on 14 August 1919. Delays ensued and when work re-commenced early on Monday 11 April 1921, on a contract to build 195 houses, a ministry directive arrived at noon sanctioning only fifty. By May 1922, 32 of those 50 were complete, and the remainder being painted or plastered, while work had begun on another twenty.[15] The estate was completed by several small contracts, 30 in 1923-4, including those around the 'square' in Berwick Avenue, another 30 in the summer of 1924, and 62 in 1924-6. In 1937, when the estate was commended for its orderly appearance and its community spirit, it comprised more than 200 homes. Old people's bungalows were added in the 1950s.[16] The roads are narrow and were clearly designed before it was anticipated that tenants might own motorcars. Round Hill Green provides a large area of open space. Differences in the design of houses and in the quality of brickwork show how the optimism of the post-war period was chastened by economic necessity and political dogma.

Greenfields

Coton Hill was in St Mary's parish, but most of the wedge of land beyond the railway bridge between Ellesmere Road and the Old River Bed was an enclave of St Julian's. In 1875 the only houses along the road to Ellesmere beyond the railway bridge were the mansions, Greenfields, and Upper Greenfields. Most of the houses between the bridge and Greenfields were constructed between 1880 and 1900. The terrace on the west side beyond the bridge dates from 1887, and the semi-detached pair May Villa and York Villa (Nos 38/40) from 1893, the year of the marriage of the Duke of York to Princess Mary of Teck. They are ornamented with stained glass upper lights in the windows, finials on the attic dormers and moulded brick string courses below the eaves and the window sills. May Villa has encaustic floor tiles between the ground- and first-floor windows, where York Villa has terracotta roundels. Henry Treasure, the builder, built Wood Street along the approach to his timber works. It was taken over by the corporation in 1892. Elm Street was built by John Gethin of Frankwell during the 1880s and ultimately totalled 20 houses. In 1887, when half the cottages were built, and only five occupied, the drains failed to function and Gethin was charged with failing to follow the agreed plans.[17]

A feature of the streets called Greenfields, acknowledged in the 1930s, was that 'the whole district was planned before one house had been built'. The property had belonged to John Maddock, an attorney who had married Hannah Ashby, niece of John Ashby the lawyer who built the *Lion* hotel. Their grandson George Ashby Maddock took the name Ashby, and lived chiefly on his estate at Naseby, Northants. In 1880 he offered 80 building lots comprising the Greenfields Freehold Building Estate, promising that roads would be laid out to create 'one of the most attractive suburbs in the town'. Most lots failed to sell, but streets, named after characters associated with the Battle of Shrewsbury, were laid out in 1881, and Ashby put 99 plots on the market early in 1882. Again, they were greeted with apathy, and the estate developed slowly. Sewers were completed in 1886-7, and the corporation adopted Greenfields and Hotspur streets in 1888.[18]

The appearance of the estate, short terraces with some detached houses, mostly of two storeys, of different dates and varying styles, with eccentric street numbering, suggests that it developed slowly, as a convenient investment vehicle for small-scale speculators. Most of the bricks were made on the spot, although the yellow bricks used in string courses were probably from elsewhere. Reputedly many of the houses were constructed by Thomas Pace, who began his own business in 1888, and lived at

105 Two houses built in 1893, the year of the marriage of the future King George V, York Villa and May Villa, Nos 38-40 Ellesmere Road. While the houses appear symmetrical, the decorative detail differs considerably between the two.

106 The Greenfields estate, while the only substantial housing development in Shrewsbury to be laid out by a landowner, was nevertheless a working-class community, in which railwaymen were the principal occupational group. Some houses were built in short terraces, others in semi-detached pairs, like this example, adorned with the polychrome string courses much favoured by Shrewsbury builders in the 1880s and '90s.

107 A few houses in Greenfields were detached, but were built on narrow plots, like this example in Hotspur Street, which meant that their surroundings were not especially spacious.

Stockton Cottage, Greenfields Street, from 1890. Yew Tree Cottage in Falstaff Street is inscribed 1881, but most dated buildings are later, houses of 1888, 1889 and 1891 in Hotspur Street, 1889, 1891 and 1895 in Percy Street, and 1890, 1897 and 1898 in Falstaff Street. The names of Gladstone Terrace and Hawarden Cottage (No 18) in Falstaff Street, Primrose Cottage (57 Hotspur Street) and Cecil Cottages (Nos 28-9 Percy Street) reflect political feelings, while houses named after Clive, Halford, Hope, Nordley and Stockton mirror the movement of migrants from the country-side into the county town. By 1891 there were 38 houses in Greenfields Street, 38 in Hotspur Street, 24 in Percy Street and ten in Falstaff Street, a total of 110 houses. Ten years later there were 210 houses on the estate. There have subsequently been small-scale additions. Maddock's mansion, Greenfields or Broom Hall, was the home by 1871 of William Patchett, stationmaster, then Superintendent of the Joint Railways from 1848 until 1890. The house accommodated Belgian refugees during the First World War, and was the designated site of a secondary school whose construction was halted by the outbreak of war in 1939. A towering Cedar of Lebanon remains as evidence of its ornamental gardens.[19]

Wesleyans evangelised Greenfields from a tent in the summer of 1890, and opened a temporary iron church on 12 September of that year, that was replaced in 1908 by a red brick chapel, with a spire-capped tower.[20] The temporary chapel stimulated complaints of Anglican lethargy, and the Revd Thomas Auden, vicar of St Alkmund's, was responsible for building a mission room, with Lilleshall Co. brick walls and a porch floored with Maw's tiles, consecrated in February 1892. A Church Army officer worked with the congregation in the 1890s.[21]

Thomas Pace was one of the founders of the Greenfields Bowling Club. A tennis club whose courts were approached between Nos 7 and 9 Falstaff Street was flourishing in the 1930s. The Greenfields & District Horticultural Society was formed in 1894, but was dissolved after the death of a bandsman from Silverdale when a platform collapsed at the show of 1898. Morris & Co. and the Co-operative Society opened shops on the estate, and the latter still bears the society's inscription.[22]

Several suburban mansions lined Ellesmere Road beyond Greenfields in 1880. More were built in the following decades and gaps between them were filled in the 1920s and '30s. Upper Greenfields, now Lymehurst, was for a time the home of the timber merchant and Wesleyan, John Barker. After crossing the Old River Bed the Ellesmere Road climbs Cross Hill where, after several accidents, the turnpike trustees lowered the gradient in 1828-9.[23] Beyond Cross Hill the suburbs of Shrewsbury encroached on the main road only after 1960.

CHAPTER X

Castle Foregate and Beyond

A soldier returning home in 1802 during the Peace of Amiens, after 12 years with the colours, stood on the walls of Shrewsbury Castle and observed 'three noble institutions, the Jail, the Canal Port and the Manufactory [i.e. the Ditherington flax mill], each in their way serviceable to mankind, and all perfected during the war'.[1] He precisely defined the time at which Shrewsbury began to grow to the north, and identified three of the responsible agencies.

Suburbs extend further from Shrewsbury's north gate than in any other direction. By 1939 ribbon development stretched 2.5 miles (4.5 km) almost to Battlefield Church, and even in 1914 there was scarcely a gap in the line of buildings as far as the tollhouse at the Heath Gates, a distance of 1.3 miles (3 km). This growth was spasmodic – spurts of building were generated by the establishment of industrial concerns, and were interspersed with periods of low activity. This is the most proletarian of Shrewsbury's suburbs, but its houses have been built by varied agencies. Most of the northern suburbs were in St Mary's parish, but there were several enclaves of other parishes, and patterns of life in recent centuries were shaped in part by medieval boundaries.

Celia Fiennes, approaching Shrewsbury from Whitchurch in 1698, related that she passed over a 'causey' raised above marshy ground.[2] The present density of buildings makes it difficult to appreciate that there was a near-swamp between the River Severn and the Bagley Brook, crossed by an embankment that can still be observed at Ann's Hill, or by the *Comet* (now the *Coach*) public house.

John Speed's map shows that Shrewsbury had two north gates, one on the town wall between the Castle and the River Severn, the other further up Castle Gates. Only a fragment of the outer gate remained in the early 19th century, and the topography of the area was transformed when Castle Gates was lowered in the 1820s, and when Thomas Penson's Tudor Revival railway station was built in 1848-49.[3] The station building was originally of two storeys with its forecourt, at the level of the platforms. The ground floor was inserted and the courtyard lowered during large-scale rebuilding in 1899-1901.[4] The ramp on the southern side of the yard indicates the earlier level.

Facing the station, the Ruabon brick building capped by a belvedere opened on 8 August 1885 as the Welcome Coffee House, a temperance hotel competing with contemporary gin palaces, with ground-floor bars, a dining room above, and sleeping accommodation on the second and third floors.[5] The adjacent three-storey Italianate building was a showroom for Thomas Corbett of the Perseverance Ironworks, whose name appears on its Chester Street elevation. The *Station Hotel* was *The Grapes*, until the 1930s, and behind it were seven houses forming Grapes Passage.[6] The *Shrewsbury Chronicle* building, designed by Frank Shaylor, opened in August 1926.[7] Two bays of the adjacent three-bay building, probably of early 19th-century date, have been occupied for at least 150 years by the *Albion Vaults*, the resort in 1871 of Irish hawkers of drapery.

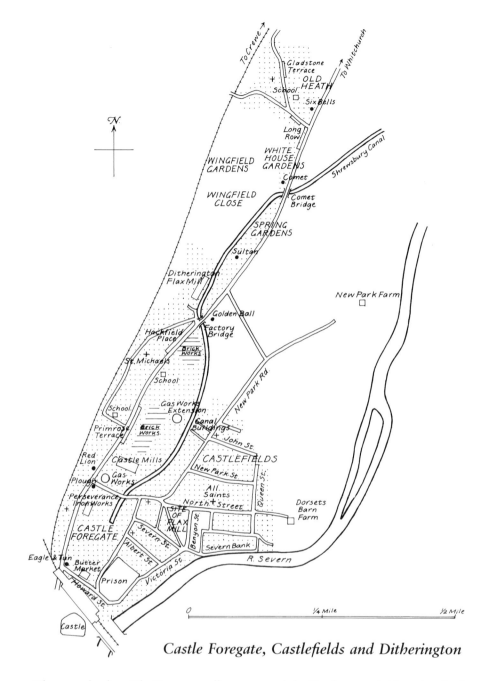

Castle Foregate, Castlefields and Ditherington

The ramp leads to The Dana, a walkway around the Castle motte laid out late in the
18th century by the Revd Edmund Dana, incumbent of Wroxeter.[8] The Dana crosses the
railway by a bridge with Gothic vaulting and, where it emerges into daylight, provides
a panorama across Shrewsbury's northern and eastern suburbs, and an opportunity to
appreciate the impact of railway construction. The level outside the prison entrance
extended to the foot of the Castle motte, and sloped gently downwards to the Castle

Foregate. The extra-mural suburb of Castle Hill, a maze of alleyways, cottages and workshops mostly owned by John Bishton Minor, was a reputed resort of criminals and prostitutes. There was an upsurge of disorder, in which a loud prostitute called Mary Whitehouse was prominent, as the demolition began in 1846-7 prior to the construction of the railway, during which 109 houses were demolished in Castle Hill, Howard Street and Castle Foregate, displacing 356 people.[9]

The Lancasterian School, the most notable of the buildings consumed by the railway, stood east of The Dana.[10] The educationalist Joseph Lancaster lectured in Shrewsbury in 1811, attracting interest from citizens, including Charles Bage, who designed a school with the appearance of a factory that opened with 233 pupils on 14 October 1812. When demolition was threatened, the school moved to the Union Wharf until 12 June 1851, when new premises were completed in Beacall's Lane. The school, designed by Edward Haycock I, was built to an E-plan. The north wing was replaced by A.B. Deakin in 1889-90, the central section by W. Scott Deakin in 1896 and the south wing in 1906. The inscription 'Established 1813' refers to the formal establishment of the charity on 10 July of that year.[11] The school, known as the Shrewsbury British School from 1896, the Shrewsbury Higher Grade School from 1891 and the Lancasterian School from 1906, always enjoyed a high reputation. The building is now used by the prison service.

Quarter Sessions established a prison in School House Lane in 1705, but the cessation of transportation to the Carribean during the American War of Independence caused overcrowding. Under the influence of the reformer John Howard, who visited Shrewsbury on 10 February 1788, the Shropshire magistrates built a new gaol, designed by John Hiram Haycock, with advice from the influential prison architect William Blackburn. It was authorised by Act of Parliament in 1786 and completed in 1793. Thomas Telford, county surveyor from 1787, supervised the final stages of construction. After it ceased to be a county responsibility in 1878 the prison was rebuilt, and the entrance is almost all that remains of the original complex. The bust of John Howard, by John Bacon, who carved Howard's statue in St Paul's Cathedral, was presented by two county magistrates, and unveiled on 4 August 1795.[12] The bay on the uphill side of the entrance was originally a 'lazarette', a place of reception for diseased inmates. Above the porter's lodge on the downhill side was the drop where prisoners sentenced to death were hanged. Some executions, like that of Josiah Mister in 1841, condemned for the attempted murder of a commercial traveller at the *Angel* in Ludlow, and of Edward Cooper, for the murder of his crippled son in 1863, attracted as many as 10,000 people, who were criticised for the levity of their demeanour. Even after public executions ceased in 1868, crowds assembled to witness the raising of a black flag when a condemned prisoner was hanged within the walls.[13]

Howard Street was laid out when the prison was built. By 1834 it had a 'respectable and architectural appearance', and six years later its 22 houses included some 'fitted up in a style of elegance seldom equalled or surpassed'. The Shrewsbury Mechanics' Institute was built there in 1833 but, like the genteel houses, was demolished to make way for the railway. In June 1835 the annual procession of stage coaches from the *Lion* witnessed the laying of the foundation stone of the Buttermarket.[14] Designed by Fallows & Hart as a wholesale market for the county's dairy produce, it stood at the terminus of the Shrewsbury Canal, whose wharf filled the area bounded by New Park Road and Beacall's Lane. When the canal opened in 1797 it extended only to Trench in the Coalbrookdale Coalfield, but in 1835 it was linked to the national waterways network. The market, opened in 1836, had direct access to the canal that

108 The gatehouse, the only surviving building of the gaol built for Quarter Sessions in the late 1780s. Executions took place on the roof of the bay to the left, and attracted large crowds until the surrounding arena was destroyed by the building of the railway station. In Shrewsbury, as in other county towns, the gaol was one of the first buildings constructed beyond the medieval limits.

was extended from the middle of the basin almost to Howard Street. From 1846 the canal was owned by the London & North Western Railway, who in 1859 constructed a line through a tunnel under Howard Street, opening into sidings extending across the wharf. After the opening of the general market in 1869 the butter market became a railway warehouse, which purpose it served for almost a century. On census night in 1881 four narrow boats were moored at the basin – *Moor Hen*, *Daisy*, *John Best* and vessel No 9593 – all crewed by much-travelled boat people. Traffic diminished until the wharf was formally closed in 1922.[15]

The Foregate

Castle Foregate is an area of ancient settlement. Two hundred early 10th-century coins were found during the construction of a garage for the Co-operative Society in 1936. John Speed shows that the area was built up in the early 17th century as far as the junction with New Park Road. The population of the area, inhabited chiefly by the labouring classes, grew fivefold between 1563 and 1668. Nevertheless Rocque's map of 1748 suggests that ornamental gardens lay behind some properties on both sides of the street. Before the Reformation many of the plots on the eastern side of the street were probably fees of the chantry of the Virgin in the collegiate church of St Mary, and passed to the Crown before being sold to speculators in 1589 and 1637.[16] The properties that extend along the eastern side of the street from Howard Street to New Park Road appear to be medieval burgage plots.

Castle Foregate was a resort of Irish migrants, 44 of whom were living on the eastern side in 1851 and 111 in 1861. It had many public houses, the *Eagle & Tun* (No 94), the *Old House at Home* (No 87), *Thrashers* (No 86), the *Crown* (No 78), the *Britannia* (before the 1850s the *Engine & Tender*, No 76), the *Bell* (No 74), the *Crown and Anchor* (No 69), the *Black Horse* (demolished in the 1870s and never numbered), and the *Plough* (No 55). The *Eagle & Tun*, an elegant three-storey structure, probably built between 1790 and 1820, had two bays in its Castle Foregate elevation,

109 The *Eagle & Tun* tavern on the corner of Howard Street and Castle Foregate, probably built when Howard Street was laid out in the late 1780s or early 1790s when the prison was built. The photograph was taken when the buildings awaited demolition to allow the widening of the railway – the sale to which the lot numbers refer took place in April 1900, and the materials were sold from Thomas Pace's yard at the end of May. The photograph shows that the adjacent buildings were tiny cottages.

110 Castle Foregate in the 1880s, showing Hall's Passage, Picken's Court, Bell Passage and Prees's Row.

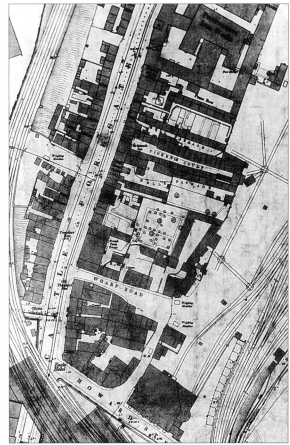

and five bays, with pedimented pavilions at each end facing Howard Street, one above a wagon arch beyond which stables accommodated more than 40 horses. From 1832 its landlord was Thomas Lunt, a farmer, host on market days to carriers from north Shropshire, and caterer for the town's great occasions. The inn was demolished when the railway tracks were re-aligned in 1897-1901. Photographs show adjoining buildings to have been two-storey timber-framed structures.

Some of the worst accommodation in 19th-century Shrewsbury was in four courts leading off Castle Foregate, where more than 300 people were living in 1861. Prees's Row had been built by 1832, but Hall's Passage (or Shut, or Buildings), Picken's Court and Bell Passage (or Shut) were probably constructed during the 1830s. The first two were approached through openings in a three-storey house that appears to date from the mid-18th century, probably the dwelling behind which Rocque depicted ornamental gardens. The *Britannia* inn occupies the central bays and is flanked by two archways lined with Ruabon bricks and ornamented with terracotta capitals and 'keystones', probably in the 1890s. The arch on the town side gave access to Hall's Passage, and the other to Picken's Court. Bell Passage, north of the *Bell* inn, probably disappeared when the Co-operative Society built a shop extending over several former properties in 1915. Prees's Row was approached through the entrance that remains between the former Co-op shop and No 70 Castle Foregate.

Hall's Passage consisted of 14 houses in two parallel terraces, the more southerly of which was demolished by 1901, and the other during slum clearance in the 1930s. Picken's Court takes its name from William Picken, keeper of *The Old House at Home* in 1841 and owner of the nearby Phoenix Foundry. He and his blacksmith son lived in the court in 1861. Picken's Court belonged to Richard Maddox, the department store owner, and consisted of 29 dwellings, two workshops and a block of 16 privies, when he died in 1892.[17] Census returns record 14 unoccupied dwellings in 1891, and by 1901 the more southerly range had been demolished. The other remained, as Britannia Place, until the 1950s. In 1871, 40 of the 134 occupants had been born in Mayo, Tipperary, Roscommon, West Meath, Kerry and Galway. All the dozen or so houses in Bell Passage remained in the mid-1920s, but they had been cleared by 1939. Its 73 occupants in 1871 included seven born in Co. Limerick and 20 from Co. Mayo. Prees's Row was consistently less overcrowded than the other courts, and was probably demolished when the Co-op shop was built in 1915.

The frontage between the former *Crown and Anchor* inn (No 69 Castle Foregate) and the *Plough* is occupied by the buildings of the Perseverance Ironworks, the creation of Thomas Corbett, son of a Wellington ironmonger, who at the age of 20 became agent in Shrewsbury for Bernhard Samuelson, a manufacturer of agricultural implements in Banbury. In 1867 Corbett began to make his '*Eclipse*' winnower in a workshop in Chester Street, and soon employed nearly 40 men. In 1868-9 he purchased from Henry Treasure a builder's yard in Castle Foregate that was the nucleus of his ironworks, which

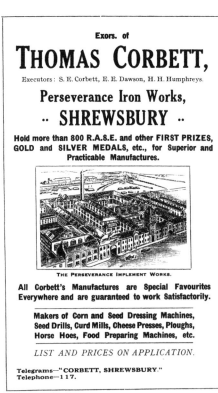

Exors. of

THOMAS CORBETT,

Executors: S. E. Corbett, E. E. Dawson, H. H. Humphreys.

Perseverance Iron Works,

·· SHREWSBURY ··

Hold more than 800 R.A.S.E. and other FIRST PRIZES, GOLD and SILVER MEDALS, etc., for Superior and Practicable Manufactures.

THE PERSEVERANCE IMPLEMENT WORKS.

All Corbett's Manufactures are Special Favourites Everywhere and are guaranteed to work Satisfactorily.

Makers of Corn and Seed Dressing Machines, Seed Drills, Curd Mills, Cheese Presses, Ploughs, Horse Hoes, Food Preparing Machines, etc.

LIST AND PRICES ON APPLICATION.

Telegrams—"CORBETT, SHREWSBURY."
Telephone—117.

111 The Perseverance Ironworks, developed by Thomas Corbett. This advertisement dates from the 1920s when the foundry was run by Corbett's executors, but the block is certainly much older, for boats had ceased to reach the canal basin in the background by that time.

by 1900 had a street frontage of 83 yards (76 m). The move to the new premises was celebrated with a treat for the foundrymen in March 1869. Wood's map of 1838 shows one or two cottages on the town side of the *Plough*, to the south of which stood three large houses with gardens extending to the Coal Wharf. One of these (No 60) was occupied in 1871 and 1881 by Thomas Corbet himself, and in 1901 by his son Edwin. The oldest part of the works is a four-bay building, bearing the date 1871, and the inscription 'Speed the Plough' above a wagon arch. To the south is a block dating from 1873, and adjoining it the clock tower and another range inscribed 1876. North of the 1871 building is a later five-bay range in red brick with blue brick dressings, with its windows divided by small cast-iron columns inscribed 'Cor-

112   A portrait of Thomas Corbett.

bett', that probably replaced the Corbetts' house. A ten-bay building on the western side of Castle Foregate dating from 1884 was also part of the enterprise. The Perseverance Works encountered difficulties after the First World War, and in 1929 Corbett's executors sold the site for £6,500 to Morris & Co. for their oil blending business. The *Plough* inn, an ancient hostelry, is probably the only timber-framed building remaining in the Castle Foregate.[18]

Back-to-Backs

Coal Wharf Square, behind the *Plough*, was one of two back-to-back developments in Shrewsbury built around the time the canal was opened in 1797. The 'square' comprised a back-to-back terrace and a row of through houses, 38 dwellings in all. The 1841 census records 154 people living in 34 occupied houses, a mean of 4.5 per house. In 1851 there were 141 occupants in 35 inhabited houses, 26 of whom were employed at the Ditherington flax mill. Ten years later 151 people occupied 36 of the 38 houses. Thereafter the occupancy rate and the number of inhabitants fell. Only 28 houses were occupied in 1891 and 30 in 1901, when the mean was 3.8 per house. The square was 'reconstructed' between 1910 and 1916, and ten of the 11 remaining houses were occupied in 1938.

The other back-to-backs were Canal Buildings, two terraces, each of 24 dwellings, between New Park Road and the canal about 500 yards from Coal Wharf Square, next to the *Bowling Green Inn*. Wood's map suggests that the terraces were in different ownerships. A notice in 1838 offered for sale 24 'recently built' brick and slate houses comprising Lower Canal Buildings. In 1841, 236 people were living in 44 occupied houses, a mean of 5.4 per house. One was Bridget Cain, an Irishwoman working at the flax mill, with her six Irish-born children. More than 200 people were recorded in the rows in each of the subsequent censuses up to 1891, and 194 lived in 43 occupied houses in 1901. By 1891 the southerly range was called Stanley Terrace, and the other gained the inappropriate name of Poplar Avenue. Between 1902 and 1925 dwellings were

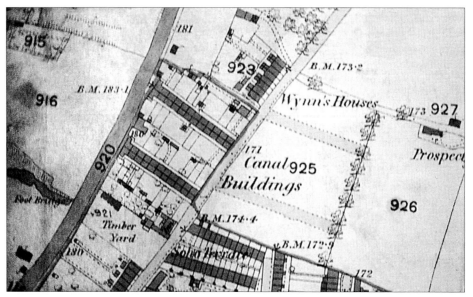

113 The two terraces of back-to-back houses that made up Canal Buildings, probably built in the 1820s.

amalgamated to form 'through' houses, 13 in Poplar Avenue and 12 in Stanley Terrace, a form of surgery also practised in Birmingham, where reconstructed terraces were called 'Nettlefold Courts'. A Salopian who passed them daily en route from Sundorne to the Lancasterian School in the 1950s still knew them as the 'back-to-backs'.[19]

Castle Foregate: The Western Side

The western side of Castle Foregate from Chester Street to the *Red Lion* inn (No 53) was a detached part of the parish of St Alkmund, bounded to the west by the Bagley Brook. In the Middle Ages most of it belonged to the Corbets of Moreton Corbet.[20] The frontage was built-up by the late 16th century, but the plots were shorter than those on the eastern side of the Foregate. In the 1830s the only one that extended to the brook was Chapel Court, at the end of which stood a meeting-house, opened on 28 February 1828 by a schismatic Baptist group from the congregation assembling in Claremont Street. In 1841 there were about 40 dwellings. Properties between Chapel Court and Cross Street were bounded by an ornamental garden, while there was a field between the brook and the properties north of Chapel Court. In 1848 the railway to Chester isolated the properties at the Chester Street end, and caused the demolition of others, while the line to Crewe, opened in 1858, cut short the property boundaries. The Bagley Brook was culverted beneath freight yards, and more properties were demolished to give access to the depot alongside the line to Chester. The re-alignment of the railway junction in 1897-1900 caused the demolition of Nos 14-20. The Baptist Chapel was taken down in 1858, and after worshipping in temporary accommodation the congregation re-joined the Claremont Street Church in 1872.[21]

The number of dwellings in the area increased between 1841 and 1851 probably due to the building of courts, that are named only in the 1871 census. Court No 1 was Grapes Passage, south of the railway. No 2, perhaps Lindley's Court with five houses, stood between Nos 22 and 23 Castle Foregate, No 3, perhaps Beacall's Court with six, between Nos 24 and 25, No 4 between Nos 25 and 26, all south of the entrance to the G.W.R. yard. To the north was No 5, which had gone by 1890, and the entrance to No 6, probably Leake's Court, with four houses, between Nos 37 and 38. There were three lodging houses in the area in 1851, with a total of 34 inmates, of whom 13 were Irish-born.

Few old buildings remain in the area. The detached early 19th-century shop (No 27) was long occupied by newsagents. The *Rock & Fountain* (No 32) is recorded in the 1871 census, but was later rebuilt. Jones's Terrace (Nos 42-49), eight two-storey cottages, with a polychrome string course below the eaves, and yellow brick bands at window sill levels, dating from the 1880s, is probably named after Thomas Jones, landlord of the *Red Lion*, which was replaced by dwellings in 2004, although it had long been de-licensed.

St Michael's Street

Gas lighting was introduced to Shrewsbury at the two flax mills in 1811. A public gas company was established on 13 January 1820, built a gas works at the junction of St Michael Street and New Park Road, and inaugurated a public supply on 8 September 1820. The works extended to the Shrewsbury Canal, the source of coal for the retorts, and by 1851 it had three gasholders. A three-storey polychrome brick office block was built in 1884, of which only the ground floor, currently part of a gymnasium, remains. The works was extended in the late 19th century with the construction of a large gasholder north of the Castle Mills and new retorts were added in 1920.

The connection of the Shrewsbury Canal to the national waterways network in 1835 stimulated the principal carriers of sundries traffic to establish warehouses in the town. John Wood's map of 1838 shows Pickford, Henshall, Johnson and Whitehouse occupying premises on the Canal Wharf, and Tilston & Co., Fairhurst & Co., and Crowley Hicklin & Co. working from warehouses on a plot north of the gasworks, approached from St Michael Street. The carrying companies ceased trading after the opening of railways, and in the early 1850s the site was adapted by Richard and William Blakeway as the Castle Mills, where two beam engines drove nine sets of stones. The Blakeways also built Castle Terrace, seven three-storey houses fronting

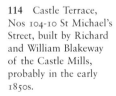

114 Castle Terrace, Nos 104-10 St Michael's Street, built by Richard and William Blakeway of the Castle Mills, probably in the early 1850s.

St Michael Street (Nos 104-10), the southernmost spanning with an arch the approach to the warehouses. These are imposing dwellings, uncharacteristic of Shrewsbury's northern suburbs. The first householders included a corn dealer, a maltster, a gas engineer, a retired farmer, a miller's clerk and a Scottish travelling draper. A branch canal served the Castle Mills, whose owners diversified into malting. Soon after 1900 William Jones & Son adapted the whole premises for malting and filled in the canal branch.[22] Malting continued until 1986 and one malthouse remains among the houses of Cornmill Square.

A strip of allotments, on some of which were glasshouses, extended along the roadside north of Castle Terrace until the 1880s, and behind them were brickfields. Advertisements from the 1830s drew attention to clay beds in the area, and canal boats provided coal. Clay was worked without powered mills and bricks were fired in temporary clamps until after 1884 when kilns and mills were erected. Between 1886 and 1907 the brickmakers, Thomas Williams and his family built Primrose Terrace, eight groups of four houses, forming a continuous terrace along St Michael's Street, where there had previously been allotments.[23] The phasing of construction can be appreciated through butt joints between the eight groups, bricks of different qualities, variations in patterns of doors and windows, and four types of cream-coloured chimney pot. Beyond the terrace were older houses built by 1861, five in Minor's Houses, 13 in Williams's Buildings, and several belonging to Edward Edwards, a boatbuilder. The St Michael's Street Board School, designed by A.E. Lloyd Oswell, was built north of Minor's Houses in 1897, while the adjoining recreation ground, extending to the line of the canal, is reclaimed brickyard. In the 20th century the brickfield behind Primrose Terrace was used by the gas company, but in 2006 it is occupied by the Castle Mews housing development.

The Factory Bridge, bearing a plaque recording its name, its number, 47, and its rebuilding in 1913, carries the main road over the canal. An enclave of St Julian's parish on the canal bank comprised two inns, the *Robin Hood* and the *Golden Ball*, two houses, a blacksmith's shop, and a wharf, which in 1841 was handling coal from the mine at Uffington. Hallcroft Court occupies the site. The adjacent old people's bungalows, at the extremity of New Park Close, occupy the sites of 17 prefabs built in 1947 on land that was once part of Golden Ball Farm.[24]

Simpson's Square

The growth of the area west of the turnpike road and north of Castle Foregate, bounded from 1858 by the railway to Crewe, was initially stimulated by the opening of the flax mill in 1796-97. There were over a hundred houses in the area in 1841, about 220 in 1861 and 1871 and 270 are shown on the Ordnance Survey map of 1884. The area occupied in 2006 by flats was the site of Simpson's Square, built by John Simpson, a quadrangle of 24 dwellings of irregular size, with privies in the centre, and the *Black Horse* inn on the corner nearest the town. John's Row, named after Simpson's son, was a terrace of ten dwellings, which, with several houses around the gardens at the rear and three in Lawley's Passage, almost made up another square.[25] To the north lay Wrekin Terrace, an L-shaped range of 14 houses set back from the road behind two detached houses with gardens. Near to John's Row and adjacent to the *Fox* public house in 1871 was a flour dealer's shop named 'the People's Warehouse'.

The school of St Mary and St Michael was opened in 1832. In front of it were two terraces, each of five houses, known as Oakley's Square in the 1830s, but later as

Derfald Court. The school building served as a municipal lodging house between 1935, when slum clearance in Bridge Street led to the closure of a common lodging house, and 2000. The front part, after an extension across the site of Derfald Court, became Shrewsbury's British Restaurant in August 1942, offering a meal with two vegetables for seven pence. On the site occupied in 2002 by the fire station stood Prospect Place, a terrace of ten houses built in the 1860s, and behind it an older terrace of nine houses extending round the corner from Derfald Street into Crewe Street, probably once called Chune's Row.[26]

Immediately to the west were ten houses with long gardens extending to Crewe Street. A terrace of 17 dwellings, known as Dolphin Row and built by 1851, extended along the turnpike road to the *Dolphin* inn. Beyond the site of the demolished row is Montford Place (Nos 49-54), a terrace of early 19th-century three-storey cottages with classically-styled doorcases. Next to Montford Place was St Michael's Terrace, a straggling range of 28 varied cottages including six back-to-back dwellings, and a salt warehouse. In 1871 No 3 was a brothel kept by Maria Diggory, a 45-year-old widow. No 55 St Michael's Street, to the north, was the clerk's house for the Ditherington flax mill, built by John Simpson with the same extra-large bricks used in the early mill buildings. The terrace of four houses, named Ann's Hill after Simpson's daughter (Nos 56-9) and constructed before June 1800, was the flax mill's first apprentice house. Behind Ann's Hill is the former church of St Michael, designed by John Carline, and consecrated on 24 August 1830, with a chancel added in 1873. Huge blocks of Grinshill stone make up much of the churchyard wall. A terrace of 14 three-storey and 16 two-storey houses (Nos 61-90), built soon after 1850 and known as Hackfield Place, extends along the main road to the corner shop (Nos 91-92), which is built of extra-large bricks, and is probably contemporary with the flax mill.[27]

The road past the school, once School Lane, and the access from the north to St Michael's church were joined to form a loop off the main road, the whole of which was was known as Derfald Street in the 1880s. By 1891 all but the former School Lane had been re-named Crewe Street, which included Meadow Terrace, a terrace of 19 dwellings on the northern side, and the 11 houses forming Robin Hood Terrace, built before 1861, on the southern side. One 19th-century terrace (Nos 1-7) remains.

The Flax Mill

The Ditherington flax mill stimulated the growth of Shrewsbury's northern suburbs. It is a significant structure, internationally, as the first multi-storey iron-framed building, and nationally as part of the factory-based linen industry that grew up from 1780. The creator of this industry, who consciously compared his role with that of Richard Arkwright in cotton-spinning, was John Marshall, son of an insignificant Leeds linen merchant, who, in 1832 in the first general election after the Great Reform Act, was elected, together with Lord Macaulay the historian, member for the West Riding, the most prestigious of parliamentary constituencies. Marshall and his partners employed from 1787 the flax-spinning frames patented by John Kendrew and Thomas Porterhouse of Darlington, soon replacing them with machines designed by their mechanic, the subsequently eminent mechanical engineer Matthew Murray. Their first factory north of Leeds was water-powered, but in 1791 they constructed a steam-powered mill south of the city centre, which became the nucleus of a complex whose architectural highlight was Temple Mill, built in the Egyptian style in 1838-41 by Ignatius Bonomi.

Marshall ended his agreement with his original partners in 1793, forsaking them for Thomas and Benjamin Benyon of Shrewsbury, who matched his £9,000 capital with a similar sum of their own. The Benyons lived in Quarry Place, traded Welsh flannel, and, like Marshall, were Unitarians. In the spring of 1796 the partners decided to build a mill in Shrewsbury, and admitted to the company Charles Bage, surveyor and wine merchant, the son of Robert Bage who managed a Derbyshire paper mill and wrote novels. Charles Bage was interested in masonry arches and in the constructional use of iron, about which he corresponded with William Strutt of Belper, who had used iron components as a means of rendering cotton mills resistant to fire. He also knew William Reynolds, the ironmaster, and Thomas Telford, who shared with him the results of experiments at the Reynolds's Ketley Ironworks in connection with the construction of Longdon Aqueduct on the Shrewsbury Canal.[28]

In September 1796 the partners bought from John Mytton of Halston a plot of seven acres in Child's Fields. They used less than half of it for mill buildings, and the rest remained pasture 90 years later. Bricks were made from clay excavated on the site, and the members of the iron frame were cast at William Hazledine's foundry in Coleham. The first of the two steam engines in the main mill was installed in August

115 The Ditherington flax mill shortly after it had been converted to a maltings by William Jones & Son. The photograph shows the canal still in water, with a narrow towpath after the single-storey extension had been added to the main mill building, increasing the area available for laying out barley for malting and bringing about the demolition of the mill's boilers.

116 The Ditherington flax mill complex from the west showing the end gable of the Hackling Block, the dye-house of the 1850s, and a 20th-century concrete silo built by the malting company. The wall in the middle distance runs alongside a railway siding off the line to Crewe.

117 A pillar that is evidence of the takeover of the flax mill site by William Jones & Son in 1898.

1797, and was working by the following November. The building was reported to be complete on 1 September 1797. More buildings were added to the complex over the next 15 years. The key to their phasing is the use of over-large bricks in buildings known to have been erected by June 1805, and of standard bricks in those of later date.[29]

Flax, from the Baltic, Flanders, Friesland, Ireland and Normandy, was delivered to the mill in bundles and stored in the flax warehouse. On removal it was heckled (i.e. combed) in the cross-wing that joins the northern end of the main building. Heckling separated the long fibres, the *line*, from the coarse ones, the *tow*, *noggs* or *hurds*. The former went to the fourth storey of the main mill for carding and to the floor below for spinning, while the tow was carded on the ground floor and spun on the first floor. The flax was bleached or dyed in the buildings along the western edge of the site, and the finished products despatched from a warehouse that formerly stood by the entrance. In the early years some linen and canvas were woven at Ditherington, perhaps on the attic floor of the main mill, but by the mid-1820s the factory concentrated on making thread for the manufacture of clothing and footwear, while Marshall made linen fabrics at Leeds. In the 1830s a new process, wet spinning, was introduced and the pattern of production changed. The ground floor of the main mill was divided between a fitters' workshop and a wood-working shop, making reels for thread, and the dyehouse was completely rebuilt in the 1850s. Steam for the engines at either end of the main mill came from boilers on the bank of the Shrewsbury Canal.[30]

Marshall & Co., while encountering difficulties in the 1870s and 1880s, was still reckoned 'the largest firm of flax spinners in Europe', when the founder's grandsons, entranced by rural pursuits in the Lake District, announced in October 1885 that they were winding-up the company. Production at Ditherington ceased on 21 October 1886, soon after the closure of the Leeds factory, and attempts to continue with locally-raised capital proved unavailing. More than a decade later the mill was adapted as a maltings by William Jones & Co., whose name, with the date 1898, appears on a pillar adjoining the railway siding. Except for an interval during the Second World War, when the building was a barracks for training infantrymen, malting continued until 1987. William Jones & Co. replaced the boiler house on the canal bank with a lean-to malting floor alongside the ground floor of the main mill, and erected the pyramidal kiln and the tower housing hoisting equipment at the northern end.[31]

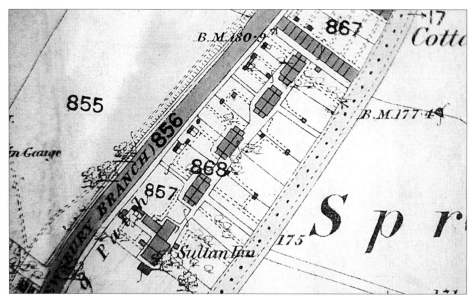

118 Spring Gardens, the area between the Shrewsbury Canal and the turnpike road to Whitchurch, showing the four blocks of cluster houses north of the *Sultan Inn*, built for the nearby Ditherington flax mill.

When Marshall and his partners purchased the site, John Mytton, the vendor, agreed to construct between the canal and the turnpike road four blocks of what are known in Derbyshire as cluster houses, each containing four dwellings, and to lease them to the millowners from Lady Day 1797 at an annual rent of £80. This was the beginning of a process by which Spring Gardens, the area enclosed by the Shrewsbury Canal and the turnpike road between the Factory and Comet bridges, became filled by the 1850s with more than 100 dwellings.[32] Mytton agreed to build four blocks but eventually eight were constructed, four on either side of a group of communal buildings, including the *Sultan Inn*, and a Congregational chapel.[33] The cluster houses had large gardens, as in Belper and Darley Abbey, where similar blocks remain. Traditionally they accommodated supervisors and skilled employees. Council flats replaced the cluster houses to the north in the late 1950s. The two blocks south of the *Sultan* had been demolished by the 1880s and their site is occupied by the bus garage, opened on 11 November 1920. In 1929 its two northerly bays replaced the inn, which had been de-licensed in 1918.[34] The site of the other two cluster

119 St Michael's Gardens, a terrace of 12 houses built between 1830 and 1850, photographed *c*.1969, not long before they were demolished.

house blocks was used for parking buses from the 1950s. There were eight terraces in Spring Gardens at right angles to the main road. Two formed Haughmond Square (or View), while the others, in south-north order were Bodkin Row, Edwards's Buildings, Kent Row, Horseman's Square, Spring Cottages and Far Garden Place.

Two terraces south of Ditherington Mill, close to the site occupied by Marshall's Court, were associated with the factory in popular memory because William Jones & Co. owned them from the 1920s, but they had no direct connection with the flax mill. The first originated early in the 19th century as two separate blocks, acquired in 1828 by Robert Davies, a linen weaver, who by 1859 had created from them a terrace of six houses called Davies's Buildings. They were demolished before 1965. A curving terrace of 12 houses known as St Michael's Gardens, built between 1830 and 1850, remained until the 1970s.[35]

Castlefields

The suburb of Castlefields was shaped by New Park Road, an ancient lane providing access to farmland between the River Severn and the turnpike road, by Shrewsbury's second flax mill constructed in 1804, and by the town's Freehold Land Society. Some houses were demolished during re-development in the 1960s, but many features remain of the historic landscape.

New Park Road was the spine of Castlefields, although most of its housing was obliterated during re-development.[36] It led to New Park Farm, a three-bay brick house, described as 'newly erected' in 1795, probably built by Edward Elsmere, a farmer whose family owned much of the riverside land that had formerly belonged to the Myttons. The first substantial housing along the road comprised the back-to-back houses known as Canal Buildings, and the adjacent *Bowling Green Inn*.[37] By 1850 semi-detached villas, two of them later extended into short terraces called Smith's Buildings and Walker's Buildings, lined the road from the *Canal Tavern* to the back-to-backs. New Park Terrace, a cul-de-sac comprising two terraces of 14 and seven houses, running north to the canal, was begun in the 1860s. On the opposite side 24 houses including six in Holt Place and eight in Langford Place were built around the junction with the track that became North Street. By 1881 the most northerly houses in New Park Road were Wynn's Cottages, which remain, and only a small amount of filling-in followed before the First World War. To the south New Park Road gave access to New Park Street, Soho Terrace, Victoria Terrace and Lindley Street. Argyll Street and John Street had been laid out by 1881. By 1901 there were 23 houses in Argyll Street and 38, including the recently-erected Pretoria Terrace, in John Street, where an uneven pattern of numbering reflects its slow growth.

120 The *Canal Tavern*, one of the few 19th-century buildings that remain on New Park Road. The line of the Shrewsbury Canal was just behind the building.

121 A sketch of the Castlefields flax mill.

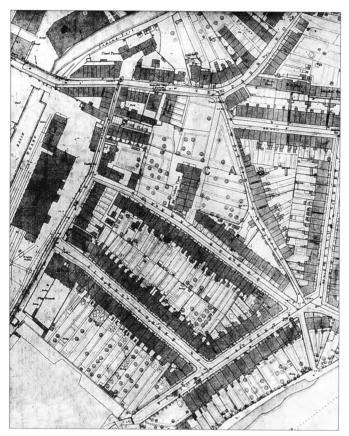

122 The Castlefields area in 1882. The three roads leading off New Park Road, North Street, Water Street and the track towards Cadran Place follow those that gave access to the Castlefields flax mill, whose main building was close to Benyon Street. Victoria Street, Albert Street and the south-western side of Severn Street comprised the first estate of the Shrewsbury Freehold Land Society, built on allotment gardens in the early 1850s. The large block on the opposite side of Severn Street is the iron-framed former flax warehouse of the mill, while Cadran Place, replaced by council flats in the 1950s, was probably the mill's apprentice house.

Thomas and Benjamin Benyon and Charles Bage terminated their flax-spinning partnership with John Marshall in 1804, and set up a business parallel to the one they had left, with mills in Leeds and at Castlefields, Shrewsbury. The latter complex was larger than the Ditherington mill, with an iron-framed main mill measuring 208 x 35 ft (63.7 x 10.8m), and many subsidiary buildings. Bage withdrew from the partnership in 1815-16. Thomas Benyon died in 1833 and his brother in 1834, and it appears that there was family discord over the succession. The mill was sold in the mid-1830s, and most of the buildings were demolished by 31 May 1837.[38] Subsequently the land was

123 The iron-framed former flax warehouse of the Castlefields flax mill, now Nos 5-8a Severn Street. Above the windows are herringbone lintels similar to those visible in the adjacent two-storey house, and it is likely that the houses on either side were built when windows were inserted in the former warehouse when it was adapted as a weaving workshop, probably in the late 1830s or 1840s. The building was a meeting place for Wesleyan Reformers in 1851, and was used for linen weaving until the 1870s.

used for brickmaking, and a scatter of houses appeared on the periphery.

At the corner where New Park Road turns north, a place still called New Factory Yard in 1871, three tracks, now North Street, Water Street and Cadran Place, fanned out towards the mill. Water Street led to the flax warehouse, dyehouse and bleachworks, and the western end of North Street to the boilers and gas works. Cadran Place, reputedly the apprentice house of the flax mill, subsequently contained ten apartments, and was replaced by council flats in 1956.[39]

The iron-framed flax warehouse of the Castlefields Mill now comprises Nos 5-8a Severn Street. After the mill closed the warehouse was adapted for linen weaving by Sacheverell Harwood.[40] He was succeeded by Robert Minns, a Yorkshireman whose widow was continuing his business in 1871. Flax warehouses usually had few windows, and the herringbone lintels above the windows of Nos 5-8a Severn Street suggest that the building was converted to housing when the eight houses to the east, which have similar lintels, were built, probably in the early 1840s.

The Shrewsbury Freehold Land Society, founded in 1851, purchased Benyon's Gardens, the 48 allotments in the area bounded by the prison, Beacall's Lane, the flax warehouse, and the River Severn, and during 1853 sought tenders for roads and sewers.[41] Victoria Street, Albert Street and the southern side of Severn Street were built by 1861, and are characteristic of Freehold Land Society developments. Plots were allocated by ballot, but since individuals could acquire more than one plot (although the number was restricted) they became vehicles for small-scale speculation rather than owner-occupied homes. The south side of Severn Street indicates the variety of

124 The characteristic mixed housing of a Freehold Land Society estate on the south-western side of Severn Street.

building. Nos 29-30 are a two-storey pair with a front of whitish brick, but red brick in the side elevations and herringbone lintels. No 31 and No 32 are single houses, while Nos 33-34 form a pair with segmental lintels over windows and doors. Nos 35-6 make up a taller pair, built of more vividly red bricks than their neighbours, with semi-circular brick arches over the doors, and herringbone lintels above the windows. Nos 37-8 have pointed arches above the doors and dentil courses below the eaves. Nos 39-42 form a terrace, Nos 43 and No 44 are single houses, while No 45, the former *Plough* public house, is a three-storey building that until 2002 had a prominent bow window. The doorways of Nos 46-8 have tiny canopies supported by scrolls. Nos 49-50 have pedimented doorcases, similar to those of Nos 7-12 Beacall's Lane round the corner. Householders in Albert Street in 1871 included a railway goods agent, a pawnbroker's assistant, a solicitor's managing clerk, an 86-year-old supernumerary Wesleyan minister, a soda water agent, a photographer, a retired farmer and a woman keeping a respectable lodging house. The Lancasterian School and the United Methodist chapel occupied plots at the west end of Albert Street.

Dorsett Street and Benyon Street, near the site of the main building of the mill, formed the core of the Freehold Land Society's second estate in Castlefields. Tenders were sought for roads and drains in the summer of 1854 and the ballot took place on 3 October.[42] By 1861 thee were eight houses in Dorsett Street and 36 in Benyon Street, the latter occupied by 151 people, a mean occupancy rate of 4.2. Heads of households including seven women of modestly independent means and eight railwaymen, with two cabinet makers and two upholsterers, a coal agent, a schoolmaster, a 'gentleman', a retired tailor, a haulier, a pawnbroker, a cow keeper, a labourer in the flax mill, a solicitor's managing clerk, a currier who kept a provision shop, a draughtsman, a civil engineer's assistant, a gunmaker, a stone mason, a pianofortemaker, a gardener and a carpenter. Twelve houses accommodated 21 lodgers, four of whom were railwaymen, and there were live-in domestic servants at Nos 10, 11 and 16. The department store owner Richard Maddox owned Nos 8-11 when he died in 1892.[43]

The Dorsetts Barn estate, on the riverbank between the Dorsett Street and New Park, was created in the mid-17th century, acquired after 1812 by Robert Burton of Longner Hall, and offered for sale in 1860.[44] The stock of Whitfield's Nursery, which occupied part of the site, was sold in the spring of 1866. The Freehold Land Society laid out streets during the summer, and the ballot for more than 100 plots took place early in 1867.[45] The estate comprised the southern side of North Street, called New North Street in 1871, Queen Street, where there were about 20 houses in 1871, West Street, Burton Street and New Park Street. The dates on two adjacent houses in North Street, 1868 on Hope Cottage, No 62 and 1876 on Howth House, No 63, show that the development of a Freehold Land Society estate could be protracted. Dorsetts Barn Farm was incorporated into the suburban landscape, and is still approached, past farmworkers' cottages, by a track, known in 1891 as Capper's Lane after the farmer, William Capper.

Some freehold land society developments had 'front rows' streets of spacious plots usually facing a main road. In Castlefields the front row was Severn Bank, overlooking the river. There were nine houses but eight empty plots in 1884, and only three dwellings were added in the next 17 years. The house at the eastern end became the vicarage for All Saints, while other occupants included the Holt family, the wine merchants, and Elizabeth Jones, a widow who kept a boarding school, which in 1891 accommodated 36 girls aged between nine and 18, and three governesses.

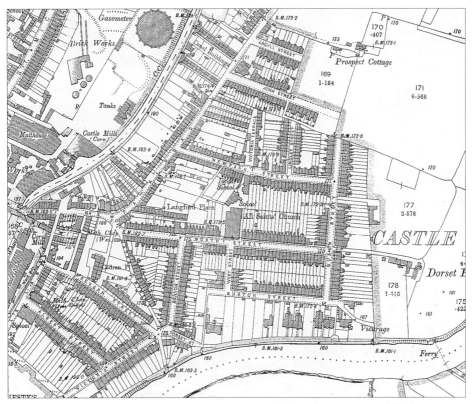

125   The later stages of development by the Freehold Land Society in Castlefields.

While the Freehold Land Society had a dissenting ethos, Castlefields was profoundly influenced by the Church of England. The 'Model Cottages', Nos 21-26 North Street, dated 1863, in bright red brick with blue and yellow brick string courses, appear to have been built by the Anglican-orientated Salopian Society for improving the Condition of the Industrious Classes.[46] To the east the 1871 census recorded a 'Temporary Iron Church', a mission hut measuring 83 ft x 28 ft (25 x 7m) that was dedicated at the initiative of the Revd T.M. Bulkeley Owen on 15 December 1870. Owen became acquainted with the navvies who built the railway through Ellesmere, and, encouraged by Archdeacon John Allen, missioned railwaymen in Shrewsbury. The foundation stone of the church of All Saints, designed by Edward Haycock II, was laid on 25 September 1875 and it was consecrated the following year. It was built of Shelvock stone, over the temporary building, which was removed through the west door. The ethos was Tractarian. Initially Owen tried to separate men and women, but the preponderance of females in the congregation made this impractical. Processions of robed clergy, and the surpliced choir, carrying banners made by women members of the congregation, were memorable.[47] Owen ended his formal connection with All Saints in 1877, and subsequently lived as squire of Tedsmore. The All Saints Institute in Queen Street was built in 1899, and tennis courts and bowling greens were added in 1922. An infant school was built between the church and New Park Street.[48]

The Wesleyan Chapel on New Park Road was built in 1837, part of the irregular building activity that took place in Castlefields after the flax mill was demolished. There were only 46 adults at the best-attended service on census Sunday in 1851. An ornate front was added in 1893. The building was sold in 1973 and subsequently demolished.[49] The other Methodist chapel in Castlefields resulted from a schism in the Wesleyan congregation at St John's Hill. Wesleyan Reformers met in the linen manufactory in Severn Street from 1 October 1850, and the Revd James Everett, a national leader of the reform movement, laid the foundation stone of a chapel in Albert Street in April 1853. The chapel bears the inscription 'Methodist Free Church 1853', although the United Methodist Free Church was not formed until 1857, when reformers came together with groups who had previously seceded from the Wesleyan Connexion.[50] The Gospel Hall in John Street was established in 1880 by a wealthy dentist, Charles Gibbs Nightingale of Severn Bank, and led for many decades by his sons.[51]

Castlefields was linked to Ditherington in the early 1920s by a thoroughfare branching off New Park Road named Sultan Road after the inn that faced its junction with the main road. The houses lining the road, built by the corporation in 1924-6, were designed so that their rents could be afforded by the lowest-paid workpeople. The council houses along the western side of New Park Road beyond Wynn's Cottages and in New Park Close were built in 1935-36.[52] New Park Road now gives access to late 20th-century developments, amongst which stands the 18th-century New Park Farm.

Beyond the Comet

The bridge carrying the turnpike road over the Shrewsbury Canal, that takes its name from the *Comet* inn, marks the beginning of the area historically known as Ditherington. Immediately beyond the *Comet* is the approach to Shrewsbury's first council estate, built under the Housing of the Working Classes Act of 1890. The 63 houses forming the 'garden suburb' of Wingfield Gardens were begun in 1913 but construction was delayed by the death of the contractor in January 1914. Building recommenced in May, and 45 houses were occupied by December. The estate was named after Col C.R.B. Wingfield of Onslow Park, who was mayor in 1913-14. Councillor Herbert Harries, a saddler from High Street, was credited with instigating the project.[53] The houses, which cost about £13,500, were built on a triangular plot, and designed in the 'Garden City' style by the Shrewsbury architect, A.E. Williams, who took pride in eliminating the 'unsightly rear extensions' of tunnel-back houses. Grouped in pairs and blocks of three and four, around a green lined with alternate lime and London plane trees, the Wingfield Gardens houses are rendered and have prominent gables in steeply-sloping chalet-type roofs.

126 Houses on Wingfield Gardens, the first estate built by Shrewsbury Borough Council, designed by A.E. Williams and completed in 1915.

127 The terrace called Mount Pleasant built by William Hazledine in the 1830s on the site of the kennels of the Shropshire Hunt at Ditherington, that stood in isolation, over the railway tracks from the ancient settlement on Old Heath, until they were surrounded by houses in the 1960s.

The houses on either side were built in the 1930s. White House Gardens, constructed in 1934-35, occupies a plot made up of a small field, two acres of abandoned clay pits and several enclosures around the White House, a villa on the main road that for a time was used as a clinic. The road was extended to join Long Row in the 1960s. The 120 houses in Wingfield Close were built in 1937-38, on land purchased by Marshall, Benyon & Bage in 1795-96, which in the mid-19th century was divided into 52 allotments.[54] Most of the houses on the two estates are grouped in fours.

The name 'Ditherington' was first applied to part of the Old Heath that belonged to Shrewsbury Corporation but lay outside the borough boundary. This was the settlement west of the main road approached by Long Row, named after a terrace of 15 cottages now demolished. By 1624 there was a bowling green alongside the main road, which in 1657 was kept by a 'brickman', who built a cottage on the edge of the green that may have been the ancestor of the *Six Bells*. In the 1770s the corporation began to sell its properties and by 1832 Ditherington was a scattered settlement of squatter-like cottages within small enclosures. Criminals were executed on a gallows on the borough boundary until 1794.[55] In the 1830s William Hazledine erected five three-storey houses called Mount Pleasant on a property where in 1825 Sir Bellingham Graham had set up kennels for the hounds of the Shropshire Hunt. The kennels had a short life, but the elegant terrace remains, surrounded by semi-detached houses of the 1960s in Weston Drive. Hazledine owned 27 nearby cottages, including 11 described in 1841 as 'newly-built'.[56] By 1840 there were more than 60 houses in the area and the settlement expanded to 75 houses in 1855, about 85 in 1861 and more than 100 by 1871. By 1881 there were about 130, approximately the same number that remained before the clearance of 62 houses was sanctioned in 1957.[57] The names of the houses suggest that this was an area where small-scale speculators flourished – they included Palmer's Houses, Craig's Houses, Hammond's Houses, Walker's Houses, Gwynn's Houses, Bull's Houses, Morgan's Houses, the Chain Row and Club Row, perhaps built by some form of building society. The buildings that survived the clearances included the 14 cottages of the 1870s called Haughmond Terrace, the *Compasses* pub, and the infants' school, now a community centre. The Primitive Methodist chapel of 1844 has disappeared.[58] Brickmaking continued in the area at least until the 1860s – a legacy of pits and waste tips remained a century later – and there were several malthouses, as well as a linen bleaching 'factory' kept in 1851 by one Joseph Lee.[59] A travelling showman was parked on open ground on census night in 1861.

On Ditherington Road north of Long Row are the *Six Bells*, which has a Ruabon brick front on an earlier building, a pair of concrete block houses (Nos 61/63), and

Grove Villa, once the premises of a coachbuilder. The estates approached along Mount Pleasant Road comprise a mixture of private and local authority houses, built from the mid-1950s, with the exception of Hazledine's terrace, from which the road takes its name. The eastern side of the main road is a mixture of shops and inter-war private housing. Comet Drive is a cul-de-sac built by Fletcher Estates in 1956-7.[60]

The Twentieth-Century Suburbs: Harlescott, Sundorne

The Heathgates island dates from 1964 and marks the first junction on the roads from Castle Foregate to Preston Brockhurst, Shawbury and Shreyhill, managed by a turnpike trust from 1756. By 1777 the trust also controlled Harlescott Lane and Featherbed Lane, linking the Ellesmere Road with Uffington and Atcham. The trust's tollgate in Castle Foregate was moved to Heathgates between 1790 and 1793.[61] The tollkeeper's cottage remained in 1924 when the occupants were robbed by burglars from Liverpool.[62] The *Heathgates* public house overlooking the island opened in October 1936.[63] To the west is the Heath Lodge or Old Heath council estate of 86 houses, built in 1938-9.[64]

The outer suburb beyond, in the triangle between the L.N.W.R. line to Crewe, Harlescott Lane and Featherbed Lane, and Sundorne Road, was shaped by developments during the First World War. In the centre stood a farmstead, called Old Heath Farm in the 19th century, but The Meadows by 1938, approached by a track from Sundorne Road. Until 1934 most of the area lay in Atcham Rural District whose council had ambitions in the 1920s for a 'new town'. In 1925 a plan was published for houses and factories extending over 3,000 acres between the Ellesmere Road and Uffington, which would cause the county town to be known as 'Shrewsbury near Harlescott'.[65] The only significant outcomes of these aspirations were the building of Harlescott Crescent and the adjacent Chatwood factory in 1925, and the construction of a sewage works for the houses in the area, opened in January 1928, about 250 yards south of Sundorne Road, between the River Severn and the canal.[66] From 1 April 1934 the borough boundary was extended and house-building in Harlescott accelerated.

New developments challenged existing ecclesiastical as well as political boundaries. The new houses in Harlescott in the 1920s were remote from the parish church of St Alkmund, and in 1924 the Revd J.E.G. Cartledge, experienced in mission work at Ashington, Northumberland, chaplain to Shrewsbury prison, and an army chaplain in the First World War, was given charge of a 'conventional district'. He held services in the Sentinel works canteen and baptised babies in his house in Sentinel Gardens. On Whit Sunday 1925 a temporary Church of the Holy Spirit, with a timber frame and asbestos cladding, was opened on land given by Hugh Corbet of Sundorne Castle in Featherbed Lane, south of the crescent of houses (Nos 1-14) built in the 1930s.[67] Cartledge left in 1928 to become vicar of Oakengates, where he organised international student camps and achieved distinction as an historian. Foundation

128 The distinctive turret of the Church of the Holy Spirit, Roselyn, consecrated in 1936, and replaced in 1961 by the larger church on Meadow Farm Drive.

Harlescott and Sundorne

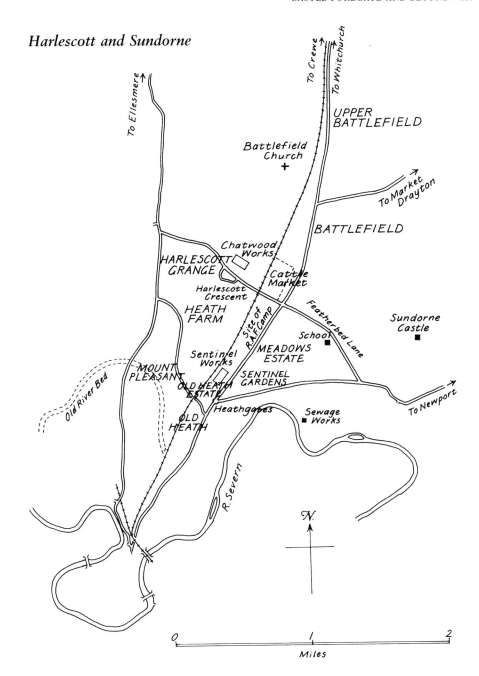

stones for a permanent church in Roseway, designed by Herbert North, were laid in November 1935, and it was consecrated on Armistice Day 1936. The building, now a social club, has rendered walls, with a high-pitched roof of turquoise tiles, and a low belfry.[68] It proved too small after the Second World War and was replaced in 1961 by the Church of the Holy Spirit in Meadow Farm Drive. The building in Featherbed Lane was adapted as a church hall but subsequently demolished.

The Impact of the Great War

The Sentinel Waggon Works was built beyond Heathgates between the road to Whitchurch and the railway to Crewe during the First World War. The Glasgow engineering company, Alley & MacLellan, took responsibility in 1903 for the development of a steam-powered road vehicle, built at Horsehay, Shropshire, by Daniel Simpson. The company lacked space for wartime production, and its manager, Shropshire-born George Woodvine, chose to build a new factory in Shrewsbury. The buildings, designed by A.E. Lloyd Oswell, were erected from March 1915. A new company, Sentinel Waggon Works Co. Ltd, formed in 1917, prospered during the 1920s, and employed over 1,000 people in 1934, but went into liquidation the following year. Steam waggons faced competition from motor lorries, and the steam railcars for which the factory supplied motive power were not wholly successful. A new company was formed in 1936 which prospered as a sub-contractor, making machine tools, Bren gun carriers, kitchen and bathroom units for 'prefabs', motor buses and motor lorries.[70] Rolls Royce Ltd. acquired the company in 1956 and used the factory primarily to make diesel engines. After the collapse of the Rolls Royce company in 1971 it passed to Rolls Royce Motors and was sold to Perkins plc in 1985. Parts of the Sentinel factory are used by Doncasters Aeromotive, and the administration block, with the figure of a sentinel above its gateway, remains, but production was moved to a plant west of the railway in the 1980s and a supermarket occupies much of the site.

The Sentinel Gardens estate was built from 1919 for employees at the waggon works, and comprised just over 100 houses on Albert Road, First Terrace, First Avenue and the eastern side of Whitchurch Road, The buildings are in Garden City style, in pairs or blocks of four, many with dormers breaking into the roof lines, mostly rough cast, and roofed with clay tiles, some of them large pantiles. Capital for construction was borrowed at high rates of interest, and rents were consequently high.[71] Corrosion in pipes caused the estate's district heating system to be abandoned in the late 1920s, but its water tower remains in Albert Road.

The next significant housing development in Harlescott was also a company village. Early in 1924 the Chatwood Safe Co. of Bolton, Lancashire, confirmed that it would move to a site on Harlescott Farm that belonged to its parent company, Hall Engineering. Work began on the factory (the current Stadco and Churchill works) in the summer of 1925. Assistance from the R.D.C. enabled the company to build for its workpeople an estate of 44 gabled, semi-detached houses, designed by William Green of

129 Garden City-style (although much altered) houses on the Sentinel Gardens estate of the early 1920s.

Birmingham, with high-quality brickwork and woodwork, grouped around a tennis court, and called Harlescott Crescent. The estate stood in isolation until the 1960s.[72]

The 60-acre property beyond the Sentinel works was acquired during the First World War by the Royal Flying Corps (from 1918 the Royal Air Force) as its road transport depot and retained for 14 years after the Armistice. The depot included workshops, a power house, 11 barrack blocks, canteens and a cinema.[73] During the 1920s RAF personnel featured in many aspects of life in Shrewsbury. A band and a concert party from Harlescott performed at a fête at Darwin's birthplace in 1922; an RAF team played hockey against local sides, while townspeople watched amateur dramatics and films in the depot cinema and athletics on the sports field, and played on the tennis courts. RAF personnel appeared before magistrates on charges ranging from bigamy through robbery to riding bicycles without lights. In 1924 Shrewsbury magistrates announced their

130   The water tower in Albert Road that was part of the district heating system of the Sentinel Gardens estate, abandoned in the late 1920s.

determination to stop fights between RAF and civilians, but brawling continued in Castle Foregate.[74] The depot closed early in 1932, stimulating speculation about its future. In the autumn it was suggested that a zoo might be an appropriate use.[75]

Early in 1934, with the expansion of its boundaries imminent on 1 April, Shrewsbury Borough Council purchased the 38 houses comprising the married quarters of the RAF depot, on the east side of the main road, together with a seven-acre playing field extending to Featherbed Lane.[76] The two-storey, rendered houses, with dormers breaking into clay tile roofs, and ground-floor bow windows remain in Harlescott Close, Haughmond Avenue, Roselyn and Whitchurch Road.

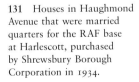

131   Houses in Haughmond Avenue that were married quarters for the RAF base at Harlescott, purchased by Shrewsbury Borough Corporation in 1934.

132 Houses on Rydal Avenue, built by Fletcher Estates Ltd in the mid-1930s, between which can be seen buildings of the RAF road transport base of the First World War. Fletchers had demolished similar buildings to make way for the houses.

133 'Maisonettes', blocks of four dwellings with external staircases giving access to those on the upper storeys, built on the eve of the Second World War on Sundorne Road.

Less than two weeks after the extension of the boundary, the Blackpool-based house builders A. & G.R. Fletcher announced they had acquired the site of the RAF camp for house-building. Initially they bought eight acres, but took options on and subsequently purchased the remainder. Some depot buildings were adapted for industrial users, the best-known of them the Lilywhite Laundry Co. Fletcher Estates opened a sales office before the end of April 1934, and displayed marketing skills of a kind previously unknown in Shrewsbury. They had a show house, offered semi-detached houses at prices from £495 to £625, and sold an average of four per week.[77]

The Fletcher houses are characteristic of those built by speculative developers in the 1930s. Most have rendering between the ground-floor and first-floor windows, integral porches and roofs of clay tiles, and some have corner windows, oriel windows above front doors, and wrap-round 'turret' windows. Liberal use was made of mass-produced stained glass. Building was progressing in 1939, and the impact of the German invasion of Poland on 1 September can be sensed in Kendal Road, where 40 characteristic Fletcher houses were completed, but the remaining ex-RAF buildings were re-occupied by the War Office, and stayed in military use until the 1990s.

Harlescott expanded in other ways in the 1930s. In 1931 Salop County Council, which was responsible for education outside the borough, opened a school on Featherbed Lane (now Harlescott Junior School).[78] The magistrates gave authority in 1937 for the *Harlescott* public house on the site of the RAF depot hospital.[79] Cars were auctioned at Harlescott Garage on the main road.[80] An application was made to build a crescent of 14 houses on Featherbed Lane in 1934, but it remained incomplete in 1939, and the gaps were filled after the Second World War.[81] Sundorne Avenue, Sundorne Crescent and Sundorne Road, as the far as the drive to The Meadows farm, were built up by 1938. Nos 33-55 Sundorne Road are a mixture of rough- and smooth-cast pairs, with semi-circular arched porches like Norman church doorways, but the houses off the main road are plain semi-detached pairs. In 1939 the builder L.T. Taylor offered semi-detached villas with bay windows for £499, while an estate agent advertised 'maisonnettes', two-storey flats in blocks of four that have the appearance of semi-detached pairs (Nos 117-77 Sundorne Road, Nos 1-8 Corndon Road). They have rendered walls, hipped roofs with clay tiles, and substantial overhangs on the eaves, sheltering the external staircases to the first-floor dwellings.[82]

A Second War and After

The Harlescott area saw many changes during the Second World War. A boy growing up in a Fletcher house looked across Kendal Road in June 1940 to the ex-RAF buildings to see unshaven soldiers straight from troop trains, having been rescued from Dunkirk.[83] The Ministry of Supply built the cold storage depot alongside the railway north of Harlescott Lane.[84] Between the railway and the road to Whitchurch was a military camp, part of it occupied after 1945 by detachments of the ATS, who left on 29 February 1948. A rumour that it was to accommodate single men working at the Sentinel factory, some of them Poles, so incensed local opinion that a group of family men without accommodation of their own, led by Thomas G. Ryder, president of the local branch of the Amalgamated Engineering Union, obtained a key to the site, cut through barbed wire fences, and drove in seven or eight lorries containing furniture. Families moved in to 22 huts and remained there as squatters, paying rents, for many months. Most were allocated prefabs and the last of them went to improved ex-military huts at Monkmoor in the autumn of 1951.[85]

The council purchased the nine-acre camp late in 1950 intending to use it as a cattle market, but because detachments of the RAOC and RASC remained in occupation, the market was built in two stages.[86] Construction began early in 1956, and the section for attested and dairy cows opened on 18 July 1956.[87] It was acknowledged that the decision to move in two stages was mistaken, and it was not until 7 April 1959 that all the new facilities, including the *Shropshire Lad* restaurant, were brought into use, the last sale in the old Smithfield having been held on 31 March.[88]

Most of the industrial concerns responsible for the post-war manufacturing boom in Shrewsbury were located at Harlescott. The Sentinel works employed about 2,000 workers in 1947, when it was manufacturing diesel lorries and equipment for the mechanisation of the newly-nationalised coal industry. Its expansion was hindered by the lack of housing for skilled workers.[89] The Chatwood Works, whose exemplary houses in Harlescott Crescent had been sold to their tenants in 1949, employed 750 in 1953.[90] A machine tool factory, established in 1953 in Featherbed Lane by J.C.R. Woodvine, prospered, and was taken over in 1956 by William Asquith Ltd.[91] Industrial expansion of a different kind took place on Harlescott Lane between the road to Whitchurch and the railway, where there was a saw mill in the inter-war period. A factory designed for the production of clothing by Corsets Silhouette Ltd, and employing 500 people, opened in the summer of 1956 and was highly successful.[92]

The Royal Show of 1949 took place on a 130-acre site between Sundorne Road and the Shrewsbury Canal, extending from a point east of Sundorne Avenue to the Pimley Manor drive. Car parks at the Monkmoor Sewage works were linked with the showground by temporary bridges over the river and the canal.[93] After the show, while the army moved out of its camps on the Whitchurch Road, a military presence grew on the showground. Construction of a drill hall began early in 1951, during that year houses for soldiers were built in Meadow Close, and in 1956 work began on a Territorial Army centre on Sundorne Road.[94]

The town council acquired 73 acres of the showground in 1950. Most of it was used as playing fields, but it also provided a route for a sewer that passed under the river to the Monkmoor treatment works, that was necessary before large-scale housing development.[95] The first council houses in Harlescott, apart from the ex-RAF married quarters, were 50 aluminium prefabs for Sentinel workers constructed on Albert Road and Corndon Crescent in 1947.[96] In 1950 the council acquired Meadows Farm, which gave it control of almost all the undeveloped land between the two main roads and Featherbed Lane. Early in 1951 contracts were let for groundwork on the Meadows estate, which was completed when tenants moved into the 624th house in March 1954. Wates of Norbury built 212 pre-cast concrete houses, now clad in brick, and marked the completion of their contract by giving a dinner to councillors.[97] Fletcher Estates built Ebury Avenue in 1953-4. The local authority constructed blocks of flats from 1956, and a 16-bungalow old people's 'village' at Moston Green was opened on 30 January 1958.[98] An infant school and Shrewsbury's first purpose-built secondary modern school (the Sundorne School) were completed off Corndon Crescent in 1954.[99] A Methodist hall opened on 6 December 1958, and Anglican and Roman Catholic churches were consecrated in 1961.[100]

Ribbon development along the main road beyond the Harlescott crossroads has ancient origins. The *Red Lion* inn, a profitable establishment in 1851, was sold with a newly-constructed villa and six nearby houses in 1872.[101] Its green was the home of the Battlefield Bowling Club. The commercial premises west of the road have been rebuilt many times, and include several former filling stations. On the eastern side are 16 houses (Nos 98-128), most of them built by 1938, including five of concrete block construction. Further 20th-century ribbon development, in an ancient roadside slang, extends on that side of the road through Upper Battlefield, the furthest extent of the Shrewsbury suburbs

CHAPTER XI

Reflections

A writer in 1836 summarised the essence of suburbs:

> there is almost always something new, raw and sprawling about it [...] The place
> [...] wants completeness and unity. You see houses whose sides betray that they
> were intended to have others stuck upon them – all yawning, ghastly, unskinned
> and irregular; you see infant shrubberies struggling in awkward parcels amidst
> lots of yet-to-be occupied ground, and clumps of fine places and squares looking
> down upon old half-ruined villages, which the spreading town has taken by surprise
> [....] Here and there, flanking the genteel streets, are dull, plebeian bricky rows,
> full of poor grocers and taverners, and which seem to have sprung up only for the
> annoyance of the gentlefolk.[1]

Shrewsbury's suburban landscapes reflect the same bursts of activity interspersed
with spells of lethargy than can be observed elsewhere. Analysis of the town's growth
shows that most farm land was put to passing uses, dairy holdings, allotments, brick
fields, sports fields, military depots, before houses were built on it, a process that was
often protracted. The power of 'events' in the wider world can be seen in many places,
and the impacts of the war with France of 1793-1815, and the two World Wars were
particularly powerful. The social pressures that created suburbs are also evident in
Shrewsbury. The outward movements, of those seeking tranquil respectability away from
the nocturnal bawdiness of Mardol, or moving to a clean council house away from the
squalor of Barker Street, are comprehensible. The suburbs also accommodated people
moving in from the countryside. Historians who criticise suburbs as destructive of civic

134 The Armoury on
London Road was built
during the wars with
Napoleon's France, and
served many purposes
before the main building
was removed in the
1920s. The cottages that
surround it have been
occupied by civilian
families since 1882.

pride and of the countryside perhaps show insufficient understanding of Victorian rural society.[2] A government commission in 1871 drew attention to the 'infamous character of the cottages' in the Shropshire countryside, 'tumbledown and ruinous, not water tight, very deficient in bedroom accommodation and in decent sanitary arrangements'.[3] Conditions in the Atcham union were 'the worst of any in this part of England'.[4] To migrants from the countryside, like the young Thomas Pace, the meanest of suburban dwellings, even No 8 Severn Square, could appear attractive.

Most of the small houses built in the first century covered by this study have been demolished, court houses in Frankwell, and Castle Foregate, two-storey terraces in Coleham and at Old Heath, and cluster houses in Spring Gardens. Most of those built after 1850 remain, and few in Shrewsbury would now agree with the sentiment that 'Nobody will be sorry when most of the six million Victorian houses still in use have followed the mud and timber huts of the medieval peasantry and the reeking rookeries of the Georgian towns into oblivion'.[5] Houses on Freehold Land Society estates and those built by the local authority and private builders in the 1920s and '30s appear likely to remain occupied for many decades. Neither in Shrewsbury nor in England as a whole have they become the slums predicted by aesthetes in the 1930s.

It is not difficult to denigrate the suburbs of any town by comparing them with 18th-century Bath or with perceptions of classical Athens. Microstudies, like the topographical chapters of this book, can easily become obsessed with trivia. Yet the significant as opposed to the trivial details of suburban landscapes are evidence of broader patterns of history. The best evocation in English literature of an urban fringe appears at the beginning of *Brideshead Re-visited*:

> Here the tram lines ended [...] This was the extreme limit of the city. Here the close, homogenous territory of housing estates and cinemas ended and the hinterland began.

135   One of the two hangars that remain from the RAF's Monkmoor airfield of the First World War. They are known as 'Belfast hangars' because of the system of construction used in the wooden roof trusses, which originated in shipyards in that city. One of the hangars was a sports centre in the 1920s and '30s but, after housing an RAF salvage team in the Second World War, both are now in commercial use.

136 Buildings of the First World War RAF base at Harlescott that were re-occupied by the military during the Second World War, and remained in use for storage for more than 40 years afterwards.

Evelyn Waugh describes an army camp on the edge of Glasgow in 1939, its battalion offices in a farmhouse scheduled for demolition, amid mutilated old trees, approached by half a mile of concrete road between bare clay banks, with open drainage ditches on either side, and the municipal lunatic asylum over the way.[6] Suburban landscapes reflect kaleidoscopic patterns of human history.

It is possible to observe in Shrewsbury the enterprise of the Industrial Revolution, the surge of middle-class political aspirations of the 1850s, the tragedy of the Great Famine in Ireland, the philanthropic impulses of the Tractarian movement, the direct influence of a lecture by Raymond Unwin, the immediate consequences of Adolf Hitler's invasion of Poland, and the long, slow process of recovery after 1945. In that period the concept of planning was popular, and planning legislation has subsequently achieved much in Shrewsbury. It ended the process of lining the 1933 by-pass with houses, and has ensured that the Ditherington flax mill, a Grade I listed building, will not be demolished. Nevertheless, long-term plans are altered by events, by economic booms or slumps, by fuel crises, technological innovations, wars or changes in fashion. Mankind's great architectural achievements are relatively rare, and should be celebrated for their uniqueness. There are features of quality in the suburban landscapes of most towns, in Kingsland or Wingfield Gardens in Shrewsbury, for example, that deserve proportionate celebration. If most suburbs appear disjointed it is because human history is disjointed. If some suburban landscapes provide only modest aesthetic pleasures, they equally provide evidence of the significant events of the past.

The Population of the Borough of Shrewsbury 1801-1961

Source: Census returns

	Population as recorded in census	Percentage increase or decrease by decade	Percentage increase over 40 years
1801	14,739		
1811	16,606	12.26	
1821	19,602	18.04	
1831	21,297	8.64	
1841	18.285	-14.14	24
1851	19,681	7.63	
1861	22,163	12.61	
1871	23.406	5.61	
1881	26.478	13.12	45
1891	26.967	1.84	
1901	28,395	5.29	
1911	29,389	3.50	
1921	31,006	5.50	45
1931	32,372	4.40	
1951	44,919	38.76 (20 years)	
1961	49,566	10.34	60

This table does not take into account boundary changes.
No census was taken in 1941.

References

Abbreviations:

ATS.	Auxiliary Territorial Service
BISF.	British Iron & Steel Federation (house)
B.P.P.	British Parliamentary Papers
E.S.J.	Eddowes's Salopian Journal
G.W.R.	Great Western Railway
KSLI.	King's Shropshire Light Infantry
L.N.W.R.	London & North Western Railway
P.S.N.W.R.	Potteries, Shrewsbury & North Wales Railway
RAF	Royal Air Force
RAOC	Royal Army Ordnance Corps
RASC	Royal Army Service Corps
R.D.C.	Rural District Council
RFC	Royal Flying Corps
S.A.	Shropshire Archives
S.A.B.C.	Shrewsbury & Atcham Borough Council
S.C.	Shrewsbury Chronicle
S.& M.R.	Shropshire & Montgomeryshire Railway
S.N.& Q.	Shropshire Notes & Queries
T.C.S.V.F.C.	Transactions of the Caradoc and Severn Valley Field Club.
T.S.A.S.	Transactions of the Shropshire Archaeological Society (also Shropshire History and Archaeology)
V.C.H.	*Victoria County History*
W.J.	*Wellington Journal*
W.M.J.E.A.	West Midlands Joint Electricity Authority

Chapter 1 – Suburbs

1. Thompson, F.M.L., ed., *The Rise of Suburbia* (1982); Harrison, M., *Bournville: Model Village to Garden Suburb* (1999); Slater, T., *Edgbaston: A History* (2002); Spiers, M., *Victoria Park, Manchester* (1976).
2. Oliphant, M.,*Chronicles of Carlingford: Phoebe Junior* (1989), pp. 81, 90-1, 211.
3. Hardy, T., *The Life and Death of the Mayor of Casterbridge* (edn. 1978), p.250.
4. Dyos, H.J., *Victorian Suburb: a study of the growth of Camberwell* (1961).
5. Beresford, M., *East End, West End: The Face of Leeds during Urbanisation 1684-1842* (1988).
6. Chalklin, C., *The Provincial Towns of Georgian England: A study of the building process 1740-1820* (1974), pp.57, 68.
7. Girouard, M., *The English Town* (1990); Muthesius, S., *The English Terraced House* (1982); Saint, A., ed., *London Suburbs* (1999); Chapman, S.D., *The History of Working Class Housing* (1971); Upton, C., *Living Back-to-Back* (2005).
8. Gaskell, S.M., *Building Control* (1983); Tarn, J.N., *Working-class Housing in 19th- century Britain* (1971); C.G.Powell, *An Economic History of the British Building Industry 1815-1979* (1980).
9. Sharp, T., *Town Planning* (1940), p.53; Tubbs, R., *Living in Cities* (1942), p.33; Betjeman, J., *First and Last Loves* (1952), pp.54-5, 64.
10. Oliver, P., Davis, I. and Bentley, I., *Dunroamin: The Suburban Semi and its Enemies* (1981).
11. Hunt, T., *Building Jerusalem* (2005), pp.416-53.
12. Owen, H., *Journey from Obscurity* (1963), vol.1, pp.124-5; Hibberd, D., *Wilfred Owen* (2002), pp.10-1, 44.

Chapter 2 – Contexts

1. Toghill, P., *Geology in Shropshire* (1990), pp.130-1; Trinder, B., *Industrial Archaeology in Shropshire* (1996), pp.77-82.
2. Toghill, P., *Geology in Shropshire* (1990), pp.167-9.
3. Morey, C. and Pannett, D., 'The Origin of the Old River Bed', *Shropshire Conservation Trust Bulletin* No 35 (1976), pp.7-12.
4. S.A., Tithe Apportionments and Maps.
5. *Shrewsbury Chronicle* (15 April 1864; 16 Nov.1866; 14 Jan. 1881).
6. See above p.102.
7. Stamper, P., *Historic Parks and Gardens of Shropshire* (1996), p.70; *Shrewsbury Chronicle* (26 Jan. 1849; 19 July, 25 Oct 1867; 14 Nov. 1873; 20 Feb. 1880; 30 Jan. 1885; 12 Sep. 1890); Murrell, H., *Hilda Murrell's Nature Diaries* (1987), pp.9, 11.

8. *Shrewsbury Chronicle* (14 Sep. 1827; 11 Jan. 1850; 18 Feb. 1898).

9. *Shrewsbury Chronicle* (1 March 1833; 2 March 1866; 13 Oct. 1876).

10. *Chambers's Edinburgh Review*, vol. IV, 1836, p.359.

11. *Shrewsbury Chronicle* (24 Aug., 7 Sep. 1883; 21 March 1884; 2 Nov. 1894).

12. *Shrewsbury Chronicle* (12 Jan. 1917).

13. *Shrewsbury Chronicle* (20 June 1941; 12 June 1942).

14. Macaulay, T.B., *The History of England from the accession of James II* (1921), p.262.

15. Phillips, T., *The History and Antiquities of Shrewsbury* (1779), p.69.

16. Trinder, B., *The Industrial Archaeology of Shropshire* (1996), pp.137-8.

17. Scarfe, N., *Innocent Espionage: the La Rochefoucauld Brothers' Tour of England in 1785* (1995), pp .90-1; Hoare, Sir R. Colt, *The Journeys of Sir Richard Colt Hoare through Wales and England* (1983), p.67.

18. *Shrewsbury Chronicle* (17 Sep. 1790); Minshull, T., *The Shrewsbury Visitor's Pocket Companion* (1803), p.28.

19. Hoskins, W.G., *Local History in England* (1959), pp.177-8.

20. Minshull, T., *The Shrewsbury Visitor's Pocket Companion* (1803), p.48; Lawson, J.B., 'The Architect of Millington's Hospital', *Shropshire Newsletter* No 42 (1972), p.10.

21. Anon, 'The English Bastille', *Social Science Review* vol.3 (1865), p.193, quoted in Driver, F., *Power and Paupers: the workhouse system 1834-84* (1993), p.1.

22. Loveday, J., *John Loveday of Caversham* (1984), p.62.

23. Minshull, T., *The Shrewsbury Visitor's Pocket Companion* (1803).

24. Rutherford, M., *Catherine Furze* (1936), p.12.

25. *Shrewsbury Chronicle* (14 Jan. 1825); Cobbett, W., *Rural Rides* (1957), vol.2, pp.273-5.

26. Trinder, B., *The Industrial Archaeology of Shropshire* (1996), p.147; *Eddowes's Salopian Journal* (25 April 1838).

27. Richard Astley – Edward Ferguson, 12 Jan. 1838. I owe this ref to James Lawson. *Eddowes's Salopian Journal* (21 July 1841).

28. See below: pp.45, 56, 130.

29. Evason, C. and Marsh, P., 'Shrewsbury's Country Carriers', Trinder, B.,*Victorian Shrewsbury* (1984), pp. 50-6; *Shrewsbury Chronicle* (2 May, 13 June 1890).

30. *Shrewsbury Chronicle* (11 Nov.1910); Robinson, Son and Pike, *Shrewsbury Illustrated* (1894), p.37; MacDonald, W., *An Illustrated Guide to Shrewsbury* (1897), p.46.

31. Butt, J., 'Red Lights in Roushill', Trinder, B., *Victorian Shrewsbury* (1984), pp.66-77.

32. *Shrewsbury Chronicle* (24 July 1914; 6 June 1919).

33. *Shrewsbury Chronicle* (1 Feb.1946), for list.

34. *Shrewsbury Chronicle* (26 Aug. 1955; 4 May 1956; 19 July 1957).

35. *Shrewsbury Chronicle* (14 March, 11 July, 22 Aug., 12 Dec., 26 Dec. 1958).

Chapter 3 – Networks

1. The boundaries are well-depicted on Tisdale, T., *Map of the town and borough of Shrewsbury* (1875).

2. *Shrewsbury Chronicle* (3 Feb. 1871; 5 Oct. 1945).

3. Butt, J., 'First Steps in Public Cleanliness', Trinder, B., *Victorian Shrewsbury* (1984), pp.57-65.

4. Ranger, W., *Report to the General Board of Health* (1854); *Shrewsbury Chronicle* (8 April, 16 Sep. 1853; 12 May, 9 June 1854).

5. *Shrewsbury Chronicle* (17 Feb. 1854; 8 Feb. 1856).

6. *Shrewsbury Chronicle* (25 Jan. 1856; 4 Sep., 18 Dec. 1863).

7. *Shrewsbury Chronicle* (4 Sep. 1868).

8. *Shrewsbury Chronicle* (6 May, 2 Dec. 1864; 19 May 1865).

9. *Shrewsbury Chronicle* (4 July 1862). See below pp.19-20, 85.

10. Cromarty, R., 'The water supply in Shrewsbury 1550-1835', *T.S.A.S.*, vol. 75 (2000), p.41; *Shrewsbury Chronicle* (3 Feb., 10 Feb. 1871; 7 July 1905; 5 Jan. 1906).

11. *Shrewsbury Chronicle* (15 Oct., 19 Nov. 1897; 21 Oct. 1898).

12. *Shrewsbury Chronicle* (2 Dec. 1853).

13. *Shrewsbury Chronicle* (3 Dec. 1920).

14. *Shrewsbury Chronicle* (20 Feb., 17 March 1903).

15. *Victoria History of Shropshire*, vol.3 (1979), pp.169-71; Walsh, V. J., 'The Diary of a Country Gentleman: Sir Baldwin Leighton, Bt.', *T.S.A.S.*, vol. 59 (1971-2), 127-69.

16. *Shrewsbury Chronicle* (3 March, 10 March, 7 April, 21 April, 21 July 1871).

17. For Besford House, see below pp.91-3; *Shrewsbury Chronicle* (24 Sep., 10 Dec 1926; 28 Jan. 1927).

18. *Shrewsbury Chronicle* (25 Sep. 1908).

19. *Victoria History of Shropshire*, vol. 3 (1979), pp.186-7; *Shrewsbury Chronicle* (24 Jan. 1913).

20. *Victoria History of Shropshire*, vol. 3 (1979), pp.188-92; *Shrewsbury Chronicle* (24 Jan. 1913).

21. *Shrewsbury Chronicle* (27 Feb. 1903; 24 April, 24 July 1931; 9 Feb., 28 Dec. 1945).

22. Trinder, B., *The Industrial Archaeology of Shropshire* (1996), pp.188-9, 252-5.

23. *Eddowes's Salopian Journal* (2 July, 17 Sep. 1828); *Shrewsbury Chronicle* (4 June 1828).

24. *Eddowes's Salopian Journal* (7 April 1824).

25. *Eddowes's Salopian Journal* (30 Nov. 1825); *Shrewsbury Chronicle* (3 March 1826).

26. *Shrewsbury Chronicle* (21 March 1789; 11 Dec. 1812; 29 Jan. 1841).

27. B.P.P. 1824 IX, Appendix B; 1826-27 VII; 1828 IX; 1829 V; 1830-31 IV; 1831-32 XXIII; 1837 XXXIII; Ironbridge Gorge Museum, *The Shelton Tollhouse*, Information Sheet No 5, nd.

28. *Victoria History of Shropshire*, vol.3 (1979), pp.193-5; *Shrewsbury Chronicle* (14 Feb., 7 March 1930; 6 Feb., 13 March 1931; 14 April 1933; Trumper, D., *A Glimpse of Old Shrewsbury* (2003), p.83.

29. 7 Ed. VII c 54; *Shrewsbury Chronicle* (9 May, 8 Aug., 7 Nov. 1913; 13 Feb., 18 Sep. 1914; 9 July 1954); *Victoria History of Shropshire*, vol.3 (1979), p.197; vol.8 (1989), pp.264-5.

30. *Victoria History of Shropshire*, vol.3 (1979), pp.209-18.

31. Cromarty, R., 'The water supply in Shrewsbury 1550-1835', *T.S.A.S.*, vol. 75 (2000), pp.15-21, 23-5, 28-35.

32. Cromarty, R., 'The water supply in Shrewsbury 1550-1835', pp.36-9; Butt, J., 'Not a drop to drink: the water supply in Shrewsbury' (unpublished typescript); *Eddowes's Salopian Journal* (2 June 1830); *Shrewsbury Chronicle* (23 July 1861; 7 Nov. 1902; 29 Jan., 8 Oct., 5 Nov. 1909; 14 June 1912).

33. *Shrewsbury Chronicle* (28 Jan. 1916; 26 June 1931; 15 April, 28 Oct. 1932; 21 Sep. 1934; 5 July, 27 Sep. 1935; 14 Feb. 1941).

34. *Shrewsbury Chronicle* (14 Aug. 1874; 13 July, 16 Nov. 1894; 10 Jan., 13 March, 5 June, 7 Aug. 1896).

35. *Shrewsbury Chronicle* (30 Aug. 1895; 12 Aug. 1898; 12 May 1899; 9 March, 18 May, 16 Nov. 1900; 4 Jan. 1901; 16 May, 14 Nov. 1902; 13 Nov. 1903; 20 May 1904; 22 June 1951).

36. *Shrewsbury Chronicle* (11 Dec. 1903; 3 June 1932; 2 Feb. 1934; 7 Sep. 1934).

37. Jones, C., 'Electricity Supply in Shropshire before Nationalisation', *Industrial Archaeology Review*, vol. 18 (1996), pp.201-22; *Shrewsbury Chronicle* (24 Nov. 1893; 13 Dec. 1895; 15 Oct., 19 Nov. 1897; 21 Oct. 1898; 21 July 1899; 27 Dec 1901; 14 Feb., 12 Oct. 1902; 28 Jan. 1938; 27 July 1956).

38. *Salopian Notes and Queries*, vol .2 (1893), p.64; *Shrewsbury Chronicle* (21 Nov. 1862; 13 Feb, 14 May 1880; 14 Oct. 1904; 26 May 1916); *Eddowes's Salopian Journal* (13 Sep.1882); Blackwall, A.H., *Historic Bridges of Shropshire* (1985), p.94; Lee, M.J., 'Cherry Orchard', Trinder, B., *Victorian Shrewsbury* (1984), pp.125-6; Carr, A.M., *Shrewsbury as it was* (1978), p.64; Trumper, D., *Shrewsbury: a Second Selection* (1995), p.30. For Kingsland Bridge, see below p.110, for Burr's leadworks see p.87.

39. Minshull, T., *The Shrewsbury Guide and Salopian Directory* (1786); *Shrewsbury Chronicle* (8 April, 16 Sep. 1898; 28 Dec. 1900; Atcham Parish Register; Trinder, B., *The Industrial Archaeology of Shropshire* (1996), pp.55-6.

40. For the Shropshire & Montgomeryshire Railway see pp.49-50. The 'drop stations' at Abbey Foregate and Underdale Road were not intended to serve local passengers.

41. Bagshaw, *Shropshire* (1851), p.120; *Shrewsbury Chronicle* (9 Jan. 1852; 6 Nov. 1903; 3 Mar., 7 April 1911; 5 May 1916).

42. Klapper, C., *The Golden Age of Tramways* (1961), pp.57-58, 152; *Shrewsbury Chronicle* (13 Aug.1897). Towns of the same order of size as Shrewsbury in 1901 that had tramway systems included Dover, Lancaster, Lincoln, Lowestoft and Peterborough.

43. The section on bus transport that follows draws heavily on the research of Chris Warn.

44. *Shrewsbury Chronicle* (4 April, 1 Aug., 8 Aug. 1913; 7 May 1915).

45. *Shrewsbury Chronicle* (10 May 1929; 16 April 1937; 12 Aug. 1938).

46. *Shrewsbury Chronicle* (1 Aug. 1941; 16 Oct. 1942; 12 Feb. 1943; 21 Sep., 30 Nov., 21 Dec. 1956; 4 Jan. 1957); Walker, W.B., *Salop & County ABC Railway and Omnibus Guide* (1947).

47. *Shrewsbury Chronicle* (3 March, 10 Sep. 1948; 18 Feb. 1949; 3 March, 10 March, 17 March, 24 March, 14 April, 21 April, 4 Aug. 1950; 18 Jan. 1952); Trumper, D., *Shrewsbury: the Twentieth Century* (1999), p.93.

48. *Shrewsbury Chronicle* (10 Oct. 1913; 24 June, 19 Aug., 2 Sep. 1932; 21 April 1933; 16 Nov. 1934; 18 Jan., 29 March 1935).

49. Watson, N., *A Family Business* (1995), p.186; *Shrewsbury Chronicle* (19 May 1950).

50. *Shrewsbury Chronicle* (19 Sep. 1873; 16 April 1875; 3 April 1896).

51. *Shrewsbury Chronicle* (26 Jan. 1934; 28 Jan. 1938).

52. Rutherford, M., *The Revolution in Tanners Lane* (1887), p.157.

53. Field, C., *Church and Chapel in Early Victorian Shropshire* (2004), pp.72-80; Cox, J.V., 'Simplicity without meanness', *T.S.A.S.*, vol. 72 (1997), pp.52-97; *Shrewsbury Chronicle* (2 May 1902).

54. Barker, J., *Shrewsbury's Free Churches* (1914), maps; Morris, W.E., *A History of Methodism in Shrewsbury* (1960), pp.36-7.

55. *Eddowes's Salopian Journal* (27 Feb. 1884); *Shrewsbury Chronicle* (21 March 1930; 24 Oct. 1930; 24 March 1939).

56. *Shrewsbury Chronicle* (18 April, 5 Dec. 1924; 22 May, 13 Nov. 1936; 27 Feb. 1948; 19 Feb. 1960; Leonard, J., *Churches of Shropshire* (2004), p. 154.

57. *Shrewsbury Chronicle* (14 Jan., 2 Dec., 9 Dec. 1955; 14 Sep. 1956; 26 Aug. 1960).

58. How, F.D., *The Revd. Thomas Mainwaring Bulkeley-Owen: a Memoir* (1914), pp. 8, 65, 76, 88, 99, 104.

59. *Shrewsbury Chronicle* (1 May 1942).

60. *Shrewsbury Chronicle* (27 Oct. 1905, 20 Jan. 1928: 28 June 1929; 16 Sep 1932); Morris, *A History of Methodism* (1960), p.22; Cox, 'Simplicity without meanness', p.77; Field, *Church and Chapel in Early Victorian Shropshire*, p.74.

61. *Shrewsbury Chronicle* (13 Oct., 21 Oct. 1870; 26 May, 2 June 1871; 27 Oct. 1905, 16 Sep. 1932; Cox, 'Simplicity without meanness', p.77.

62. *Shrewsbury Chronicle* (21 March, 27 June 1879; 14 Sep. 1945).

63. *Shrewsbury Chronicle* (3 Aug. 1945; 12 Dec. 1952; W. Leary, *Ministers and Circuits in the Primitive Methodist Church* (1990), p.175.

64. *Shrewsbury Chronicle* (27 March 1863); Binfield, C., *So Down to Prayers* (1977), pp. 163-5.

65. Cox, 'Simplicity without meanness', p.81; *Shrewsbury Chronicle* (19 Feb., 23 April 1909).

66. Pattison, A., *On Severn Shore* (2004), p.61.

67. *Shrewsbury Chronicle* (14 Dec. 2002); Leonard, *Churches of Shropshire* (2004), p.159.

68. Minshull, T., *The Shrewsbury Guide* (1786), p.ix; Minshull, T., *The Shrewsbury Visitor's Pocket Companion* (1803), p.26; Clark, P., *The English Alehouse* (1983), pp.279-80.

69. *Victoria History of Shropshire*, vol. 2 (1973), pp.166-71; *Shrewsbury Chronicle* (24 Feb.1871; 15 Feb. 1878; 23 Nov. 1900).

70. *Shrewsbury Chronicle* (20 Sep. 1878; 2 Sep. 1881; 3 April 1891).

71. *Shrewsbury Chronicle* (21 May 1852; 24 Feb. 1854; 28 Sep. 1855; 7 March 1884).

72. *Victoria History of Shropshire*, vol. 2 (1973), pp.195-6; *Shrewsbury Chronicle* (5 Sep., 21 Nov. 1862; 18 Aug. 1865; 3 Aug. 1866).

73. *Victoria History of Shropshire*, vol. 2 (1973), pp.156, 197, 200; *Eddowes's Salopian Journal* (26 May, 11 Aug., 1 Sep., 8 Sep., 12 Oct. 1886; *Shrewsbury Chronicle* (20 March 1874; 1 Jan. 1875; 20 Dec. 1878; 9 Feb. 1894; 30 May 1895; 26 Aug. 1910).

74. *Shrewsbury Chronicle* (18 Aug. 1865; 6 Jan. 1882; 10 Feb. 1905).

75. Henshaw, J., *Passing Shots* (2003), pp. 9-14, 24-7.

76. *Shrewsbury Chronicle* (23 Dec. 1892; 25 May 1934).

77. *Victoria History of Shropshire*, vol. 2 (1973), pp.201-3; *Shrewsbury Chronicle* (19 June 1868).

78. Pidgeon, *Memorials of Shrewsbury* (1837), pp.185-7;

Shrewsbury Chronicle (4 May 1832; 7 Feb. 1896; 23 May 1902).

79. Minshull, T., *The Shrewsbury Guide* (1786), p.16.

Chapter 4 – Building

1. Moran, M., *Vernacular Architecture in Shropshire* (2003), pp.213-76; Lawson, J.B., 'Harnage Slates', *T.S.A.S.*, vol. 64 (1985), pp.116-18; Toghill, P., *Geology in Shropshire* (1990), pp. 130-1, 146-8; Scard, A., *The Building Stones of Shropshire* (1990), pp.27-34, 65.

2. Miller, M., *Letchworth: the first Garden City* (2002), p.28; *The Book of English Trades and Library of the Useful Arts* (1821), pp. 49-50.

3. Ex inf. Bill Champion; Lichfield Record Office, inventory, Thomas Tither, St Julian's, ex.18 Aug.1684.

4. *Shrewsbury Chronicle* (19 April 1850, 30 Aug. 1850); *Salopian Shreds & Patches* (11 Dec. 1878); *Eddowes's Salopian Journal* (14 May 1879).

5. Trinder, B., *The Industrial Archaeology of Shropshire* (1996), pp.67, 80; Robinson, Son and Pike, *Shrewsbury Illustrated* (1894), pp.37, 47, 113; MacDonald, W., *An Illustrated Guide to Shrewsbury* (1897), p.47; *Shrewsbury Chronicle* (15 March 1867; 21 Jan. 1870; 29 Sep. 1916); *Eddowes's Salopian Journal* (31 Dec. 1884).

6. *Shrewsbury Chronicle* (27 March, 1 May 1925; 20 Sep. 1946).

7. *Shrewsbury Chronicle* (12 July 1867; 21 Jan. 1870).

8. *Shrewsbury Chronicle* (12 July 1867; 16 Nov. 1945); *Eddowes's Salopian Journal* (31 Dec. 1884); Cossons, N. and Trinder, B., *The Iron Bridge* (2002), p.51.

9. Trinder, B., *Barges and Bargemen* (2005), p. 77; MacDonald, *Illustrated Guide to Shrewsbury* (1897), p.47.

10. Trinder, *Industrial Archaeology of Shropshire* (1996), pp. 26-30; Crocker, *The Post Office Shrewsbury Directory* (1886-7), p.24; *Shrewsbury Chronicle* (5 July 1867).

11. Wilding & Co., *Shropshire: a beautiful English county* (1914), p.121; Trinder, *Industrial Archaeology of Shropshire* (1996), p.68; *Shrewsbury Chronicle* (6 Oct.1939).

12. Trinder, *Industrial Archaeology of Shropshire* (1996), p. 118.

13. 'A Modern Mineral Railway: the East & West Yorkshire Union Railway', *Railway Magazine*, vol. 7 (1900), pp.113-17.

14. Stratton, M. and Trinder, B., *Twentieth Century Industrial Archaeology* (2000), pp. 135-8; Vale, B., *A History of the UK Temporary Housing Programme* (1995), pp. 107-8; *Shrewsbury Chronicle* (16 Sep. 1949).

15. *Shrewsbury Chronicle* (9 Dec. 1949; 12 March 1954; 15 Feb. 1957; 6 Sep. 1957); Trumper, D., *Shrewsbury: the Twentieth Century* (1999), p. 92.

16. *Shrewsbury Chronicle* (24 June 1955).

17. Quartermaine, J., Trinder, B. and Turner, R., *Thomas Telford's Holyhead Road* (2003), pp. 15-6, 24-6, 148.

18. Lawson, J.B., 'The Architects of Millington's Hospital', *Shropshire Newsletter* 42 (1972), p.10; Mercer, E., *English Architecture to 1900: the Shropshire Experience* (2003), pp. 187-8.

19. *Shrewsbury Chronicle* (7 Jan 1791; 5 May, 12 May 1882); *Eddowes's Salopian Journal* (19 April 1871); Mercer, E., *English Architecture to 1900: the Shropshire Experience* (2003), pp.223, 232, 328-9.

20. *Shrewsbury Chronicle* (20 Feb. 1786; 11 Feb. 1791, 28 Oct. 1791; 24 July 1903); *Shropshire Magazine* (March 1960), pp.17-8 (April 1960), pp.15-6.

21. Lawson, J.B., 'Thomas Telford in Shrewsbury', Penfold, A., *Thomas Telford: Engineer* (1980), pp.2-3.

22. Quartermaine, J., Trinder, B. and Turner, R., *Thomas Telford's Holyhead Road* (2003), pp. 15-6, 90; *Shrewsbury Chronicle* (27 May 1791; 1 March 1793; 27 July 1866); Trinder, B., 'Ditherington Flax Mill – a Re-evaluation', *Textile History*, vol. 23 (1992), pp.204-5; Hobbs, J.B., *Shrewsbury Street Names* (1954), p.106.

23. Quartermaine, J., Trinder, B. and Turner, R., *Thomas Telford's Holyhead Road* (2003), pp.22, 24; *Shrewsbury Chronicle* (22 Sep. 1809; 7 July 1815); *Eddowes's Salopian Journal* (5 July 1815; 19 June 1816).

24. *Shrewsbury Chronicle* (4 Jan. 1850; 11 May 1866; 2 Feb., 16 March 1877).

25. Mercer, E., *English Architecture to 1900: the Shropshire Experience* (2003), p.329; *Shrewsbury Chronicle* (5 June 1835; 4 March 1842; 15 Dec. 1843; 15 March, 22 Nov. 1844)

26. *Shrewsbury Chronicle* (9 Aug. 1940).

27. *Shrewsbury Chronicle* (1 April 1881; 14 Nov. 1930).

28. *Shrewsbury Chronicle* (20 June, 14 Nov. 1930).

29. MacDonald, *Illustrated Guide to Shrewsbury* (1897), p.47; *Shrewsbury Chronicle* (22 Jan. 1869; 16 May 1869; 28 Nov. 1873; 2 Dec. 1881; 27 Jan. 1882; *Salopian Shreds & Patches* (11 Dec. 1878).

30. *Shrewsbury Chronicle* (27 April 1900; 19 Oct. 1923; 4 March 1927; 7 April 1933). There is some confusion over Pace's birthplace, usually said to be Brierley Hill, Staffs., but given as Madeley, Shropshire in the 1871 census.

31. *Shrewsbury Chronicle* (1 Feb. 1935).

32. *Shrewsbury Chronicle* (12 Jan. 1906).

33. *Shrewsbury Chronicle* (28 Sep. 1923).

34. *Shrewsbury Chronicle* (14 Jan. 1831).

35. *Shrewsbury Chronicle* (12 July 1901).

36. *Shrewsbury Chronicle* (1 Feb. 1935).

37. *Shrewsbury Chronicle* (13 April 1934; 20 Dec.1991); Letter, G.R. Fletcher to B.Trinder, 11 Nov. 1982, copy in S.A.

38. *Shrewsbury Chronicle* (3 Aug. 1934; 22 Nov. 1935; 20 March, 1 May, 3 July 1936).

39. *Shrewsbury Chronicle* (2 Oct. 1953; 12 Feb., 9 April 1954).

40. Chapman, S.D., *The History of Working Class Housing* (1971), pp. 221-46; Brown, C., *Shoe Town: New Town* (1990), pp.21, 31-4, 75-8; Trinder, B., *Victorian Banbury* (1982), pp.98-100; *Shrewsbury Chronicle* (24 Oct., 31 Oct.1851).

41. *Shrewsbury Chronicle* (25 Feb., 8 April, 17 June 1853); *Eddowes's Salopian Journal* (13 Sep. 1854).

42. Lee, M.J., 'Cherry Orchard', Trinder, B., *Victorian Shrewsbury* (1984), pp. 119-22; *Shrewsbury Chronicle* (12 March, 8 Oct. 1858; 18 Feb. 1859).

43. *Shrewsbury Chronicle* (16 March, 6 April 1860).

44. *Shrewsbury Chronicle* (9 March, 30 March 1866; 15 Feb. 1867; 3 April, 30 Oct. 1868; 2 Feb. 1869; 15 Sep. 1871;18 Oct. 1872).

45. *Shrewsbury Chronicle* (15 Sep. 1871; 2 May, 12 Sep. 1873).

46. If this figure does not accord with the number of 'plots' allocated in ballots, it is because many 'plots' came to be occupied by more than one house.

47. *Shrewsbury Chronicle* (11 March 1864; 28 April 1865; 16 Feb. 1866; 14 Nov. 1913).

48. *Shrewsbury Chronicle* (11 Aug. 1871; 26 July 1872; 25 June 1875; 14 July 1876; 1 Dec.1881); *Eddowes's Salopian Journal* (31 Aug. 1853).

49. Brown, C., *Shoe Town: New Town* (1991), p.116.

50. *Shrewsbury Chronicle* (27 April 1900).

51. *Shrewsbury Chronicle* (24 Feb., 17 March, 15 Dec.1911; 5 Jan., 12 Jan., 26 Jan., 8 March, 15 March, 19 July 1912.

52. Stratton and Trinder, *Twentieth Century Industrial Archaeology* (2000), p.126; *Shrewsbury Chronicle* (13 Dec. 1918; 14 March 1919).

53. *Shrewsbury Chronicle* (5 May 1919, 6 June, 11 April, 17 Oct.1919; 9 July, 12 Nov. 1920).

54. *Shrewsbury Chronicle* (3 Jan., 11 May, 22 June, 21 Sep. 1923;12 Dec 1924; 30 Oct. 1925; 12 Feb. 1926).

55. *Shrewsbury Chronicle* (16 May 1919; 13 March, 31 July 1925; 5 Oct. 1928; 15 Feb. 1929).

56. *Shrewsbury Chronicle* (15 Feb., 13 Sep. 1929; 12 Dec. 1930).

57. *Shrewsbury Chronicle* (19 Feb., 12 March 1926; 29 April 1927; 6 April 1928; 26 July, 2 Aug. 1929; 15 Jan. 1932).

58. *Shrewsbury Chronicle* (23 March 1928; 4 Jan. 1929).

59. *Shrewsbury Chronicle* (8 April 1927; 6 April 1928; 12 April 1929; 18 Dec. 1936).

60. *Shrewsbury Chronicle* (26 March 1937; 13 Jan., 17 March 1939).

61. *Shrewsbury Chronicle* (19 June, 31 July 1931; 29 July 1932; 12 Feb. 1937).

62. *Shrewsbury Chronicle* (19 June 1931; 3 Nov., 15 Dec. 1933; 16 March 1934; 8 Feb., 11 Oct. 1935).

63. *Shrewsbury Chronicle* (19 May, 26 May 1934; 21 June 1935; 18 Sep. 1936; 26 March 1937; 15 Jan 1937; 11 Nov. 1938)

64. *Shrewsbury Chronicle* (12 Feb. 1937; 28 Sep. 1938; 13 Jan. 1939).

65. *Shrewsbury Chronicle* (13 Dec. 1940).

66. *Shrewsbury Chronicle* (3 Sep.1880; 15 March 1889; 24 Oct., 14 Nov. 1890; 7 Jan., 11 Nov. 1898; 11 Oct. 1901; 20 Feb. 1903; 5 Jan., 18 Oct. 1912; 5 May 1919; 12 Nov. 1920; 15 Jan. 1932; 16 Aug 1935; 10 March 1939).

67. *Shrewsbury Chronicle* (16 Nov. 1945; 26 March 1954).

68. See below pp.133, 167; *Shrewsbury Chronicle* (26 March 1954).

69. *Shrewsbury Chronicle* (10 Nov., 13 Dec. 1944; 16 Feb.1945).

70. *Shrewsbury Chronicle* (17 Aug., 12 Oct. 1945).

71. Stratton and Trinder, *Twentieth Century Industrial Archaeology* (2000), pp.136-7; *Shrewsbury Chronicle* (16 Oct. 1945; 12 April, 7 June, 9 Aug., 27 Sep. 1946).

72. *Shrewsbury Chronicle* (17 May 1946; 13 June, 1 Aug. 1947; 16 April, 10 Sep.1948; 29 April 1949).

73. *Shrewsbury Chronicle* (13 Dec. 1946; 14 Feb. 1947; 16 April 1948).

74. *Shrewsbury Chronicle* (16 Nov. 1945; 27 Sep. 1946; 14 Feb., 30 May, 13 June 1947; 30 July 1948).

75. *Shrewsbury Chronicle* (1 Aug., 31 Oct. 1947; 16 April, 10 Sep., 10 Dec. 1948; 11 Feb., 18 Feb. 1949; 26 Oct. 1951).

76. *Shrewsbury Chronicle* (18 March, 22 July 1949; 4 Aug., 13 Oct. 1950; 30 Oct. 1953; 12 March 1954).

77. Stratton and Trinder, *Twentieth Century Industrial Archaeology* (2000), p.138; *Shrewsbury Chronicle* (10

Dec. 1948; 29 April, 7 Oct. 1949; 18 Jan., 17 Oct. 1952; 18 June 1954).

78. *Shrewsbury Chronicle* (18 June 1954; 13 May, 18 Nov. 1955; 6 Jan. 1956).

79. *Shrewsbury Chronicle* (15 June, 28 Sep.1956; 15 Feb., 6 Sep. 1957).

80. *Shrewsbury Chronicle* (30 Sep. 1955; 6 Jan., 15 June, 30 Nov. 1956; 6 Sep. 1957; 5 June 1959, 16 Oct. 1959; 1 Jan. 1960).

81. *Shrewsbury Chronicle* (30 Nov. 1956; 17 Oct. 1958; 6 March, 5 June 1959; 11 March, 29 April 1960).

82. *Shrewsbury Chronicle* (27 July 1956; 26 July 1957; 7 Feb., 11 April, 18 April 1958).

83. *Shrewsbury Chronicle* (1 Aug., 28 Nov. 1958; 30 Jan., 3 April, 3 July 1959).

84. *Shrewsbury Chronicle* (19 Dec. 1958; 5 June 1959).

85. *Shrewsbury Chronicle* (14 Nov. 1952; 8 June 1956; 28 Nov. 1958).

86. *Shrewsbury Chronicle* (26 Oct 1956; 15 Aug. 1958; 22 May 1959; 5 Aug. 1960).

87. Orwell, G., *The Road to Wigan Pier* (1962), p.59.

Chapter 5 – The Abbey Foregate

1. Baker, N., ed., *Shrewsbury Abbey* (2002), pp.15, 206-9, 216-18; *Victoria History of Shropshire*, vol. 2, pp.30-7.

2. Blackwall, A.H., *Historic Bridges of Shropshire* (1985), pp.97-8; Ward, A.W., *The Bridges of Shrewsbury* (1935), pp.41-81; Carr, A.W., *Shrewsbury: a Pictorial History* (1990), pp.135-43.

3. S.A., 6000/14941; *Shrewsbury Chronicle* (28 April 1871; 27 Oct. 1876; 1 April 1887; 18 Jan., 8 Feb. 1889; 18 April 1902; 24 July 1903).

4. Moran, M., *Vernacular Buildings of Shropshire* (2003), pp.259, 274; Trumper, D., *Shrewsbury: a second selection* (1995), p.10.

5. Cox, J.V., 'Simplicity without meanness', *T.S.A.S.*, vol. 72 (1997), p.86; *Shrewsbury Chronicle* (3 Oct., 10 Oct., 19 Dec. 1862; 3 June 1864; 24 Nov. 1899); *Eddowes's Salopian Journal* (15 April 1863). For a sketch of the temporary building see S.A. 399/14.

6. *Eddowes's Salopian Journal* (25 Oct.1871).

7. Baker, *Shrewsbury Abbey* (2002), pp.47-68, 178-89, 208-9; Nightingale, J., *The Beauties of England and Wales* (1813), vol.13, pp.85-6; Cromarty, D., *Everyday Life in Medieval Shrewsbury* (1991), pp.8-10; Tisdale, T., *Town of Shrewsbury* (1850).

8. Baker, *Shrewsbury Abbey* (2002), pp.9, 40-3; *Victoria History of Shropshire*, vol. 2, pp.30-7; *Shrewsbury Chronicle* (31 July 1863); Stamper, P., *Historic Parks and Gardens of Shropshire* (1996), pp.9-10, 73; Ionides, J., *Thomas Farnolls Pritchard* (1999), p.290; Moran, *Vernacular Buildings of Shropshire* (2003), p.251; Carr, A.M., *Shrewsbury: a Pictorial History* (1994), p.152.

9. Stamper, P., *Historic Parks and Gardens of Shropshire* (1996), pp.71-8.

10. Trinder, *Industrial Archaeology of Shropshire* (1996), pp. 195-7; Holyhead Road reports, B.P.P. 1824 IX; B.P.P. 1834 XL; B.P.P. 1837 XXXIII; Evason, C., 'Downhill Journey', Trinder, B., *Victorian Shrewsbury* (1984), pp.78-9; *Eddowes's Salopian Journal* (22 March 1836); S.A. Holy Cross Tithe Map (1842).

11. *Eddowes's Salopian Journal* (7 April 1841; 23 March 1853; 15 Sep. 1886; 17 Nov. 1886); A Harrison, *West Midland Trustee Savings Bank 1816-1966* (1966), pp.5-9; *Hereford Journal* (29 Oct. 1851; 14 Jan. 1852);

Shrewsbury Chronicle (15 April 1932; 3 June 1932).

12. Fiennes, C., *The Journeys of Celia Fiennes* (1947), p. 227; Stamper, P., *Historic Parks and Gardens* (1996), pp.38-9; Baker, *Shrewsbury Abbey* (2002), pp.45-6; *Eddowes's Salopian Journal* (14 Aug.1839; 20 Oct.1841); *Shrewsbury Chronicle* (22 May 1840); S.A. Watton Colln., vol.4, pp.163, 174.

13. Baker, *Shrewsbury Abbey* (2002), pp.41-3; Owen, M., 'Before Beringar', *Shrewsbury Civic Society Newsletter*, Summer 1993, pp.5-6; *Shrewsbury Chronicle* (27 Feb., 24 July 1863).

14. Tonks, E.S., *The Shropshire & Montgomeryshire Railway* (1972), pp.12, 24, 37, 51; *Shrewsbury Chronicle* (23 Sep.1921; 27 July 1934).

15. Tonks, E.S., *The Shropshire & Montgomeryshire Railway* (1972), pp.57, 93; *Shrewsbury Chronicle* (17 Nov.1944).

16. *Shrewsbury Chronicle* (4 Dec.1863; 25 Nov. 1864; 2 Dec. 1864; 9 Dec.1864; 12 May 1865; 16 April, 23 April 1869; 7 July 1876; 28 Dec. 1877).

17. *Shrewsbury Chronicle* (19 Nov.1880; 11 Nov.1881; 4 July 1890); Trinder, B., *Industrial Archaeology of Shropshire* (1996), p.63.

18. Trinder, B., *A History of Shropshire* (1997), p.130; *Shrewsbury Chronicle* (12 May 1899; 20 Oct., 27 Oct. 1899; 17 March 1911; 24 Oct. 1919; 13 Feb. 1920).

19. Lloyd, *Inns of Shrewsbury* (1942), p.14; S.A., Watton Collection, vol. 4, p.448, vol.6, p.300; Auden, H.M., 'Social Life in the Abbey Foregate', *T.C.S.V.F.C.*, vol. 9 (1932-4), pp.253-5; *Shrewsbury Chronicle* (5 Feb. 1847; 23 April 1909); Trumper, D., *Yesterday's Shrewsbury* (2002), p.88, shows the building *circa* 1960.

20. *Shrewsbury Chronicle* (13 Dec. 1929; 18 Jan., 21 June 1935); Moran, *Vernacular Architecture of Shropshire* (2003), p. 242; Trumper, D., *Shrewsbury: the Twentieth Century* (1999), pp.32, 70.

21. *Shrewsbury Chronicle* (17 Oct. 1873; 22 Jan. 1904).

22. Lloyd, *Inns of Shrewsbury* (1942), p.18; *Shrewsbury Chronicle* (14 Dec. 1838; 30 Oct. 1903; 22 Jan. 1904; 17 March 1933). For the brush factory see below p.84.

23. *Eddowes's Salopian Journal* (29 Jan. 1879).

24. Auden, H.M., 'Social Life in the Abbey Foregate', *T.C.S.V.F.C.*, vol. 9 (1932-4), pp.254-6; Carr, A.M., *Shrewsbury as it was* (1978), p. 40; Lichfield Joint Record Office, inventory of Mary Hampton, Abbey Foregate (1662-3); *Shrewsbury Chronicle* (21 March 1958; 11 March 1960).

25. Wood, J., *Map of Shrewsbury* (1838); Smith, thesis, pp.344-7; *Shrewsbury Chronicle* (21 Feb. 1862).

26. *Shrewsbury Chronicle* (27 July 1888; 15 March 1901; 14 July 1905; 24 Feb. 1922).

27. Forrest, H.W., *Old Houses of Shrewsbury* (1972), p.87; Mate, W., *Shropshire* (n.d., *c.*1900), vol.1, p.61; *Shrewsbury Chronicle* (12 Aug. 1831; 1 July 1842; 28 July 1854; 16 Dec. 1887; 14 Oct. 1892); *Eddowes's Salopian Journal* (28 June 1848).

28. *Shrewsbury Chronicle* (1 July 1842; 27 July 1894); Trumper,D., *Shrewsbury: a second selection* (1995), p.17; S.A. 6229/6237.

29. Baker, *Shrewsbury Abbey* (2002), pp.210-1; Trumper, D., *Shrewsbury: the Twentieth Century* (1999), p. 89.

30. Owen, H. and Blakeway J.B., *A History of Shrewsbury* (1825), Vol. 1, p.583; *Shrewsbury Chronicle* (2 April, 9 April, 24 Sep. 1774)

31. *Shrewsbury Chronicle* (16 April, 15 Aug. 1847; 11 Jan. 1856).

32. *Shrewsbury Chronicle* (14 May 1858; 3 May 1867; 7 Jan., 28 Jan. 1880; 13 July 1956); Trumper, D., *Shrewsbury: a second selection* (1995), p.19; Lloyd, *Inns of Shrewsbury*, p. 9.

33. Moran, *Vernacular Architecture of Shropshire*, pp.245, 274-5; *Shrewsbury Chronicle* (9 Nov. 1894), Carver, M., 'Early Shrewsbury: an Archaeological Definition in 1975', *T.S.A.S.*, vol. 59 (1978), p. 238; Lloyd, *Inns of Shrewsbury*, p.9. For illustrations of buildings demolished see Trumper, D., *Shrewsbury: a second selection* (1995), p. 18.

34. *Shrewsbury Chronicle* (5 Dec., 12 Dec. 1851; 2 March 1855; 10 Jan. 1862; 13 Jan. 1865; 23 Oct. 1903); *Eddowes's Salopian Journal* (17 Feb. 1841; 22 Nov., 29 Nov. 1871).

35. Morris, L., *The Country Garage* (1985), p.25; for illustration see Trumper, D., *Shrewsbury: the Twentieth Century* (1999), p.19.

36. Moran, *Vernacular Architecture of Shropshire* (2003), p.274; J.T.Smith thesis, pp.249-53; Trumper, D., *A Glimpse of Old Shrewsbury* (2003), p.133; *Shrewsbury Chronicle* (2 April 2003).

37. Trumper, D., *Shrewsbury: a second selection* (1995), p.19; *Eddowes's Salopian Journal* (5 April 1871); *Shrewsbury Chronicle* (23 Nov. 1855; 7 March 1856; 23 March 1866; 22 Nov. 1907).

38. Lloyd, *Inns of Shrewsbury* (1942), p.9; *Shrewsbury Chronicle* (17 Nov. 1871; 22 Oct. 1886).

39. Wood, J., *Map of Shrewsbury* (1838); *Shrewsbury Chronicle* (17 Aug. 1841; 21 April 1882; 24 July 1903).

40. *Ex inf.* Bill Champion; Forrest, *Old Houses of Shrewsbury* (1972), pp. 89-90; *Shrewsbury Chronicle* (17 Nov. 1865; 7 Feb. 1868; 7 April 1871).

41. *Shrewsbury Chronicle* (12 Nov. 1869; 21 Sep. 1888; 9 Aug. 1907).

42. Baker, *Shrewsbury Abbey* (2002), pp. 215-6; *Shrewsbury Chronicle* (28 Oct. 1892; 13 Sep. 1901; 29 June 1906). For Waters see Brook, F. and Allbutt, M., *The Shropshire Lead Mines* (1973), pp.30-1, 64.

43. *Shrewsbury Chronicle* (13 Jan., 9 March 1888; 28 April 1911).

44. *Shrewsbury Chronicle* (17 June 1910; 7 May 1920; 25 Sep. 1953).

45. *Shrewsbury Chronicle* (27 April 1956).

46. Lee, M.J., 'Cherry Orchard: the growth of a Victorian Suburb', Trinder, B., ed., *Victorian Shrewsbury* (1984), p.115.

47. *Shrewsbury Chronicle* (5 June 1903).

48. *Eddowes's Salopian Journal* (10 July, 24 July, 13 Nov. 1872; 5 Feb., 19 Feb., 19 March, 23 July, 6 Aug. 1873).

49. *Eddowes's Salopian Journal* (17 Nov.1886); *Shrewsbury Chronicle* (16 June 1933). The two engine houses are shown on Tisdale, T., *Town of Shrewsbury* (1850).

50. *Shrewsbury Chronicle* (23 Oct. 1863; 16 Nov. 1934; 8 March 1935; 15 March 1957); Lee, 'Cherry Orchard' (1984), pp.124-5.

51. Carr, A.M., *Shrewsbury as it was* (1978), p.64; Trumper, D., *Shrewsbury: a second selection* (1995), p. 30.

52. Lee, 'Cherry Orchard' (1984), pp.125-7; *Shrewsbury Chronicle* (3 July 1885); *Eddowes's Salopian Journal* (17 Feb., 12 May, 8 Dec. 1893).

53. Lee, 'Cherry Orchard' (1984), p.122; Pidgeon, H., *Memorials of Shrewsbury* (1837), p.179; *Shrewsbury Chronicle* (4 July 1818; 20 June 1845; 6 July 1860; 26

June, 3 July 1863; 1 July 1864; 17 July 1868; 6 Aug. 1869).

54. *Eddowes's Salopian Journal* (27 Feb. 1884); *Shrewsbury Chronicle* (26 Aug.1955).

55. Hibberd, D., *Wilfred Owen* (2002), p. 61.

56. *Shrewsbury Chronicle* (12 Oct. 1860; 6 Feb. 1880; 16 May 1902; 21 April, 28 April, 14 July 1905; 12 Jan. 1917; 26 May 1922; 29 Jan., 12 Feb., 16 April 1937; 16 Sep. 1938).

57. *Shrewsbury Chronicle* (20 Oct. 1933).

58. Lee, 'Cherry Orchard' (1984), pp. 117-22; *Eddowes's Salopian Journal* (13 Sep. 1854, 3 Jan. 1855); *Shrewsbury Chronicle* (5 Dec. 1817; 18 May 1855; 12 Oct. 1860).

59. *Shrewsbury Chronicle* (26 May 1922; 16 March, 21 Sep. 1928; 9 Aug. 1935; 29 May 1936; 10 Dec. 1937; 24 Mar. 1939).

60. *Shrewsbury Chronicle* (25 June 1926).

61. *Shrewsbury Chronicle* (19 Sep. 1862; 6 June 1873; 19 June, 31 July 1931; 29 July 1932; 19 May 1934; 26 July 1957; 5 June 1959; 1 Jan. 1960; 22 April 1960).

62. Neal, T., *Shropshire Airfields* (2005), pp. 69-72; *Shrewsbury Chronicle* (12 July 1912; 6 June 1919; 5 March 1920; 1 Dec. 1922; 11 Sep. 1925); Trumper, D., *Shrewsbury: a second selection* (1995), p 32.

63. *Shrewsbury Chronicle* (9 Sep. 1927; 5 June 1931; 20 May 1932; 20 Jan. 1933; 2 June 1939).

64. *Shrewsbury Chronicle* (13 March 1936; 16 Sep. 1949; 2 April 1954).

65. *Shrewsbury Chronicle* (23 May 1919; 5 March, 17 Dec. 1920; 1 Dec. 1922; 23 Nov. 1923; 1 June 1928; 5 July 1957); Trumper, D., *Shrewsbury: a second selection* (1995), p.31; Roberts, M.K., *In Retrospect: a short history of the Royal Salop Infirmary* (1981), pp.85-8.

66. *Shrewsbury Chronicle* (23 July, 3 Sep., 22 Oct., 19 Nov. 1948; 16 Feb., 12 Oct. 1951; 26 March 1954).

67. *Shrewsbury Chronicle* (16 Aug. 1861; 6 July 1883; 19 March, 14 May 1909); Lee, 'Cherry Orchard' (1984), p.117.

68. Evason, C., 'Downhill Journey: Stage Coaching in Shrewsbury 1833-61', Trinder, B., ed., *Victorian Shrewsbury* (1984), pp.78-94; *Eddowes's Salopian Journal* (7 Feb. 1838); *Shrewsbury Chronicle* (23 Feb. 1838; 6 March 1846; 8 Sep. 1848).

69. Hibberd, *Wilfred Owen* (2003), pp. 60-1; Owen, H., *Journey from Obscurity* (1963), vol.1, pp.167-72.

70. Baker, *Shrewsbury Abbey* (2002), pp.211-3; ex inf. Bill Champion; Butler, S., *Life and Letters of Samuel Butler* (1896), vol. 1, pp.10, 166; Lee, 'Cherry Orchard' (1984), p.118; Moran, *Vernacular Architecture of Shropshire* (2003), pp.263-4; Forest, *Old Houses of Shrewsbury* (1972), pp.88-9; *Shrewsbury Chronicle* (28 Feb. 1896).

71. *Shrewsbury Chronicle* (23 June 1916; 5 Dec. 1919; 23 Jan., 7 May, 10 Dec. 1920; 16 June 1922; 13 April 1923; 2 Oct. 1931; 4 Jan., 29 March 1935; 3 Jan., 7 Feb., 14 March 1947); Trumper, *Shrewsbury: the Twentieth Century* (1999), p. 74.

72. Butler, S., *Life and Letters of Samuel Butler* (1896), vol. 1, p.351, vol.2, p.52; *Shrewsbury Chronicle* (13 Nov. 1903).

73. *Shrewsbury Chronicle* (11 Aug. 1899; 8 May 1903; 28 Sep. 1923; 2 Mar. 1928).

74. *Victoria History of Shropshire*, vol. 2, p.177; *Shrewsbury Chronicle* (18 May, 14 Sep.1832; 22 Feb.,

8 March, 5 April, 27 Sep. 1839; 20 Jan. 1843). See above pp.53-5 (Int.).

75. *Shrewsbury Chronicle* (14 Sep., 21 Sep. 1838; 18 July 1845; 21 Aug. 1846; 7 July 1854); *Eddowes's Salopian Journal* (10 May 1848).

76. *Shrewsbury Chronicle* (21 Nov. 1856; 15 May 1857; 12 March 1869; 15 Nov. 1878).

77. *Shrewsbury Chronicle* (16 Jan. 1885; 20 Jan., 3 Feb., 17 Feb. 1888; 29 March, 10 May 1895); *Eddowes's Salopian Journal* (15 Feb. 1888); *Salopian Shreds and Patches*, vol 8 (1887-8) p.52; Brown, C., *Northampton 1835-1985, Shoe Town: New Town* (1990), pp.101-2.

78. *Shrewsbury Chronicle* (4 Feb. 1876; 2 May 1884; 8 July 1887; 22 May 1891); *Eddowes's Salopian Journal* (18 Dec. 1878).

79. *Shrewsbury Chronicle* (14 April, 19 May 1911; 10 May, 17 May 1912; 16 Mar. 1945); Trumper, *Shrewsbury: a Second Selection* (1995), p.20.

80. *Shrewsbury Chronicle* (16 May 1919; 6 March, 13 March, 31 July 1925).

81. *Shrewsbury Chronicle* (17 Dec. 1926; 6 April, 15 May, 5 Oct. 1928; 4 Jan., 15 Feb., 2 Aug, 13 Sep. 1929; 15 Jan. 1932)

82. *Shrewsbury Chronicle* (2 Aug., 13 Sep. 1929; 29 Aug. 1930; 18 Sep. 1934; 1 Feb. 1935; 12 Feb. 1937).

83. Lee, 'Cherry Orchard' (1984), p.127; *Eddowes's Salopian Journal* (23 March 1842); *Shrewsbury Chronicle* (1 July 1842; 1 May 1914).

84. *Shrewsbury Chronicle* (1 Aug., 8 Nov. 1912; 9 May, 8 Aug., 7 Nov. 1913).

85. *Shrewsbury Chronicle* (16 Feb., 16 March 1945).

86. *Shrewsbury Chronicle* (31 Jan., 1 Aug. 1958; 18 March 2004); Stratton, M. and Trinder, B., *Twentieth Century Industrial Archaeology* (2000), p.136. A Uni-Seco prefab is preserved at the Imperial War Museum, Duxford.

87. *Shrewsbury Chronicle* (16 Oct. 1945; 12 April, 7 June, 27 Sep. 1946; 29 April 1949; 26 Oct. 1951).

88. *Shrewsbury Chronicle* (9 Aug., 20 Sep., 27 Sep., 18 Oct., 1946; 13 June 1947; 16 April, 10 Sep. 1948).

89. Stratton and Trinder, *Twentieth Century Industrial Archaeology* (2000), p.137; *Shrewsbury Chronicle* (13 Dec. 1946; 2 Jan., 10 Sep. 1948; 26 Oct 1951; 14 Jan., 2 Dec., 9 Dec. 1955; 4 Aug. 2004); Pattison, A., *On Severn Shore* (2004), p.6.

90. S.A., Watton Collection, vol.1, p.115, vol.6, p.345; *Shrewsbury Chronicle* (21 March 1817; 20 Sep.1818; 12 Oct.1860).

91. 91. 12 Geo.I c.9 (1725); 25 Geo.II c.49 (1752); *Shrewsbury Chronicle* (13 Aug., 12 Nov., 17 Dec. 1915).

92. S.A. possesses pictures of both the interior and exterior of Nearwell. *Shrewsbury Chronicle* (22 Jan. 1904; 19 March 1943; 7 June 1946).

93. Mate, W., *Shropshire* (n.d., c.1900), vol.1, p.46; *Eddowes's Salopian Journal* (22 Feb. 1871); *Shrewsbury Chronicle* (8 July 1910; 10 Feb. 1911; 19 April 1946; 3 July 1953). *Ex inf.* Les Dolamore.

94. *Shrewsbury Chronicle* (8 Feb. 1957).

95. *Shrewsbury Chronicle* (4 April 1862; 7 Nov. 1884; 30 Jan. 1885; 12 Sep. 1890; 24 Jan., 31 Jan. 1908; Murrell, H., *Hilda Murrell's Nature Diaries 1961-1938* (1987), pp. 9-11. For Olroyd see below p.73.

96. Bagshaw, *Shropshire* (1851), p.100; *Shrewsbury Chronicle* (6 Nov. 1840; 1 Jan. 1841; 7 Sep. 1849).

97. *Shrewsbury Chronicle* (20 May 1927; 17 Dec. 1937; 27 May 1938; 28 July 1939).

98. Baker, *Shrewsbury Abbey* (2002), p. 211; Field, C., *Church and Chapel in Early Victorian Shropshire* (2004), p.72; *Shrewsbury Chronicle* (March 1861; 5 April, 12 April 1872; 13 Dec. 1895); Bryan, W.T., *St Giles Church* (1979).

99. *Shrewsbury Chronicle* (7 Sep. 1838, 28 Jan., 18 Feb. 1842; 9 Feb. 1844; 9 May 1851; 20 Aug. 1852; 4 April 1862; 5 April, 10 May 1867).

100. 'Notes and Queries', *ex inf.* H E Forrest, *Shrewsbury Chronicle* (10 July 1914).

101. *Shrewsbury Chronicle* (31 Aug. 1832).

102. Nightingale, J., *Beauties of England and Wales* (1813), Vol.13, pp. 164-65; *Shrewsbury Chronicle* (4 Sep., 11 Sep. 1840; 29 April 1887; 1 Jan., 26 Feb. 1915); *Eddowes's Salopian Journal* (5 Dec. 1827; 7 Sep. 1881; 2 Feb. 1887).

103. *Shrewsbury Chronicle* (16 Feb. 1883; 2 Jan. 1942; 20 March, 10 July, 13 Nov. 1959; 9 Sep. 1960); *Eddowes's Salopian Journal* (12 Feb. 1879).

104. *Shrewsbury Chronicle* (12 Oct. 1934; 12 July 1946).

105. *Shrewsbury Chronicle* (14 March 1947; 7 Sep. 1951; 9 March 1956).

106. *Shrewsbury Chronicle* (8 April 1904; 5 Feb. 1909; 12 July 1946; 3 Dec. 1948; 13 May 1949); Philpot, B.M, *A Name: a Man: A House* (1982), p.11.

107. *Shrewsbury Chronicle* (5 April 1889; 25 Oct. 1929).

108. *Shrewsbury Chronicle* (20 Feb. 1874).

109. Tisdale, T., *Map of Shrewsbury* (1875); *Shrewsbury Chronicle* (26 Jan. 1872; 20 Feb. 1880).

110. Salop County Council, *Twenty Years: Education in Shropshire 1945 to 1965* (1965), p.67; *Victoria History of Shropshire*, vol. 4 (1989), p.264; *Shrewsbury Chronicle* (3 Aug. 1934; 11 April 1919; 20 Feb. 1925; 13 June 1958; 14 Nov. 1958).

111. Ex inf. John Swannick. *Shrewsbury Chronicle* (11 April 1919; 30 Dec.1927).

112. *Shrewsbury Chronicle* (17 March 1882; 17 March 1899; 29 March 1901; 2 Jan. 1903; 20 Jan. 1911; 17 Dec. 1937).

113. *Shrewsbury Chronicle* (5 Oct. 1866; 19 Jan. 1877; 10 Nov. 1905).

114. *Shrewsbury Chronicle* (30 March 1906).

115. *Shrewsbury Chronicle* (28 July 1939; 18 March 1949; 15 Feb. 1957).

116. *Shrewsbury Chronicle* (18 Nov. 1841; 3 Nov. 1854; 24 April 1896;10 Aug. 1923, 4 May 1928).

117. Hitchcock, A., *Map of Shrewsbury* (1832); *Shrewsbury Chronicle* (17 Feb. 1832; 1 Sep. 1922; 4 June 1948).

118. *Shrewsbury Chronicle* (18 Jan., 15 Aug., 17 Oct. 1952; 8 Oct. 1954). I am grateful to Mr & Mrs G. Sproston for allowing me to examine the construction of their no-fines house.

119. *Shrewsbury Chronicle* (23 Dec. 1831; 12 July 1839).

120. *Shrewsbury Chronicle* (5 Jan. 1877; 28 April 1893; 2 Sep. 1904).

121. *Shrewsbury Chronicle* (30 Oct. 1883; 2 Sep. 1887; 6 Oct. 1911; 16 Aug. 1918; 30 Sep. 1921).

122. *Eddowes's Salopian Journal* (7 March 1832).

123. *Ex inf.* Bill Champion; Watson, M. and Musson, C., *Shropshire from the air: An English County at Work* (1996), p. 56; *Shrewsbury Chronicle* (7 March 1856; 7 May 1886).

124. *Shrewsbury Chronicle* (5 Feb.1892; 7 June 1918).

125. Trumper, *Shrewsbury: the Twentieth Century* (1999), p.98; *Shrewsbury Chronicle* (28 June 1946; 30 July 1948; 22 July 1949; 25 July, 31 July 1953).

126. *Shrewsbury Chronicle* (30 March 1894; 30 Oct. 1936).

127. *Eddowes's Salopian Journal* (6 May 1857); *Shrewsbury Chronicle* (3 Jan., 24 April, 10 July 1896; 20 Jan. 1911; 6 May 1927; 19 July 1929; 3 Feb., 10 Nov. 1950).

128. *Shrewsbury Chronicle* (28 July 1939; 11 Nov. 1949).

129. Leonard, J., *Churches of Shropshire* (2004), p.159; *Shrewsbury Chronicle* (14 Dec. 2002).

Chapter 6 – Longden Coleham and Belle Vue

1. Quoted in S.A.B.C., *Coleham and Belle Vue Conservation Area*.

2. Carr, A.M., *Shrewsbury: a Pictorial History* (1994), p.141; Trumper, D., *A Glimpse of Old Shrewsbury* (2003), p.14; Blackwall, A.H., *Historic Bridges of Shropshire* (1985), pp.92-3; *Shrewsbury Chronicle* (12 March 1852; 11 July 1873; 20 Nov. 1903).

3. Hitchcock, A., *Map of Shrewsbury* (1832); Wood, J., *Map of Shrewsbury* (1838); Trinder, B., *Barges and Bargemen* (2005), pp.131-2; *Shrewsbury Chronicle* (2 Aug. 1861; 28 March 1884).

4. Lloyd, L.C., *Inns of Shrewsbury* (1942), p.16; *Eddowes's Salopian Journal* (30 Nov. 1825; 22 Feb. 1871); *Shrewsbury Chronicle* (3 March 1826; 12 Oct. 1832; 9 March 1894; 15 April 1910). The villa was probably named after Hazledine's birthplace, Moreton Corbet. For Woodlands and Chaddeslode see above pp.57, 68-9.

5. *Shrewsbury Chronicle* (17 March, 24 March 1882).

6. J. Rocque, *Plan of Shrewsbury* (1746); Carr, A.M., *Shrewsbury: a Pictorial History* (1994), p.142.

7. Trumper, D., *Yesterday's Shrewsbury* (2002), pp.95-6, 131; *Eddowes's Salopian Journal* (16 Jan. 1878); *Shrewsbury Chronicle* (3 Nov. 1905; 6 March 1908).

8. Trumper, D., *Yesterday's Shrewsbury* (2002), p.131; *Shrewsbury Chronicle* (6 Jan. 1832; 20 March 1857; 31 Jan. 1873; 1 Sep. 1899).

9. *Ex inf.* Mrs S. Cooper; Andrews, J.E., 'Taylor & Co., Clay Pipe Makers of Shrewsbury', *Shropshire Newsletter*, No 39 (1970); *Shrewsbury Chronicle* (15 Jan. 1835; 10 Aug. 1855; 23 May 1856; 23 Aug. 1861; 21 June 1872; 6 March 1936; 7 Jan. 1938).

10. Cox, J.V., 'Simplicity without meanness', *T.S.A.S.*, vol. 72 (1997), p. 91; *Shrewsbury Chronicle* (24 Oct. 1873; 25 Oct. 1878; 28 Oct. 1881; 13 Oct., 24 Nov. 1882; 15 March, 19 July 1889).

11. *Shrewsbury Chronicle* (15 Feb. 1907; 27 Nov. 1908; 4 June 1909; 12 Dec. 1913; 13 Feb., 19 June, 18 Sep. 1914).

12. Hulbert, C., *History and Description of the County of Salop* (1837), pp.307-8; Hulbert, C., *Memoirs of Seventy Years* (1852), p. 223; Pattinson, A., *On Severn Shore* (2004), pp.9, 17; Trinder, B., *Industrial Archaeology of Shropshire* (1996), pp.138-40; *Shrewsbury Chronicle* (9 Oct. 1795; 12 July 1799; 16 May 1806); *Chester Chronicle* (3 Dec. 1802).

13. Hulbert C., *History and Description of the County of Salop* (1837), pp.307-8; *Shrewsbury Chronicle* (11 May 1860; 17 May 1861; 15 Sep., 29 Sep. 1871; 25 July 1873; 23 July 1875).

14. Pattinson, A., *On Severn Shore* (2004), pp.40, 44, 49, 52; *Shrewsbury Chronicle* (13 May, 24 June 1881; 7 April 1893; 10 Jan. 1896; 2 April, 14 May, 21 May 1915); *Eddowes's Salopian Journal* (10 May 1881)

15. Pattinson, A., *On Severn Shore* (2004), pp.40, 43-4; Jones dissertation, pp.11-2; *Shrewsbury Chronicle* (1

March 1872; 24 Oct., 14 Nov. 1890; 18 March 1892; 24 June 1892); Review Publishing, *Industries of Shropshire* (1891), p.15; Robinson, Son and Pike, *Shrewsbury Illustrated* (1894), p.33.

16. Hulbert, C., *Manual of Shropshire Biography* (1839), p.8; Hulbert, C., *Memoirs of Seventy Years* (1852), pp.195, 220-1; *Shrewsbury Chronicle* (1 Jan. 1864; 3 Nov.1905); *Eddowes's Salopian Journal* (15 Feb. 1860).

17. *Shrewsbury Chronicle* (13 July, 16 Nov. 1894; 10 Jan., 7 Aug. 1896; 18 Feb., 12 Aug., 28 Oct. 1898; 12 May 1899; 16 Feb., 18 May, 16 Nov. 1900; 4 Jan. 1901); *The Music of Machinery, Vol.1, Shrewsbury Pumping Station*, Big Ben Records, MOM1.

18. *Shrewsbury Chronicle* (5 June 1835; 19 July 1861; 29 July 1904; 21 June 1907).

19. Jones dissertation, p.17; *Shrewsbury Chronicle* (6 March 1829; 19 Aug. 1898).

20. Trinder, *Industrial Archaeology of Shropshire* (1996), pp.59-60; *Shrewsbury Chronicle* (26 Jan. 1872); *Eddowes's Salopian Journal* (6 Sep. 1876; 10 April 1878; 15 Jan. 1879).

21. Blackwall, *Historic Bridges of Shropshire* (1985), p.94; *Shrewsbury Chronicle* (29 Oct. 1869; 18 Jan., 25 Jan., 15 Feb., 17 May 1878; 25 March 1960).

22. Hulbert, *Memoirs of Seventy Years* (1852), p.263; *Eddowes Salopian Journal* (2 Jan. 1828); *Shrewsbury Chronicle* (8 May 1829; 1 Aug. 1845); Robinson, Son and Pike, *Shrewsbury Illustrated* (1894), p.35.

23. Trinder, *Industrial Archaeology of Shropshire* (1996), pp.149, 161-2. For the Burr family see above, p.77, below pp.110-121.

24. *Shrewsbury Chronicle* (13 Nov. 1903; 18 March 1904; 23 March, 24 Oct. 1913).

25. Trinder, *Barges and Bargemen* (2005), pp. 131-2; Trinder, *Industrial Archaeology of Shropshire* (1996), p.51; MacDonald, W., *An Illustrated Guide to Shrewsbury* (1897), p.37; *Shrewsbury Chronicle* (16 Nov. 1923).

26. S.A.B.C., *Coleham and Belle Vue Conservation Area*.

27. See above: p.28; *Shrewsbury Chronicle* (1 March 1833; 13 Oct. 1876); Henshaw, J., *Passing Shots* (2003), p.27.

28. Griffiths, R. and Smith, P., *The Directory of British Engine Sheds*, vol.1 (1999), pp.150-1; *Shrewsbury Chronicle* (18 Nov. 1927).

29. *Eddowes's Salopian Journal* (14 Nov. 1888); *Shrewsbury Chronicle* (16 Feb. 1883; 21 May 1886; 30 Aug. 1957); Mercer, E., *English Architecture to 1900: the Shropshire Experience* (2003), pp.241-4, includes a plan of Nos 1-11 Rea Street.

30. *Shrewsbury Chronicle* (18 Nov. 1927; 25 May 1928; 22 Nov. 1935; 5 Oct. 1945; 20 March 1959; 25 March 1960).

31. *Shrewsbury Chronicle* (9 Dec. 1831; 14 June 1861).

32. Moran, M., *Vernacular Architecture in Shropshire* (2003), p. 273; Lloyd, *Inns of Shrewsbury* (1976), p.20; *Shrewsbury Chronicle* (21 Sep. 1894).

33. Pidgeon, H., *Memorials of Shrewsbury* (1937), pp.92-3; Field, C., *Church and Chapel in Early Victorian Shropshire* (2004), p.73; *Shrewsbury Chronicle* (23 Feb. 1838; 23 Aug., 30 Aug. 1861; 30 Sep. 1887); *Salopian Shreds & Patches*, vol. 8 (1887) pp.94-7.

34. *Eddowes's Salopian Journal* (4 July 1838; 17 June 1857; 19 Dec. 1866); *Shrewsbury Chronicle* (8 May 1857).

35. See above p.82.

36. *Shrewsbury Chronicle* (23 April 1852; 29 April, 20 June 1853); *Eddowes's Salopian Journal* (4 May 1853).

37. *Shrewsbury Chronicle* (15 Sep., 29 Sep., 1 Dec. 1865; 15 June 1866); *Eddowes's Salopian Journal* (6 Dec. 1865). For plan see Mercer, *English Architecture to 1900: the Shropshire Experience* (2003), p.241.

38. *Shrewsbury Chronicle* (30 March, 20 April 1866); *Eddowes's Salopian Journal* (18 April 1866).

39. *Shrewsbury Chronicle* (26 April 1907; 16 Dec. 1909; 18 Feb. 1910; 21 April, 8 Sep. 1911; 2 Jan. 1914); *Victoria History of Shropshire* (1979), Vol. 3, p.173. This paragraph draws on information supplied by the late Miss Constance Evason.

40. *Shrewsbury Chronicle* (20 Feb. 1857; 23 Aug. 1929; 14 Nov. 1930).

41. *Shrewsbury Chronicle* (3 Sep. 1852; 3 July 1914).

42. *Shrewsbury Chronicle* (28 April 1876; 3 July 1914; 29 April 1921); *Eddowes's Salopian Journal* (3 March 1869).

43. *Victoria History of Shropshire*, vol.3 (1979), p. 228; *Shrewsbury Chronicle* (3 July 1914; 29 April 1921; 29 Nov. 1946; 30 July 1948); Kingsland Grange website; Trumper, D., *Shrewsbury: a Second Selection* (1995), p.42 shows The Limes as a school, with boys playing hockey.

44. *Shrewsbury Chronicle* (14 Jan.1916).

45. *Shrewsbury Chronicle* (28 Sep. 1894; 14 June 1912).

46. Carver, M.O.H., 'Early Shrewsbury', *T.S.A.S.*, vol. 59 (1978), pp. 229-30.

47. S.A.B.C., *Coleham and Belle Vue Conservation Area*, p.3; *Shrewsbury Chronicle* (3 Feb. 1888); Lee, M.J., 'Cherry Orchard', Trinder, *Victorian Shrewsbury* (1984), p.119.

48. S.A.B.C., *Coleham and Belle Vue Conservation Area*, pp. 6-7; *Shrewsbury Chronicle* (18 June 1880; 13 March, 13 Nov. 1891; 16 June 1893; 25 May 1894; 16 Aug. 1895; 14 Feb., 15 May 1896; 14 Jan. 1916; 19 July 1929).

49. *Shrewsbury Chronicle* (21 June 1935; 29 Oct. 1937; 2 May 1958).

50. Minshull, T., *Salopian Directory* (1803), p.53; *Shrewsbury Chronicle* (6 Jan. 1804; 19 Aug. 1805; 22 March 1889; 14 Aug. 1896; 25 Sep. 1896).

51. Philpot, B.M., *A Name, A Man, A House* (1982), pp.2-4; *Shrewsbury Chronicle* (16 March, 6 April 1860).

52. Tonks, E.S., *The Shropshire & Montgomeryshire Railway* (1972), pp.7, 39; *Eddowes's Salopian Journal* (8 Aug. 1866); *Shrewsbury Chronicle* (24 July 1868).

53. Philpot, *A Name, A Man, A House* (1982), p.4; S.A.B.C., *Coleham and Belle Vue Conservation Area*, p.21; *Shrewsbury Chronicle* (19 May 1916).

54. See above (Hermitages)

55. *Ex inf.* the late Mrs Philippa Gray; *Shrewsbury Chronicle* (25 Sep. 1896; 7 April 1916).

56. *Shrewsbury Chronicle* (17 Feb., 1 Sep. 1905).

57. *Shrewsbury Chronicle* (12 Nov. 1886).

58. *Shrewsbury Chronicle* (21 March, 27 June 1879; 31 Aug. 1883; 29 Sep. 1929).

59. *Shrewsbury Chronicle* (2 Nov. 1866; 17 July 1874).

60. *Shrewsbury Chronicle* (2 March 1928; 22 Oct. 1937).

61. *Shrewsbury Chronicle* (4 Aug. 1916; 16 Feb. 1923; 13 April 1936).

62. Tisdale, T., *Town of Shrewsbury* (1850); *Shrewsbury Chronicle* (8 March 1889; 23 April, 29 Oct. 1937; 19 May 1939); Trumper, D., *Yesterday's Shrewsbury* (2002), pp. 99, 151.

63. *Shrewsbury Chronicle* (29 Oct. 1937).
64. *Shrewsbury Chronicle* (1 Oct. 1852; 25 Feb. 1853; 3 Sep. 1886).
65. *Shrewsbury Chronicle* (13 Dec. 1918; 14 Feb., 5 May, 24 Oct., 19 Dec. 1919; 14 May, 13 Aug., 1 Oct. 1920; 27 May 1921).
66. *Shrewsbury Chronicle* (6 June 1919; 12 Nov. 1920; 19 May, 25 Aug. 1922; 15 June 1923).

Chapter 7 – The Parish of Meole Brace
1. *Shrewsbury Chronicle* (5 Oct.1945).
2. *Shrewsbury Chronicle* (21 March 1930).
3. 29 Geo.II c.61 (1756); *Shrewsbury Chronicle* (17 Jan.1812).
4. Bagshaw, *Shropshire* (1851), p.511.
5. *Shrewsbury Chronicle* (13 Aug. 1790; 11 May 1838; 22 March, 28 June 1850; 18 Nov 1853; 13 July, 7 Sep. 1855; 6 Jan. 1860; 8 May 1896).
6. Lloyd, L.C., *Inns of Shrewsbury* (1972), p.13; *Shrewsbury Chronicle* (2 Aug. 1907; 22 April 1934; 11 Oct. 1937).
7. Trumper, D., *Glimpse of Old Shrewsbury* (2003), p. 97; *Shrewsbury Chronicle* (25 May 1934; 25 Dec. 1903).
8. Pevsner, N., *Buildings of England: Shropshire* (1958), pp.198-9; Leonard, J., *Churches of Shropshire* (2004), pp.149-50; *Shrewsbury Chronicle* (1 June 1866; 3 May 1867; 21 May 1869). For Juson see above p.56.
9. *Shrewsbury Chronicle* (19 April 1861; 2 Jan. 1903; 8 Jan. 1960).
10. Walley, D.M., *Around Shrewsbury* (1999), p. 87; *Shrewsbury Chronicle* (24 July, 14 Aug. 1908; 5 April 1912).
11. *Shrewsbury Chronicle* (28 March 1958).
12. Coles, G.M., *The Flower of Light* (1978), pp.63-9, 114.
13. *Shrewsbury Chronicle* (7 April 1916; 22 Oct. 1937).
14. Tonks, E.S., *The Shropshire and Montgomeryshire Railway* (1972), p.39; *Shrewsbury Chronicle* (21 Oct. 1910).
15. *Shrewsbury Chronicle* (29 May 1936; 22 Oct. 1937).
16. *Shrewsbury Chronicle* (18 June 1954; 6 May, 29 July, 16 Sep. 1955; 25 May 1956; 15 Feb., 26 July, 6 Sep. 1957).
17. *Shrewsbury Chronicle* (13 April 1936).
18. *Shrewsbury Chronicle* (26 Sep., 28 Nov. 1856).
19. Kingsland Grange website; *Shrewsbury Chronicle* (22 Dec. 1911).
20. *Ex inf.* AlanWilding; *Shrewsbury Chronicle* (29 Sep. 1939).
21. *Shrewsbury Chronicle* (28 Dec. 1928; 28 July, 5 Nov. 1937; 28 July 1939).
22. *Shrewsbury Chronicle* (19 May, 28 July 1939).
23. This section draws much from Stella Straughan's *Kingsland: a Shrewsbury Suburb* (1994), a privately-published account of research undertaken in the 'Victorian Shrewsbury' class, and on Bill Champion's research on the history of the common land and adjacent estates.
24. *Ex inf.* Bill Champion; Phillips, T., *History and Antiquities of Shrewsbury* (1779), p.202.
25. Stamper, P., *Historic Parks and Gardens of Shropshire* (1996), pp.13, 39.
26. Minshull, T., *Salopian Directory* (1786), p.ix; Minshull, T., *Salopian Directory* (1803), p.53; *Shrewsbury Chronicle* (6 March 1868; 11 Feb., 4 Mar. 1898; 2 Feb. 1934).

27. Stamper, *Historic Parks and Gardens* (1996), p.13; S.A., Watton Colln., vol.1, p.256; the mill stood in the garden of the present No 11 Ashton Road.
28. Price, P., 'The decline and fall of the Old Shrewsbury Show', Trinder, B., ed., *Victorian Shrewsbury* (1984), pp.143-9.
29. Price, 'Decline and Fall' (1984), p.149.
30. *Shrewsbury Chronicle* (7 June 1850); *Eddowes's Salopian Journal* (5 June 1850); Price, 'Decline and Fall' (1984), p.149.
31. Ionides, J., *Thomas Farnolls Pritchard* (1999), pp.71-86; Owen, H., *Some Account of the Ancient and Present State of Shrewsbury* (1808), p.333; *Shrewsbury Chronicle* (4 Jan.1907); *Salopian Shreds & Patches*, vol. 4 (1880-1), p.68.
32. Parry-Jones, W., *The Trade in Lunacy* (1972), pp. 51-2; *Eddowes's Salopian Journal* (27 Jan.1832).
33. *Victoria History of Shropshire*, vol. 3 (1979), pp.169-71; *Shrewsbury Chronicle* (3 March, 10 March, 7 April, 21 April, 21 July 1871; 15 June 1951). See above p.16.
34. Lawson, J.B., 'Thomas Telford in Shrewsbury', Penfold, A., *Thomas Telford; Engineer* (1980), p.10; *Shrewsbury Chronicle* (18 April 1856; 3 April, 19 May, 1885; 13 Feb. 1891; 26 June 1931); Oldham, J.B., *A History of Shrewsbury School* (1952), pp.141, 211; *ex inf.* Bill Champion.
35. Oldham, *History of Shrewsbury School* (1952), p.192; *ex inf.* James Lawson, Bill Champion, Bridget Downer.
36. *Shrewsbury Chronicle* (7 Oct. 1898; 18 Mar. 1904); inscription on the building.
37. Price, 'Decline and Fall' (1984), pp.145-8, 153-5.
38. Charlesworth, M., 'The "penny bridge" celebrates its 100th birthday', *Shropshire Magazine* (July 1992); Blackwall, A.H., *Historic Bridges of Shropshire* (1985), pp.94-5; Lerry, G.C., *Henry Robertson* (1949), p.38; *Eddowes's Salopian Journal* (2 Aug. 1882). I am grateful to Mr L.S. Asbury for showing me original drawings of the bridge that remain in possession of the Bridge Company.
39. *Victoria History of Shropshire*, vol.2 (1973), pp.154-5; Oldham, *History of Shrewsbury School* (1952), pp. 72, 90, 104, 125, 128-30.
40. Lawson, J.B., 'Genesis: Exodus', *Salopian Newsletter* (May 1983); Oldham, *History of Shrewsbury School* (1952), pp.131-5; *Shrewsbury Chronicle* (9 June 1876; 4 Jan. 1878; 21 July, 4 Aug. 1882).
41. *Shrewsbury Chronicle* (30 June, 21 July, 25 Aug. 1882; 15 Aug 1884.).
42. *Eddowes's Salopian Journal* (31 Dec. 1884); Charlesworth, M., *Behind the Headlines* (1994), p.52.
43. Oldham, *History of Shrewsbury School* (1952), pp.142-6; Charlesworth, *Behind the Headlines* (1994), pp. 47, 51.
44. *Shrewsbury Chronicle* (4 Jan. 1895; 14 March 1913).
45. *Victoria History of Shropshire*, vol. 3 (1979), p. 188.
46. *Shrewsbury Chronicle* (21 March 1913; 4 May 1917); Roberts, M.K., *In Retrospect* (1981), p.81.
47. *Eddowes's Salopian Journal* (14 May 1879; 31 Dec. 1884); *Shrewsbury Chronicle* (7 Feb, 1936).

Chapter 8 – Frankwell and the Roads to the West
1. Fiennes, C., *The Journeys of Celia Fiennes* (1947), p.226; Blackwall, A.H., *Historic Bridges of Shropshire* (1985), pp. 91-2; Trinder, B., *Barges and Bargemen*

(2005), p.1.

2. Cox, J.V., 'Simplicity without meanness', *T.S.A.S.*, vol.72 (1997), p.84; *Shrewsbury Chronicle* (19 May 1865).

3. 31 Geo II c.67 (1758); Trinder, *Barges and Bargemen* (2005), pp.42-4.

4. *Shrewsbury Chronicle* (22 Aug., 31 Oct., 13 Dec. 1873; 20 Mar. 1874).

5. *Shrewsbury Chronicle* (4 Dec., 11 Dec. 1874).

6. *Shrewsbury Chronicle* (15 Jan., 16 July, 23 July, 3 Sep. 1875; 15 Feb. 1876).

7. Moran, M., *Vernacular Architecture in Shropshire* (2003), pp.227, 247; Mercer, E., *English Architecture to 1900: the Shropshire Experience* (2003), p.128.

8. Gaydon, A.T., 'The Old Co-op, Frankwell, Shrewsbury', *Shropshire Newsletter* No 37 (1969); Moran, *Vernacular Architecture in Shropshire* (2003), p. 252; Trumper, D., *Shrewsbury: the Twentieth Century* (1999), p.129.

9. Moran, *Vernacular Architecture in Shropshire* (2003), pp.256-8, 265-7, 269-70.

10. Trumper, D., *Shrewsbury: the Twentieth Century* (1999), p. 79; *Shrewsbury Chronicle* (29 Jan. 1922; 28 May 1943).

11. This table draws on data assembled by Iris Harris.

12. *Ex inf.* Iris Harris.

13. *Shrewsbury Chronicle* (11 April 1913; 17 March 1933; 17 Oct. 1958).

14. *The Builder* (10 Aug. 1861); *Shrewsbury Chronicle* (16 Aug. 1861).

15. *Daily News* (2 Nov. 1912).

16. *Eddowes's Salopian Journal* (6 July 1836).

17. Trinder, B., '18th and 19th-Century Market Town Industry: An analytical model', *Industrial Archaeology Review*, vol. 24 (2002), 79-81.

18. Minshull, T., *Salopian Directory* (1786); *Shrewsbury Chronicle* (24 Dec. 1841; 5 March 1847; 30 June 1848; 3 May 1861; 21 Aug. 1868; 10 Nov. 1871; 29 Aug. 1873; 1 Feb., 19 July 1907; 29 Jan. 1922).

19. Trinder, *Industrial Archaeology of Shropshire* (1996), p.50; *Shrewsbury Chronicle* (24 March 1826; 16 Oct. 1829).

20. *Shrewsbury Chronicle* (1 Feb. 1839; 18 June, 24 Dec. 1841; 30 June 1848; 28 Jan. 1881; 22 July 1892).

21. Moran, *Vernacular Architecture in Shropshire* (2003), pp. 256-8; Minshull, T., *Salopian Directory* (1803); Trinder, *Industrial Archaeology of Shropshire* (1996), p.42; *Shrewsbury Chronicle* (27 Aug. 1841; 3 May 1861; 8 June 1923).

22. *Shrewsbury Chronicle* (21 Feb., 11 Sep., 4 Dec. 1868).

23. Rolt, L.T.C., *Railway Adventure* (1971), p.33.

24. Watson, N., *A Family Business* (1995), p.25.

25. *Shrewsbury Chronicle* (18 June 1841; 5 March 1847; 19 Aug. 1892; 2 Aug. 1907).

26. Trinder, B., *The Market Town Lodging House in Victorian England* (2001), pp. 11-7, 21-2.

27. Trumper, D., *Shrewsbury: the Twentieth Century* (1999), p.79.

28. *Eddowes's Salopian Journal* (2 April 1827); *Shrewsbury Chronicle* (26 Sep. 1879); Trumper, D., *A Glimpse of Old Shrewsbury* (2003), pp. 150-1.

29. Field, C., *Church and Chapel in Early Victorian Shropshire* (2004), p. 77; Cox, 'Simplicity without meanness' (1997), p. 82; *Shrewsbury Chronicle* (21 Oct. 1870; 26 May, 2 June 1871; 16 Dec. 1909).

30. *Shrewsbury Chronicle* (26 Feb. 1858; 18 Nov. 1910; 6 March, 27 March, 5 June 1959).

31. *Shrewsbury Chronicle* (25 March, 8 April 1910; 22 May 1914).

32. *Shrewsbury Chronicle* (5 June 1903).

33. *Shrewsbury Chronicle* (19 Nov. 1852; 15 July 1853); Carr, A.M., *Shrewsbury as it was* (1978), p.59; Trumper, D., *Shrewsbury in Old Photographs* (1994), p. 80; Hart, S., *Shrewsbury: a Portrait* (1988), p. 119.

34. Blackwall, *Historic Bridges of Shropshire* (1985), pp.95-6; *Shrewsbury Chronicle* (19 Jan. 1923; 19 Oct. 1945).

35. See above, p.36.

36. Trumper, D., *Yesterday's Shrewsbury* (2002), p. 106; *Shrewsbury Chronicle* (14 Sep. 1827; 8 Feb. 1850; 18 April 1856; 9 April 1858; 18 Feb. 1898; 20 Aug. 1954).

37. *Shrewsbury Chronicle* (1 Feb. 1935).

38. *Shrewsbury Chronicle* (23 March 1928)

39. *Shrewsbury Chronicle* (31 May 1872).

40. *Eddowes's Salopian Journal* (3 Oct. 1800; 26 Oct. 1803); *Shrewsbury Chronicle* (31 July 1840; 31 Dec. 1841; 16 March 1849; 4 March 1898); Lloyd, *Inns of Shrewsbury* (1942), p. 48.

41. For Woodward, see memorial in St Chad's church; *Shrewsbury Chronicle* (30 May 1913; 11 Feb. 1927; 14 Feb. 1930; 6 Jan. 1939).

42. *Shrewsbury Chronicle* (15 Dec. 1922; 13 July 1923; 28 Feb. 1936).

43. Henshaw, J., *Passing Shots* (2003), p.115.

44. *Shrewsbury Chronicle* (13 July 1923; 19 June 1931; 3 Nov. 1933; 16 March 1934).

45. *Shrewsbury Chronicle* (19 Aug., 26 Aug. 1910; 28 Feb. 1936).

46. *Shrewsbury Chronicle* (28 Feb. 1936).

47. *Shrewsbury Chronicle* (21 Sep. 1928; 15 Feb. 1935; 28 June 1935).

48. Oliphant, M., *Chronicles of Carlingford: Miss Marjoribanks* (1988), p.246.

49. *Shrewsbury Chronicle* (29 March, 12 April 1872).

50. S.A., D3651/531/81. I owe these references to Dr Donald Harris; *Salopian Shreds & Patches* (11 Dec. 1878); *Shrewsbury Chronicle* (8 Nov. 1878).

51. *Shrewsbury Chronicle* (6 May 1853; 28 Dec. 1951; 19 June, 3 July 1953); *Eddowes's Salopian Journal* (4 May 1853).

52. *Shrewsbury Chronicle* (2 July, 9 July 1881; 14 March 1884; 1 April 1887); *Eddowes's Salopian Journal* (24 Aug. 1881).

53. *Shrewsbury Chronicle* (19 Nov. 1937; 18 Jan. 1946).

54. Lloyd, *Inns of Shrewsbury* (1942), p.10; *Shrewsbury Chronicle* (14 Jan. 1938; 17 Feb., 28 July, 10 Nov. 1939; 18 April, 20 June 1941; 12 Oct. 1956).

55. Field, *Church and Chapel* (2004), p.77; Pidgeon, *Memorials of Shrewsbury* (1837), pp.88-91; *Shrewsbury Chronicle* (7 Dec. 1827; 4 Jan. 1828; 3 Feb. 1832; 28 June 1833; 1 May 1835).

56. *Eddowes's Salopian Journal* (29 Sep. 1815); *Shrewsbury Chronicle* (28 July 1843; 3 Nov. 1848).

57. *Shrewsbury Chronicle* (1 Dec. 1865; 8 March 1867); *Eddowes's Salopian Journal* (6 Dec. 1865).

58. *Shrewsbury Chronicle* (1 Jan. 1915).

59. *Shrewsbury Chronicle* (16 Feb., 2 March 1883; 9 Aug. 1901); *Eddowes's Salopian Journal* (14 Nov. 1888).

60. *Ex inf.* Dr Donald Harris, the late H.G.F.Foxall.

61. S.A., 2133/1199.

62. Meteyard, E., *A Group of Englishmen* (1871), pp.

256-60; S.A., Salop Fire Office Policy Book No 3, p.424, 21 Oct. 1797. I owe this reference to Dr Donald Harris.

63. *Shrewsbury Chronicle* (17 Nov. 1848; 21 March 1919; 24 March 1922); *Eddowes's Salopian Journal* (15 Nov. 1848). *Ex inf.* Dr Donald Harris.

64. *Shrewsbury Chronicle* (20 July 1832).

65. *Shrewsbury Chronicle* (21 Jan. 1831; 10 July 1840; 3 Jan. 1845; 20 Nov. 1868; 4 June 1869).

66. *Shrewsbury Chronicle* (31 July 1931); Trumper, D., *Shrewsbury: a Second Selection* (1995), p.65.

67. *Shrewsbury Chronicle* (7 Oct. 1831; 10 Jan. 1851).

68. Lloyd, *Inns of Shrewsbury* (1942), p.14; Lichfield Record Office, inventory, Edward Reynolds, St Chad, 1719.

69. *Shrewsbury Chronicle* (30 May 1930).

70. *Shrewsbury Chronicle* (24 July 1891).

71. *Shrewsbury Chronicle* (5 Nov. 1954; 11 May 1956).

72. *Shrewsbury Chronicle* (1 Oct. 1920; 26 Jan. 1934; 1 Feb.1935).

73. *Shrewsbury Chronicle* (29 July 1831; 20 Jan. 1905); *Salopian Shreds and Patches*, vol. 8 (1887-8), 12 Oct. 1887.

74. *Victoria History of Shropshire*, vol. 3 (1979), p.198; *Shrewsbury Chronicle* (18 Jan. 1901; 22 July 1932).

75. Ex inf. Dr D.C.Cox; *Wellington Journal* (20 June 1936); *Shrewsbury Chronicle* (19 Nov.1937).

76. *Shrewsbury Chronicle* (19 Nov. 1937). For the church see above, p.26.

77. *Shrewsbury Chronicle* (11 June 1915).

78. *Shrewsbury Chronicle* (7 Aug. 1908; 15 Sep., 6 Oct.1933; 29 May 1936; 19 Nov. 1937).

79. *Shrewsbury Chronicle* (31 Oct. 1947; 2 Jan., 16 Jan., 10 Sep. 1948; 9 March, 26 Oct. 1951; 5 June 1953).

80. Minshull, T., *The Shrewsbury Visitor's Pocket Companion* (1803), p.56; Mercer, *English Architecture to 1900: the Shropshire Perspective* (2003), pp.203-4; Stamper, P., *Historic Parks and Gardens of Shropshire* (1996), p.85; S.A. Watton Collection, vol.2, p.498.

81. Bagshaw, *Shropshire* (1851), p. 675; *Shrewsbury Chronicle* (2 Jan.1863; 17 Dec. 1868; 8 Jan., 5 Feb. 1869; 1 April 1870; 16 Sep. 1932); *Eddowes's Salopian Journal* (27 Jan. 1869).

82. *Shrewsbury Chronicle* (18 April 1919; 10 Feb. 1928; 19 May, 28 July 1939).

83. *Victoria History of Shropshire*, vol. 3 (1979), p. 213; Trumper, D., *Shrewsbury: the Twentieth Century* (1999), p.141; *Shrewsbury Chronicle* (3 Jan. 1947; 13 Feb., 18 June 1948; 25 July 1958).

84. *Shrewsbury Chronicle* (25 Feb. 1949; 21 April 1950).

85. B.P.P. 1824 IV; 1830-1, IV; Ironbridge Gorge Museum, Information Sheet No 3, *The Shelton Tollhouse* (n.d.) includes the specifications for the building.

86. Trumper, *Shrewsbury: the Twentieth Century* (1999), p. 69; Lloyd, *Inns of Shrewsbury* (1942), p.43; *Shrewsbury Chronicle* (2 May 1941).

87. Pidgeon, *Memorials of Shrewsbury* (1837), p.191; *Shrewsbury Chronicle* (22 Nov. 1878; 1 Sep. 1899; 4 April 1930).

88. *Victoria History of Shropshire*, vol. 3 (1979), pp.160-2, 212.

89. Field, *Church and Chapel* (2004), p.78; *Shrewsbury Chronicle* (29 June 1832; 17 Nov. 1843; 9 June 1854). The site is commemorated by the name of Chapel Cottages.

90. Fletcher, W.G.D., *A Short History of Shelton & Oxon*

(1920), pp.2-5; Tomlinson, J.W.B., *Oxon lives* (2004), p.13; *Shrewsbury Chronicle* (20 May 1853; 6 Oct. 1854; 24 Aug. 1855).

91. *Shrewsbury Chronicle* (16 July 1920).

92. Bagshaw, *Shropshire* (1851), p. 687; Tomlinson, *Oxon Lives* (2004), p.44; *Shrewsbury Chronicle* (31 July 1840; 11 Jan. 1856; 7 Jan. 1870; 2 June 1871).

93. *Victoria History of Shropshire*, vol.2 (1973), pp. 171, 177; 191; *Shrewsbury Chronicle* (12 Sep. 1851; 4 May 1855; 3 July 1868; 22 June, 3 Aug. 1888).

94. *Shrewsbury Chronicle* (14 Jan. 1831; 12 Nov. 1852).

Chapter 9 – Coton Hill and Greenfields

1. *Ex inf.* Bill Champion; Forrest,H.E., *Old Houses of Shrewsbury* (1972), p.91.

2. Trumper, D., *A Glimpse of Old Shrewsbury* (2003), p.140; Trinder, B., *The Industrial Archaeology of Shropshire* (1996), p.52; *Shrewsbury Chronicle* (22 Dec.1905).

3. Cox, J.V., 'Simplicity without meanness', *T.S.A.S.*, vol. 72 (1997), p. 81; Pidgeon, H., *Memorials of Shrewsbury* (1837), pp.185-7; *Shrewsbury Chronicle* (4 May 1832; 7 Feb. 1896; 23 May 1902; 19 Feb. 1909).

4. Trinder, *Industrial Archaeology of Shropshire* (1996) p.55; Forrest, *Old Houses of Shrewsbury* (1972), p. 91; *Shrewsbury Chronicle* (21 Sep. 1838; 14 Oct 1910; 24 April 1931).

5. Griffiths, R. and Smith, P., *The Directory of British Engine sheds* (1999), p.151.

6. *Shrewsbury Chronicle* (7 Aug. 1857; 11 Sep. 1874; 30 Jan. 1891). For Simpson see above p.34.

7. Wood, J., *Map of Shrewsbury* (1838); *Shrewsbury Chronicle* (18 Feb., 1 April 1842); *Eddowes Salopian Journal* (14 June 1848).

8. Trinder, B., *Barges & Bargemen* (2005), pp.136-7.

9. *Shrewsbury Chronicle* (26 Nov. 1847); *Eddowes's Salopian Journal* (30 March 1887).

10. 25 Geo II, c 22; 31 Geo II, c 67; Wood, J., *Map of Shrewsbury* (1838); Tisdale, T., *Map of Shrewsbury* (1875); Shropshire & West Midlands Agricultural Society, *Century of Progress* (1975), p.13.

11. *Shrewsbury Chronicle* (21 March, 24 Oct. 1930).

12. *Shrewsbury Chronicle* (1 Sep. 1876; 18 Jan. 1889; 25 Dec. 1891).

13. Pidgeon, *Memorials of Shrewsbury* (1837), p.188; *Shrewsbury Chronicle* (1 June 1894; 4 Jan., 27 Sep. 1895; 18 Sep. 1914).

14. Wood, J., *Map of Shrewsbury* (1838); *Shrewsbury Chronicle* (14 July 1933).

15. *Shrewsbury Chronicle* (14 March, 21 March, 15 Aug., 22 Aug. 1919; 12 Nov. 1920; 18 Feb., 18 March, 15 April 1921; 19 May 1922).

16. *Shrewsbury Chronicle* (24 Aug. 1923; 4 Jan., 25 Jan., 30 May, 12 Dec. 1924; 13 March 1925; 12 Feb., 15 Oct. 1926; 30 Dec. 1927; 26 Nov. 1937).

17. *Shrewsbury Chronicle* (11 Nov., 2 Dec. 1887; 18 March 1892).

18. Champion, W., 'John Ashby and the history and environs of the Lion Inn Shrewsbury', *T.S.A.S.*, vol. 75 (2000), p. 77; *Shrewsbury Chronicle* (24 Sep. 1880; 31 March, 14 April, 21 April 1882; 12 Nov. 1886; 26 Jan. 1936); *Eddowes's Salopian Journal* (13 Oct. 1880; 18 May 1881; 14 Nov. 1888).

19. *Shrewsbury Chronicle* (29 July 1887; 10 April 1891; 6 July 1900; 7 April 1933; 26 Jan. 1936).

20. Morris, W.E., *A History of Methodism in Shrewsbury*

(1960), pp.36-7; *Shrewsbury Chronicle* (23 Oct. 1908)

21. *Shrewsbury Chronicle* (7 Nov. 1890; 31 July 1891; 19 Feb., 25 Nov. 1892; 30 Dec. 1898; 19 Nov. 1920).

22. *Shrewsbury Chronicle* (2 Nov. 1894; 5 Aug. 1898; 3 Feb., 21 April 1899; 26 Jan. 1936).

23. *Shrewsbury Chronicle* (4 June 1828); *Eddowes's Salopian Journal* (2 July, 17 Sep. 1828).

Chapter 10 – The Castle Foregate and Beyond

1. *Shrewsbury Chronicle* (30 July 1802).

2. Fiennes, C., *The Journeys of Celia Fiennes* (1947), p.226.

3. Owen, H., *Some Account of the Ancient and Present State of Shrewsbury* (1808), p.75; Owen, H. and Blakeway, J.B. (1825), *A History of Shrewsbury* (1826), I, p.586.

4. Shropshire Railway Society, *Shropshire Railways Revisited* (1982), pp.2,4; Carr, A.M., *Shrewsbury as it was* (1978), p.37.

5. *Eddowes's Salopian Journal* (18 Aug. 1885).

6. Lloyd, L.C., *Inns of Shrewsbury* (1942), p.23. Grapes Passage was also Court No 1 in Castle Foregate.

7. *Shrewsbury Chronicle* (1 Jan. 1926; 13 Aug. 1926).

8. *Shrewsbury Chronicle* (29 Oct. 1830).

9. Marsh, P., 'Below the Castle Walls', Trinder, B., *Victorian Shrewsbury* (1984), pp.105-13.

10. The best source for the history of the school is in *Shrewsbury Chronicle* (26 Dec. 1930).

11. Bagshaw, S., *Shropshire* (1851), p.61; *Shrewsbury Chronicle* (1 Nov.1811; 13 June 1851); *Eddowes's Salopian Journal* (18 June 1851); Thomas thesis, pp.iii-iv; Hulbert, C., *Memoirs of Seventy Years* (1852), pp.50-1.

12. Brodie, A., Croom, J. and Davies, J.O., *English Prisons: an Architectural History* (2002), pp.30-2, 46-7, 62, 90, 150; *Victoria History of Shropshire*, vol. 3, pp. 105, 113, 125, 154-5; Nightingale, J., *Beauties of England & Wales* (1813), vol. 13, p. 145; *Shrewsbury Chronicle* (16 Feb. 1788; 3 Aug. 1795; Lawson, J.B., 'Thomas Telford in Shrewsbury', Penfold, A., *Thomas Telford: Engineer* (1980), 3-4; Johnston, H., 'Discovering the local prison: Shrewsbury Gaol in the nineteenth century', *The Local Historian*, vol. 35 (2005), pp.130-42.

13. Frost dissertation, pp. 16-39; *Eddowes's Salopian Journal* (7 April 1841); *Shrewsbury Chronicle* (10 April 1863).

14. *Shrewsbury Chronicle* (3 May 1834); *Eddowes's Salopian Journal* (11 Dec. 1839; 17 Feb. 1841); Bagshaw, *Shropshire*, pp.65-7; Marsh, 'Below the Castle Walls', pp. 108-9; Evason, C., 'Downhill Journey: Stage Coaching in Shrewsbury 1833-61', Trinder, B., *Victorian Shrewsbury* (1984), p.78.

15. Marsh, 'Below the Castle Walls', pp.21-2; *Shrewsbury Chronicle* (19 Jan. 1835); Trinder, B., *The Industrial Archaeology of Shropshire* (1996), pp.129, 178-9; C. Hadfield, *The Canals of the West Midlands* (1966), pp.162-5; John Wood, *Map of Shrewsbury* (1838).

16. Carver, M.C., 'Early Shrewsbury; an Archaeological Definition in 1975', *T.S.A.S.*, vol. 59 (1978), pp. 225-63; *Shrewsbury Chronicle* (28 Feb. 1936); Champion, W.A., 'Population change in Shrewsbury, 1400-1700' (1983), unpublished typescript, SA 6001/6821, pp.222-4.

17. *Shrewsbury Chronicle* (7 Oct. 1892; 17 March 1933); Trinder, *Industrial Archaeology of Shropshire*, p.60.

18. Trinder, *Industrial Archaeology of Shropshire*, p.61; *Eddowes's Salopian Journal* (3 March 1869); Watson,

N., *Family business* (1995), p.85.

19. Upton, C., *Living Back-to-Back* (2005), pp.1-7, 123; *ex inf.* John Smith.

20. *Ex inf.* Bill Champion; Cox, J.V., 'Simplicity without meanness', *T.S.A.S.*, vol. 72 (1997), p.75; *Baptist Magazine* (1828), p.223; S.A., Deposited Plan 336, Shrewsbury, Oswestry & Chester Junction Railway (1842).

21. Trinder, *Industrial Archaeology of Shropshire*, p.74; *Shrewsbury Chronicle* (3 June 1932).

22. *Eddowes's Salopian Journal* (10 Jan. 1838; 14 Nov. 1877); Trinder, *Industrial Archaeology of Shropshire*, p.44. For William Jones & Son, see pp.87-8.

23. *Shrewsbury Chronicle* (24 Oct. 1975)

24. *Shropshire Conservative* (24 April 1841); *Shrewsbury Chronicle* (27 Sep. 1946; 14 Feb.1947; 30 May 1947; 18 June 1948).

25. For Simpson see Introduction p.34.

26. *Eddowes's Salopian Journal* (10 Jan. 1838; 27 May 1840); *Shrewsbury Chronicle* (8 Feb. 1935; 26 Oct. 2000).

27. B. Trinder, 'Ditherington Flax Mill, Shrewsbury – A Re-evaluation', *Textile History*, vol. 23 (1992), pp.205-8; Pidgeon, H., *Memorials of Shrewsbury* (1837), pp.85-7.

28. Trinder, 'Ditherington Flax Mill', p.193.

29. *Shrewsbury Chronicle* (1 Sep. 1797); Trinder, 'Ditherington Flax Mill', pp.194-5.

30. Trinder, 'Ditherington Flax Mill', p.193; Macleod, M., Trinder, B. and Worthington, M., *Ditherington Flax Mill, Shrewsbury: a Survey and Historical Evaluation* (1988), p.218.

31. Trinder, 'Ditherington Flax Mill', pp.193-4; *Shrewsbury Chronicle* (18 May 1945).

32. Trinder, 'Ditherington Flax Mill', pp.204-8.

33. Field, C., ed., *Church and Chapel in Early Victorian Shropshire* (2004), p.75.

34. Grey, P., Keeley, M. and Seale, J., *Midland Red: a History of the Company and its vehicles from 1940 to 1970* (1979), pp.167-8; Anderson, R.C., *A History of Midland Red* (1984), pp. 15, 185; Lloyd, *Inns of Shrewsbury*, p. 45.

35. Trinder, 'Ditherington Flax Mill', p.205.

36. Trumper, D., *Shrewsbury: the Twentieth Century* (1999), p.106, for a photograph of New Park Road before re-development.

37. See above pp.147-8.

38. Trinder, *Industrial Archaeology of Shropshire*, pp.146-8; *Shrewsbury Chronicle* (9 Aug. 1837).

39. S.A., Tithe Map, St Mary's, Castle Foregate; S.A., Particulars of a very valuable property, offered for sale 21 December 1835; *Shrewsbury Chronicle* (18 Dec. 1835; 15 June, 28 Sep. 1956).

40. *Eddowes's Salopian Journal* (5 April 1843); John Wood, *Map of Shrewsbury* (1838).

41. For the Freehold Land Society see above p.37.

42. *Shrewsbury Chronicle* (16 June 1854); *Eddowes's Salopian Journal* (13 Sep. 1854).

43. *Shrewsbury Chronicle* (19 July 1892).

44. Ex inf. Bill Champion; *Eddowes's Salopian Journal* (12 Sep. 1860).

45. *Eddowes's Salopian Journal* (28 Feb., 4 April, 9 May, 6 June, 15 Aug., 19 Sep., 26 Sep., 24 Oct., 19 Dec. 1866; 16 Jan. 1867).

46. *Eddowes's Salopian Journal* (31 Aug. 1853; 12 Nov. 1856).

47. *Eddowes's Salopian Journal* (21 Dec. 1870; 8 Nov. 1876); *Shrewsbury Chronicle* (3 Nov. 1876; 2 Dec. 1927); How, F.D., *The Revd Thomas Mainwaring Bulkeley-Owen* (1914), pp.76, 88, 99, 104, 142; Scard, A., *The Building Stones of Shropshire* (1990), p.31; Leonard, J., *Churches of Shropshire* (2004), p.153.

48. *Shrewsbury Chronicle* (9 June 1922; 2 Dec. 1927; 21 Jan. 1938).

49. Cox, 'Simplicity without meanness' (1997), p.77; Field, C., ed., *Church and Chapel in Early Victorian Shropshire* (2004), p.74; Morris, W.E., *A History of Methodism in Shrewsbury* (1960), pp.34-5; *Shrewsbury Chronicle* (20 Jan.1928).

50. Cox, 'Simplicity without meanness' (1997), pp.83-4; Field, *Church and Chapel* (2004), p.75; Morris, W.E., *A History of Methodism in Shrewsbury* (1960), p.23; *Shrewsbury Chronicle* (16 Sep. 1932).

51. *Shrewsbury Chronicle* (1 May 1942); Cox, 'Simplicity without meanness' (1997), p.91.

52. *Shrewsbury Chronicle* (22 June 1923; 4 Jan., 29 Feb. 1924; 12 Feb. 1926; 21 June 1935).

53. *Shrewsbury Chronicle* (13 June, 26 Sep., 21 Nov. 1913; 13 Mar., 10 April, 22 May, 18 Sep. 1914). See above pp.36, 107 (Int).

54. *Shrewsbury Chronicle* (6 Oct. 1933; 16 March 1934; 8 Feb. 1935; 15 Jan. 1937); Trinder, 'Ditherington Flax Mill', pp.206-8.

55. Ex inf. Bill Champion; *Shrewsbury Chronicle* (21 March 1902).

56. *Eddowes's Salopian Journal* (20 Oct. 1841); *Shropshire Conservative* (23 Oct. 1841); *Victoria History of Shropshire*, vol. 2, p.169.

57. *Shrewsbury Chronicle* (30 Nov. 1956; 6 Sep.1957).

58. Field, *Church and Chapel* (2004), p.75.

59. *Shrewsbury Chronicle* (9 Dec. 1831); *Eddowes's Salopian Journal* (1 Aug. 1877).

60. *Shrewsbury Chronicle* (15 Feb.1957).

61. 29 Geo.II.c.64 (1756); Trinder, *Industrial Archaeology of Shropshire* (1996), p.254; *Shrewsbury Chronicle* (30 Aug. 1777; 7 May 1790; 24 May 1793; 29 Jan.1802).

62. *Shrewsbury Chronicle* (8 Feb. 1924).

63. *Shrewsbury Chronicle* (2 Oct. 1936).

64. *Shrewsbury Chronicle* (18 Dec. 1936; 3 Dec. 1937; 11 Nov. 1938).

65. *Shrewsbury Chronicle* (17 Aug. 1923; 12 June 1925; 15 Jan. 1926).

66. *Shrewsbury Chronicle* (20 Jan. 1928). For Harlescott Close see below p.164.

67. *Shrewsbury Chronicle* (18 April, 5 Dec. 1924; 22 May 1925). *Ex inf.* Tony Cooper.

68. *Shrewsbury Chronicle* (13 April, 20 April 1928; 12 July 1929; 7 Dec 1934; 22 Nov., 29 Nov. 1935; 13 Nov. 1936); *Wellington Journal* (14 Nov.1936).

69. Hughes, W.J. and Thomas, J.L., *'The Sentinel'*, vol.1 (1973), pp.118-20; Trinder, *Industrial Archaeology of Shropshire*, pp.63-4; *Shrewsbury Chronicle* (14 Nov. 1930; 27 Oct. 1933).

70. *Shrewsbury Chronicle* (5 Jan. 1934); Thomas, W.J. and Thomas, R.L., *'The Sentinel'*, vol.2 (1987), pp. 174-205; Trinder, *Industrial Archaeology of Shropshire* (1996), pp. 64-5.

71. *Shrewsbury Chronicle* (28 Jan., 18 Feb. 1921; 14 Nov. 1930; 2 Feb. 1923).

72. *Shrewsbury Chronicle* (17 Aug. 1923); S.A.B.C., *Harlescott (Chatwood Village) Conservation Area*, n.d. (c.1986); S.A., *The Chatwood Security* (pamphlet, n.d., *circa* 1926).

73. *Shrewsbury Chronicle* (26 Sep., 21 Nov. 1919; 14 Sep. 1932)

74. *Shrewsbury Chronicle* (21 July, 30 June 1922; 12 Oct., 14 Dec. 1923; 9 May 1924; 27 March, 29 May 1925; 2 April 1926; 7 Feb., 28 March 1930; 17 April 1931).

75. *Shrewsbury Chronicle* (24 June, 14 Sep. 1932; 13 Jan., 30 June, 6 Oct. 1933.

76. *Shrewsbury Chronicle* (5 Jan.1934).

77. Letter, G. R. Fletcher to B. Trinder, 11 Nov. 1982, copy in S.A.; *Shrewsbury Chronicle* (13 April, 20 April, 3 Aug., 17 Aug. 1934).

78. *Shrewsbury Chronicle* (24 April, 24 July 1931).

79. *Shrewsbury Chronicle* (15 Nov. 1935; 2 Oct. 1936; 3 Dec. 1937); Lloyd, *Inns of Shrewsbury* (1942), p.26.

80. *Shrewsbury Chronicle* (14 Jan. 1938).

81. *Shrewsbury Chronicle* (19 March 1934; 3 Dec. 1937. *Ex inf.* Tony Cooper.

82. *Shrewsbury Chronicle* (24 Feb. 1939; 28 July 1939).

83. *Shrewsbury Chronicle* (6 May 2005).

84. *Shrewsbury Chronicle* (30 Oct. 1953); Stratton, M. and Trinder, B., *Twentieth Century Industrial Archaeology* (2000), p.113.

85. *Shrewsbury Chronicle* (3 Mar., 21 May 1948; 12 Oct. 1951).

86. *Shrewsbury Chronicle* (13 Oct., 17 Nov. 1950; 30 Oct. 1953).

87. *Shrewsbury Chronicle* (10 Feb., 15 June, 29 June, 13 July, 20 July 1956).

88. *Shrewsbury Chronicle* (1 Feb., 2 Aug. 1957; 9 May 1958; 3 April 1959).

89. *Shrewsbury Chronicle* (27 June, 17 Oct. 1947)

90. *Shrewsbury Chronicle* (30 Oct. 1953).

91. *Shrewsbury Chronicle* (6 March, 30 Oct. 1953; 23 March 1956; 22 Feb. 1957).

92. *Shrewsbury Chronicle* (10 Oct. 1919; 4 June 1920; 26 Aug. 1955; 4 May 1956; 19 July 1957).

93. *Shrewsbury Chronicle* (25 March, 17 June, 1 July, 8 July 1949).

94. *Shrewsbury Chronicle* (2 Feb., 12 Oct. 1951; 6 April 1956).

95. *Shrewsbury Chronicle* (14 April, 21 April 1950).

96. *Shrewsbury Chronicle* (14 Feb., 13 June 1947).

97. *Shrewsbury Chronicle* (22 July 1949; 16 June, 4 Aug., 17 Nov. 1950; 9 Feb. 1951; 30 Oct. 1953; 12 March 1954).

98. *Shrewsbury Chronicle* (2 March, 15 June, 28 Sep. 1956; 10 Jan., 31 Jan., 7 Feb., 1 Aug. 1958).

99. *Shrewsbury Chronicle* (30 Oct. 1953; 24 Sep. 1954; 8 April 1955).

100. Morris, *History of Methodism* (1960), pp.37-8; *Shrewsbury Chronicle* (2 Dec. 1955; 19 Feb., 29 April, 26 Aug. 1960). See above pp.25, 162-3.

101. *Shrewsbury Chronicle* (29 Aug. 1851; 9 Aug. 1872).

Chapter 11 – Reflections

1. *Chambers's Edinburgh Journal*, vol.4 (1836), p.345.

2. Hunt, T., *Building Jerusalem* (2005), pp.447-53.

3. Commission on the Employment of Children, Young Persons and Women in Agriculture (1871), summary by Edward Stanhope, reproduced in *Eddowes's Salopian Journal* (25 Jan.1871).

4. *Eddowes Salopian Journal* (3 June 1873).

5. Kidson, P., Murray, P. and Thompson, P., *A History of English Architecture* (1965), p. 257.

6. Waugh, E., *Brideshead Revisited* (ed. 1962), p.9.

Bibliography

1. Works on suburbs and other relevant aspects of urban history:

Aikin, J., *A Description of the country from 30 to 40 miles round Manchester* (1795). London: John Stockdale

Aston, M. and Bond, J., *The Landscape of Towns* (1976). London: Dent

Barrett, H. and Phillips, J., *Suburban Style – the British Home 1840-1960* (1987). London: Macdonald

Beresford, M., *History on the Ground* (edn. 1991). London: Methuen

Beresford, M., *East End, West End: The Face of Leeds during Urbanisation 1684-1842* (1988). Leeds: Thoresby Society

Best, G., *Mid-Victorian Britain 1851-75* (1973). St Albans: Panther

Betjeman, J., *The Oxford University Chest* (1938). London: John Miles, rep. 1979, Oxford: Oxford University Press

Betjeman, J., *First and Last Loves* (1952). London: John Murray

Binfield, C., *So Down to Prayers: Studies in English Congregationalism 1780-1920* (1977). London: Dent

Borsay, P., ed., *The Eighteenth Century town: A Reader in English Urban History 1688-1820* (1990). London: Longman

Bowley, M., *Housing and the State 1919-1944* (1945). London: Allen & Unwin

Briggs, A., *Victorian Cities* (1963). London: Odhams

Brodie, A., Croom, J. and Davies, J.O., *English Prisons: an Architectural History* (2002). Swindon: English Heritage

Brown, C., *Northampton 1835-1985; Shoe Town, New Town* (1990). Chichester: Phillimore

Brown, M., *The Market Gardens of Barnes and Mortlake* (1985). Barnes: Barnes & Mortlake History Society

Burnett, J., *The Social History of Housing 1815-1986* (1986). London: Methuen

Cannadine, D., *The Pleasures of the Past* (1989). London: Collins

Chalklin, C., *The Provincial Towns of Georgian England: A study of the building process 1740-1820* (1974). London: Arnold

Chancellor, V.E., *Master and Artisan in Victorian England: The Diary of William Andrews and the Autobiography of Joseph Gutteridge* (1969). London: Evelyn, Adams & Mackay

Chaplin, R., 'Discovering Lost New Towns of the Nineteenth Century; a forgotten phase of urban growth', *Local Historian*, vol. 4 (1972)

Chapman, D., *The Home and Social Status* (1955). London: Routledge & Kegan Paul

Chapman, S.D., *The History of Working Class Housing: a symposium* (1971). Newton Abbot: David & Charles

Chesney, K., *The Victorian Underworld* (1970). London: Maurice Temple Smith

Clark, C., *The British Malting Industry since 1830* (1998). London: Hambledon

Clark, P., *The Early Modern Town: A Reader* (1976). London: Longman

Clark, P., ed., *Country Towns in Pre-Industrial Britain* (1981). Leicester: Leicester University Press

Clark, P., *The English Alehouse: a social history 1200-1830* (1983). London: Longman

Clark, P., ed., *The Cambridge Urban History of Britain, vol.II 1540-1840* (2000). Cambridge: Cambridge University Press

Clark, P. and Corfield, P., eds., *Industry and Urbanisation in Eighteenth Century England* (1994). Leicester: Centre for Urban History, University of Leicester

Corfield, P.J., *The impact of English towns 1700-1800* (1982). Oxford: Oxford University Press

Crosby, A., et al., *Jeeves Yard; A dynasty of Hitchin builders and brickmakers* (2003). Baldock: Streets Publishers

Crouch, D. and Ward, C., *The Allotment: its landscape and culture* (1997). Nottingham: Five Leaves

Darley, G., *Villages of Vision* (1975). London: Architectural Press

Daunton, M., ed., *The Cambridge Urban History of Britain, vol.III 1840-1950* (2000). Cambridge: Cambridge University Press

Driver, F., *Power and Paupers: the workhouse system 1834-84* (1993). Cambridge: Cambridge University Press

Dyos, H.J., *Victorian Suburb: a study of the growth of Camberwell* (1961). Leicester: Leicester University Press

Dyos, H.J., ed., *The Study of Urban History* (1968). London: Arnold

Dyos, H.J. and Wolff, M., eds., *The Victorian City: Images and Realities* (2 vols., 1973). London: Arnold

Edwards, A., *The Design of Suburbia* (1981). London: Pembridge

Ellis, C.W., *England and the Octopus* (1928). London: Geoffrey Bles

Finnegan, F., *Poverty and Prostitution: A study of Victorian Prostitutes in York* (1979). Cambridge: Cambridge University Press

Fraser, D., *Power and Authority in the Victorian City* (1979). Oxford: Blackwell

Gaskell, S.M., *Building Control: National Legislation and the Introduction of Local Bye-laws in Victorian England* (1983). London: Bedford Square Press

Gauldie, E., *Cruel Habitations: A History of Working-Class Housing 1780-1918* (1974). London: Allen & Unwin

Girouard, M., *The English Town* (1990). New Haven & London: Yale University Press

Godwin, G., *Town Swamps and Social Bridges* (1859, ed., A.D. King, 1972). Leicester: Leicester University Press

Graves, R. and Hodge, A., *The Long Weekend* (1940). London: Faber

Hardy, D. and Ward, C., *Arcadia for All: the Legacy of a Makeshift Landscape* (1984). Oxford: Alexandrine

Hardy, Thomas, *The Mayor of Casterbridge* (1886)

Hardy, Thomas, *Jude the Obscure* (1896)

Harrison, B.H., *Drink and the Victorians* (1971). London: Faber

Harrison, M., *Bournville: Model Village to Garden Suburb* (1999). Chichester: Phillimore

Herbert, T. and Huggins, K., *The Decorative Tile in Architecture and Interiors* (1995). London: Phaidon

Higgs, E., *Making Sense of the Census: The Manuscript Returns for England and Wales, 1801-1901* (1989). London: HMSO

Hillier, B., *John Betjeman: New Fame, New Love* (2002). London: John Murray

Hollingshead, J., *Ragged London in 1861* (ed. A.S.Wohl, 1986). London: Dent (Everyman)

Hoskins, W.G., *Midland England: A Survey of the Country between the Chilterns and the Trent* (1949). London: Batsford

Hoskins, W.G., *The Making of the English Landscape* (1957). London: Hodder & Stoughton

Hoskins, W.G., *Local History in England* (1959). London: Longman

Hoskins, W.G., *Fieldwork in Local History* (1967). London: Faber

Humphreys, R., *No Fixed Abode: a history of responses to the roofless and the rootless in Britain* (1999). London: Macmillan

Hunt, T., *Building Jerusalem: the rise and fall of the Victorian City* (2005). London: Phoenix

Jackson, A., *Semi-detached London: Suburban Development, Life and Transport 1900-39* (1973). London: Allen & Unwin

James, P. and Sadler, R., eds., *Homes Fit for Heroes: Photographs by Bill Brandt 1939-1943* (2004). Stockport: Dewi Lewis

Keating, P., ed., *Into Unknown England 1866-1913: Selections from the Social Explorers* (1976). London: Fontana

Kellett, J.R., *The Impact of Railways on Victorian Cities* (1969). London: Routledge & Kegan Paul

Kidson, P., Murray, P. and Thompson, P., *A History of English Architecture* (1965). Harmondsworth: Penguin

King, A.D., *The Bungalow: the production of a global culture* (1984). London: Routledge & Kegan Paul

Klapper, C., *The Golden Age of Tramways* (1961). London: Routledge & Kegan Paul

Le Lièvre, A., 'Capital Orchards', *Country Life* (2 November 1989)

Macaulay, T.B., *The History of England from the accession of James II* (1848, Everyman ed., 1921). London: Dent

Meakin, B., *Model Factories and Villages: Ideal Conditions of Labour and Housing* (1905). London: T.Fisher Unwin

Miller, M., *Letchworth: the First Garden City* (2002). Chichester: Phillimore

Morris, L., *The Country Garage* (1985). Princes Risborough: Shire Books

Morris, R.J. and Rodger, R., *The Victorian City: A Reader in British Urban History 1820-1914* (1990). London: Longman

Mowat, C.L., *Britain between the Wars* (1955). Methuen

Mowl, T., *Stylistic Cold Wars: Betjeman versus Pevsner* (2000). London: John Murray

Muthesius, S., *The English Terraced House* (1982). New Haven & London: Yale University Press

Oliphant, M., *Chronicles of Carlingford: Phoebe Junior* (1876)

Oliphant, M., *Chronicles of Carlingford: Miss Marjoribanks* (1866)

Oliver, P., Davis, I. and Bentley, I., *Dunroamin: The Suburban Semi and its Enemies* (1981). London: Barrie & Jenkins

Olsen, D.M.J., *The Growth of Victorian London* (1976). London: Batsford

Orwell, G., *The Road to Wigan Pier* (1937). London: Gollancz

Orwell, G., *Selected Essays* (1960). Harmondsworth: Penguin

Parry-Jones, W., *The Trade in Lunacy* (1972). London: Routledge & Kegan Paul

Powell, C., *The British Building Industry since 1800* (2nd ed., 1996). London: Spon

Prest, J., *The Industrial Revolution in Coventry* (1960). Oxford: Oxford University Press

Priestley, J.B., *English Journey* (1936). London: Heinemann

Ravetz, A., *Model Estate; Planned Housing at Quarry Hill Flats, Leeds* (1974). London: Croom Helm

Razzell, P.E. and Wainwright, R.W., *The Victorian Working Class: Selections from Letters to the Morning Chronicle* (1973). London: Cass

Richards, J.M., *Modern Architecture: an Introduction* (1940). Harmondsworth: Penguin

Richards, J.M., *Castles on the Ground: the anatomy of suburbia* (1946). London: Architectural Press

Robbins, M., *Middlesex* (1953). London: Collins

Rodger, R., *The Transformation of Edinburgh: Land, Property and Trust in the Nineteenth Century* (2001). Cambridge: Cambridge University Press

Rowntree, B.S., *Poverty and Progress: a second study of York* (1941). London: Longman Green

Rubinstein, D., ed., *Victorian Homes* (1974). Newton Abbot: David & Charles

Rutherford, M., *Catherine Furze* (1936). Oxford: Oxford University Press

Rutherford, M., *The Revolution in Tanners' Lane* (1887). London: Hodder & Stoughton

Rutland Local History Society, *Oakham in Rutland* (1982). Stamford: Spiegl

Saint, A., ed., *London Suburbs* (1999). London: Merrell Holberton/English Heritage

Sharp, T., *Town Planning* (1940). Harmondsworth: Penguin

Simmons, J., *The Railway in Town and Country 1830-1914* (1986). Newton Abbot: David & Charles

Slater, T., *Edgbaston: A History* (2002). Chichester: Phillimore

Spiers, M., *Victoria Park, Manchester; a 19th century suburb in its social and administrative context* (1976). Manchester: Manchester University Press

Stobart, J. and Lane, P., eds., *Urban and Industrial Change in the Midlands 1700-1840* (2000). Leicester: Centre for Urban History, University of Leicester

Stobart, J. and Raven, N., eds., *Towns, regions and industries: Urban and industrial change in the midlands, c.1700-1840* (2005). Manchester: Manchester University Press

Stratton, M., *The Terracotta Revival: Building Innovation and the Image of the Industrial City in Britain and North America* (1993). London: Gollancz

Stratton, M. and Trinder, B., *The English Heritage Book of Industrial England* (1997). London: Batsford/English Heritage

Stratton, M. and Trinder, B., *Twentieth Century Industrial Archaeology* (2000). London: Spon

Summerson, J., *Georgian London* (1945). London: Pleiades

Swift, R., ed., *Victorian Chester* (1996). Liverpool: Liverpool University Press

Tarn, J.N., *Working-class Housing in 19th century Britain* (1971). London: Lund Humphries

Taylor, C., *Fields in the English Landscape* (1975). London: Dent

Thompson, F.M.L., ed., *The Rise of Suburbia* (1982). Leicester: Leicester University Press

Thorns, D.C., *Suburbia* (1972). London: MacGibbon & Kee

Tindall, G., *The Fields Beneath: The History of One London Village* (1977), Maurice Temple Smith

Tressell, R., *The Ragged Trousered Philanthropists* (ed. 1955). London: Laurence & Wishart

Trinder, B., *Banbury's Poor in 1850* (1966). Banbury: Banbury Historical Society

Trinder, B., *Victorian Banbury* (1982, 2005). Chichester: Phillimore

Trinder, B., *The Making of the Industrial Landscape* (1982). London: Dent

Trinder, B., ed., *The Blackwell Encyclopedia of Industrial Archaeology* (1992). Oxford: Blackwell

Trinder, B., *The Market Town Lodging House in Victorian England* (2001). Leicester: Friends of the Centre for English Local History

Trinder, B., '18th- and 19th-Century Market Town Industry: An analytical model', *Industrial Archaeology Review*, vol. 24 (2002)

Trinder, B., *English Market Towns and their suburbs in recent centuries* (2005). Cambridge: University of Cambridge Institute of Continuing Education

Tubbs, R., *Living in Cities* (1942). Harmondsworth: Penguin

Turner, H., *Town Defences in England and Wales* (1971). London: J. Baker

Ucko, P.J. and Layton, R., eds., *The Archaeology and Anthropology of Landscape: Shaping your Landscape* (1999). London: Routledge

Upton, C., *Living Back-to-Back* (2005). Chichester: Phillimore

Urwin, A.C.B., *The Rabbit Warrens of Twickenham* (1986). Twickenham: Borough of Twickenham Local History Society

Vale, B., *A History of the UK Temporary Housing Programme* (1995). London: Spon

Vincent, D., *Victorian Eccleshall* (1982). Keele: University of Keele

Walton, J.K., *Fish and Chips and the British working class 1870-1940* (1992). Leicester: Leicester University Press

Ward, C., *Cotters and Squatters: Housing's Hidden History* (2002). Nottingham: Five Leaves

Whitehead, D., *Urban Renewal and Suburban Growth* (1989). Worcester: Worcestershire Historical Society, Occasional Publication No 5

Williams, G.R., *London in the Country: the Growth of Suburbia* (1975). London: Hamish Hamilton

Woodforde, J., *Bricks to build a house* (1976). London: Routledge & Kegan Paul

Yorke, F.R.S., *The Modern House* (1934). London: Architectural Press

2. *Works relating to Shrewsbury:*

Allen, A.O., *John Allen and Friends* (1922). London: Hodder & Stoughton

Anderson, R.C., *A History of Midland Red* (1984). Newton Abbot: David & Charles

Andrews, J.E., 'Taylor & Co., Clay Pipe Makers of Shrewsbury', *Shropshire Newsletter*, No 39 (1970)

Auden, H.M., 'Social Life in the Abbey Foregate a hundred years ago', *T.C.S.V.F.C.*, vol. 9 (1934)

Auden, H.M., 'Kingsland and its Associations', *T.S.A.S.*, vol.52 (1948)

Auden, T., The Church and Parish of St Juliana in Salop', *T.S.A.S*, 1st ser., vol.10 (1887)

Baker, N., *Shrewsbury Abbey: Studies in the archaeology and history of an urban abbey* (2002). Shrewsbury: Shropshire Archaeological and Historical Society

Baker, N., *Shrewsbury: archaeological discoveries from a Medieval Town* (2004). Shrewsbury: Shropshire Books

Barker, J., *Shrewsbury's Free Churches: their history and romance* (1914). Shrewsbury: Brown & Brinnand

Barker, P.A., Haldon, R. and Jenks, W.E., 'Excavations on Sharpstones Hill near Shrewsbury 1965-1971', *T.S.A.S.,* vol. 67 (1991)

Bassett, S.R., 'Anglo-Saxon Shrewsbury and its churches', *Midland History*, vol.16 (1991)

Blackwall, A.H., *Historic Bridges of Shropshire* (1985). Shrewsbury: Shropshire Libraries

Blakeway, J.B., *History of Shrewsbury Hundred or Liberties* (1897). Oswestry: Woodall Minshall

Bryan, W.T., *St Giles Church, Shrewsbury: a guide and brief history* (1979). Shrewsbury: privately published

Buckley, A. *et al.*, *The 125th anniversary of the Methodist Church, Belle Vue, Shrewsbury, 1879-2004* (2004), Shrewsbury: privately published

Buteux, S. and Hughes, G., 'Reclaiming a Wilderness: the prehistory of Lowland Shropshire', *T..S.A.S.*, vol. 70 (1995)

Butler, S., *Life and Letters of Samuel Butler* (2 vols., 1896). London: John Murray

Carr, A.H., *Shrewsbury as it was* (1978). Nelson: Hendon

Carr, A.H., *Shrewsbury: a Pictorial History* (1994). Chichester: Phillimore

Carver, M.O.H., 'Early Shrewsbury: an Archaeological Definition in 1975', *T.S.A.S.*, vol. 59 (1978 for 1973-74)

Cassey, E., *History, Gazetteer and Directory of Shropshire* (1871; 1874). Shrewsbury: Cassey

Champion, W.A., *Everyday Life in Tudor Shrewsbury* (1994). Shrewsbury: Shropshire Books

Champion, W.A., 'John Ashby and the history and environs of the Lion Inn, Shrewsbury', *T.S.A.S.*, vol. 75 (2000)

Charlesworth, M., 'The "penny bridge" celebrates its 100th birthday', *Shropshire Magazine*, July 1992

Charlesworth, M., *Behind the Headlines* (1994). Wells: Greenbank

Coles, G.M., *The Flower of Light: a biography of Mary Webb* (1978). London: Duckworth

Cossons, N. and Trinder, B., *The Iron Bridge: Symbol of the Industrial Revolution* (2nd ed., 2002). Chichester: Phillimore

Cox, D.J. and Godfrey, B.S., *Cinderellas and Packhorses: a History of the Shropshire Magistracy* (2005). Leominster: Logaston

Cox, J.V., '"Simplicity without meanness, commodiousness without extravagance": the Nonconformist Chapels and Meeting Houses in Shrewsbury in the Nineteenth Century', *T.S.A.S.*, vol. 72 (1997)

Cranage, D.H.S., *An architectural account of the churches of Shropshire* (1901). Wellington: Hobson

Crocker, W.G., *The Post Office Shrewsbury Directory 1882-83* (1882). Shrewsbury: Crocker

Cromarty, D., *Everyday Life in Medieval Shrewsbury* (1991). Shrewsbury: Shropshire Books

Cromarty, R., 'The water supply in Shrewsbury 1550-1835', *T.S.A.S.*, vol. 75 (2000)

Denton, J.H., *Canals and Railways: a list of plans and related documents deposited at the Shirehall, Shrewsbury* (1869). Shrewsbury: Salop Record Office

Ellis, P., *et al.*, 'Excavations in the Wroxeter Hinterland 1988-1990: the Archaeology of the Shrewsbury by-pass', *T.S.A.S.*, vol. 69 (1994)

Evans, C.J., Jenks, W.E. and White, R., 'Romano-British kilns at Meole Brace (Pulley), Shropshire', *T.S.A.S.*, vol. 74 (1999)

Evason, C. and Marsh, P., 'Shrewsbury Country Carriers', *Shropshire Magazine*, June 1980

Field, C., ed., *Church and Chapel in Early Victorian Shropshire: Returns from the 1851 Census of Religious Worship* (2004). University of Keele: Centre for Local History

Fiennes, C., *The Journeys of Celia Fiennes* (ed. C. Morris, 1947). London: Cresset

Fletcher, W.D.G., *A Short History of Shelton & Oxon* (1920). Shrewsbury: privately published

Fletcher, W.F.D., ed., *The Register of Atcham* (1916). Shrewsbury: Shropshire Parish Registers Society

Forrest, H.E., *The Old Houses of Shrewsbury: their history and associations* (5th ed., 1972). Shrewsbury: Wilding

Foxall, H.D.G., *A Gazetteer of Streets, Roads and Place Names in Shropshire* (1967). Shrewsbury: Salop County Council

Foxall, H.D.G., *Shropshire Field Names* (1980). Shrewsbury: Shropshire Archaeological Society

Gardiner, R., *Profitable Instructions for the manuring, sowing and planting of kitchin* gardens (1599), *T.S.A.S.*, 2nd ser., vol.4 (1892)

Gaydon, A.T., 'The Old Co-op (formerly the *String of Horses*), Frankwell, Shrewsbury', *Shropshire Newsletter* No 37 (1969)

Gelling, M., *The Place Names of Shropshire, part 4: Shrewsbury Town and Suburbs and the Liberties of Shrewsbury* (2004). Nottingham: English Place Names Society

Gillam, P., *Shrewsbury: a celebration* (2000). Shrewsbury: Chasing Rainbows

Girouard, M., *The English Town* (1990). London: Yale University Press

Gough, R., *The History of Myddle* (ed.D.Hey, 1981). Harmondsworth: Penguin

Grey, P., Keeley, M. and Seale, J., *Midland Red: a History of the Company and its vehicles from 1940 to 1970* (1979). Glossop: Transport Publishing Co

Grier, R.M., *John Allen: Vicar of Prees and Archdeacon of Salop: a memoir* (1889). London: Rivingtons

Griffiths, R. and Smith, P., *The Directory of British Engine Sheds*, vol.1 (1999). Shepperton: Oxford Publishing Co.

Hadfield, C., *The Canals of the West Midlands* (1966). Newton Abbot: David & Charles

Harrison, A., *West Midland Trustee Savings Bank 1816-1966* (1966). Shrewsbury

Hart, S., *Shrewsbury: a Portrait in Old Picture Post Cards* (1988). Market Drayton: S.B. Publishers

Henshaw, J., *Passing Shots: Shropshire Tennis 1885-2003* (2003). Shrewsbury: privately published

Hibberd, D., *Wilfred Owen: a new biography* (2002). London: Weidenfeld & Nicolson

Hoare, Sir R. Colt, *The Journeys of Sir Richard Colt Hoare through Wales and England 1793-1810* (ed. M.W.Thompson, 1983). Gloucester: Sutton

Hobbs, J., *Shrewsbury Street Names* (1954). Shrewsbury: Wilding

How, F.D., *The Revd.Thomas Mainwaring Bulkeley-Owen: a Memoir* (1914). London: Wells Gardner, Darton & Co.

Howell, T.J., *The Stranger in Shrewsbury* (1816). Shrewsbury: Watton

Hughes, G. and Woodward, A., 'A ring ditch and neolithic pit complex at Meole Brace, Shrewsbury', *T.S.A.S.*, vol. 70 (1995)

Hughes, W.J. and Thomas, J.L., '*The Sentinel*': A History of Alley & MacLellan and the Sentinel Waggon Works, Vol. I, 1875-1930 (1973). Newton Abbot: David & Charles

Hulbert, C., *History and Description of the County of Salop* (1837). Hadnall: Hulbert

Hulbert, C., *A Manual of Shropshire Biography, Chronology and Antiquities, including also the Rise, Course and Termination of the River Severn* (1839). Shrewsbury: Hulbert

Hulbert, C., *Memoirs of Seventy Years of an Eventful Life* (1852). Shrewsbury: Hulbert

Ionides, J., *Thomas Farnolls Pritchard of Shrewsbury: Architect and Inventor of Cast Iron Bridges* (1999). Ludlow: Dog Rose Press

James, R.E., 'The Old River Bed at Shrewsbury', *Transactions of the Shropshire Archaeological Society*, vol. 53 (1950)

Jarvis, B., 'The Scourge of cholera in 19th century Shrewsbury', *Shropshire Magazine*, April 1980

Jenkinson, A., *Shropshire's Wild Places* (1992). Little Stretton: Scenesetters

Johnston, H., 'Discovering the local prison: Shrewsbury Gaol in the nineteenth century', *Local Historian*, vol.35 (2005)

Jones, C., 'Electricity Supply in Shropshire before Nationalisation', *Industrial Archaeology Review*, vol.18 (1996)

Jones, R., *The Shrewsbury Lancasterian School 1813-1988* (1988). Shrewsbury: privately published

Kelly's Directories, *Kelly's Directory of Shropshire* (1885; 1891; 1895; 1900; 1905; 1909;

1913; 1917; 1922; 1926; 1929; 1934; 1937; 1941). London: Kelly's Directories Ltd.

Kelly's Directories, *Kelly's Directory of Shrewsbury* (1936; 1938). London: Kelly's Directories Ltd.

Kent Service, *Shrewsbury Directory* (n.d., *circa* 1955). London: Kent Service

Lawson, J.B., 'The Architects of Millington's Hospital, Shrewsbury', *Shropshire Newsletter* No 42 (1972)

Lawson, J.B., 'Thomas Telford in Shrewsbury: The metamorphosis of an architect into a civil engineer', Penfold, A., ed., *Thomas Telford: Engineer* (1980). London: Thomas Telford

Lawson, J.B., '1882 Genesis: Exodus', *Salopian Newsletter* No 92, May 1983

Lawson, J.B., 'Harnage Slates and other roofing materials in Shrewsbury and neighbourhood in the late medieval and early modern period', *T.S.A.S.*, vol. 64 (1985)

Leary, W., *Ministers and Circuits in the Primitive Methodist Church: a Directory* (1990). Loughborough: Teamprint

Lee, M.J., 'Cherry Orchard: the growth of a Victorian suburb', *Shropshire Magazine*, October/November 1980

Leland, J., *John Leland's Itinerary: Travels in Tudor England* (ed. J. Chandler, 1993). Stroud: Sutton

Leonard, J., *Churches of Shropshire & their Treasures* (2004). Leominster: Logaston

Lerry, G.G., *Henry Robertson: Pioneer of Railways into Wales* (1949). Oswestry: Woodall

Lloyd, E.N.V., *The History of Millington's Hospital* (1982). Shrewsbury: Caradoc & Severn Valley Field Club, Occasional Paper No 7

Lloyd, L.C., *The Inns of Shrewsbury* (1942). Shrewsbury: Shrewsbury Circular (Rep. Shrewsbury: Shropshire Libraries, 1976)

Loveday, J., *John Loveday of Caversham 1711-1789: the Life and Times of an Eighteenth Century Onlooker* (ed. S. Markham, 1984). Wilton: Russell

MacDonald, W., *An Illustrated Guide to Shrewsbury* (1897). Edinburgh & London: MacDonald

Mate, W., *Shropshire: Historical, Descriptive, Biographical* (2 vols., n.d., c.1900). London: Mate

Mercer, E., *English Architecture to 1900: the Shropshire Experience* (2003). Leominster: Logaston

Mercer, E., 'Whitehall, Shrewsbury', *Society of Architectural Historians of Great Britain, Proceedings of the 1988 annual conference at Newport*

Mercer, E., 'The Abbey of Holy Cross, Shrewsbury', *Society of Architectural Historians of Great Britain, proceedings of the 1988 annual conference at Newport*

Mercer & Crocker, *General Topographical and Historical Directory of Shropshire* (1877). Leicester; Mercer & Crocker

Meteyard, E., *A Group of Englishmen (1795-1815) being the records of the younger Wedgwoods and their friends* (1871). London: Longmans Green

Minshull, T., *The Shrewsbury Guide and Salopian Directory* (1786). Shrewsbury: Pryse.

Minshull, T., *The Shrewsbury Visitor's Pocket Companion or Salopian Guide and Directory* (1803). Shrewsbury: Minshull

Moran, M., *Vernacular Architecture in Shropshire* (2003). Leominster: Logiston

Morey, C. and Pannett, D., 'The Origin of the Old River Bed at Shrewsbury', *Shropshire Conservation Trust Bulletin* No 35 (1976)

Morgan, J.S., *The Colonel Stephens Railways: a Pictorial History* (1978). Newton Abbot: David & Charles

Morris, W.E., *A History of Methodism in Shrewsbury and District* (1960). Shrewsbury: Wilding

Murrell, H., *Hilda Murrell's Nature Diaries 1961-1983* (ed. C. Sinker, 1987). London: Collins

Neal, T., *Shropshire Airfields* (2005). Telford: Langrish Caiger

Neal, T. and Knowles, K., *The Great Millennium Floods: Pictures from across Shropshire and Mid-Wales* (2000). Telford: Shropshire Newspapers Ltd.

Nightingale, J., *The Beauties of England and Wales, or Original Delineations of Each County, vol.13, part 1, Shropshire* (1813). London: Harris

Oldham, J.B., *A History of Shrewsbury School* (1952). Oxford: Blackwell

Owen, Harold, *Journey from Obscurity* (1963-65, 3 vols.), Oxford: Oxford University Press

Owen, Hugh, *Some Account of the Ancient and Present State of Shrewsbury* 1808). Shrewsbury: Sandford. Reprint Manchester, E.J.Morten (1972)

Owen, Hugh and Blakeway, J.B., *A History of Shrewsbury* (1825). London: Harding Lepard

Owen, M., 'Before Beringar', *Shrewsbury Civic Society Newsletter*, Summer 1993

Owen, W., *Wilfred Owen: Collected Letters* (ed. H. Owen and J. Bell,1967). Oxford: Oxford University Press

Owen, W., *Wilfred Owen: The Complete Poems and Fragments* (ed. J.Stallworthy, 2 vols., 1983). Oxford: Oxford University Press

Paddock, E.A., *Meole Brace through the Centuries* (1958). Shrewsbury: Shrewsbury Circular

Pannett, D., 'Fish Weirs on the River Severn in Shropshire', *Shropshire Newsletter* No 44 (1973)

Pannett, D. and Trinder, B., *Old Maps of Shrewsbury* (1975). Shrewsbury: Field Studies Council

Pattison, A., *On Severn Shore: the story of the Drill Hall, Coleham, Shrewsbury* (2004). Shrewsbury: Privately published

Penfold, A., ed., *Thomas Telford: Engineer* (1980). London: Thomas Telford

Pendlebury, W.J. and West, J.M., *Shrewsbury School – Recent Years* (1934). Shrewsbury: Wilding

Pevsner, N., *The Buildings of England: Shropshire* (1958). Harmondsworth: Penguin

Phillips, T., *The History and Antiquities of Shrewsbury* (1779). Shrewsbury: Wood

Phillips, W., *Early Methodism in Shropshire* (1896). Shrewsbury: Napier

Philpot, B.M., *A Name, a Man, a House: Oakley Manor, Shrewsbury* (1982). Shrewsbury: privately published

Pidgeon, H., *Memorials of Shrewsbury* (1837). Shrewsbury: Eddowes (Rep. 1975, Shrewsbury: Salop County Library)

Pigot & Co., *National Commercial Directory for Shropshire* (1828-9). Manchester: Pigot

Price, P., 'The Decline and Fall of the Old Shrewsbury Show', Trinder, B., ed., *Victorian Shrewsbury* (1984), Shrewsbury: Shropshire Books

Price, W. and Milner, C., 'Tractarians in Shropshire', *Shropshire Newsletter* No 36 (1969)

Quartermaine, J., Trinder, B. and Turner, R., *Thomas Telford's Holyhead Road: The A5 in North Wales* (2003). York: Council for British Archaeology

Quinn, H., *Charles Darwin: Shrewsbury's Man of the Millennium: a short history and guide* (1999). Shrewsbury: privately published

Ranger, W., *Report to the General Board of Health on the Sanitary Condition of the Inhabitants of Shrewsbury* (1854). London: Eyre & Spottiswoode

Rayska, U., *Victorian and Edwardian Shropshire from Old Photographs* (1977). London: Batsford

Rees, U.M., *The Cartulary of Shrewsbury Abbey* (1975). Aberystwyth: National Library of Wales

Rees, U.M., *The Cartulary of Haughmond Abbey* (1985). Cardiff: University of Wales Press

Review Publishing, *Industries of Shropshire: Business Review* (1891). Birmingham: Review Publishing Co

Roberts, M. Keeling, *In Retrospect: a short history of the Royal Salop Infirmary* (1981). Wem: privately published

Robinson, Son and Pike, *Shrewsbury Illustrated* (1894). Brighton: Robinson, Son & Pike

Rolt, L.T.C., *Railway Adventure* (edn. 1971). London: Pan

Scard, M. A., *The Building Stones of Shropshire* (1990). Shrewsbury: Swan Hill

Scard, M.A., 'The Development and changing Organisation of Shropshire's Quarrying Industry 1750-1900', *Industrial Archaeology Review*, vol. 11 (1989)

Scarfe, N., *Innocent Espionage: the La Rochefoucauld Brothers' Tour of England in 1785* (1995). Woodbridge: Boydell

Shrewsbury Chronicle & Shropshire Libraries, *The Changing Face of Shrewsbury* (1977). Shrewsbury: Shrewsbury Chronicle & Shropshire Libraries

Shrewsbury Chronicle & Shropshire Libraries, *The Changing Face of Shrewsbury* (1981). Shrewsbury: Shrewsbury Chronicle & Shropshire Libraries

Shropshire & West Midlands Agricultural Society, *Century of Progress 1875-1975: a centenary brochure* (1975). Shrewsbury: Shropshire & West Midlands Agricultural Society

Shropshire Federation of Women's Institutes, *Shropshire: the Century in Photographs* (1998). Newbury: Countryside Press

Shropshire Railway Society, *Shropshire Railways Revisited* (1982). Shrewsbury: Shropshire Libraries

Shropshire Records & Research Unit, *Shrewsbury Then and Now* (1991). Shrewsbury: Shropshire Books

Simcox, K., *Wilfred Owen: Anthem for a Doomed Youth* (1987). London: Woburn

Stallworthy, J., *Wilfred Owen: A Biography* (1974). Oxford: Oxford University Press

Stamper, P., *Historic Parks and Gardens of Shropshire* (1996). Shrewsbury: Shropshire Books

Straughan, S., *Kingsland: a Shrewsbury suburb* (1994). Shrewsbury: privately published

Thomas, A.R. and Thomas, J.L., *'The Sentinel': A history of Alley & MacLellen and the Sentinel Waggon Works, vol. II, 1930-1980* (1987). Worcester: Woodpecker Publications

Toghill, P., *Geology in Shropshire* (1990). Shrewsbury: Swan Hill

Tomlinson, J.W.B., *Oxon lives: Memories and Predictions of a Shropshire Parish* (2004). Shrewsbury: Parish of Christ Church, Shelton and Oxon

Tonks, E.S., *The Shropshire & Montgomeryshire Railway* (1972). London: The Industrial Railway Society

Trinder, B., 'The Holyhead Road: an engineering project in its social context', Penfold, A., ed., *Thomas Telford: Engineer* (1980). London: Thomas Telford

Trinder, B., ed., *Victorian Shrewsbury: Studies in the History of a County Town* (1984). Shrewsbury: Shropshire Libraries

Trinder, B., 'Ditherington Flax Mill – a Re-evaluation', *Textile History*, vol. 23 (1992)

Trinder, B., 'The Textile Industry in Shrewsbury in the late Eighteenth Century', Clark, P. and Corfield, P., *Industry and Urbanisation in Eighteenth Century England* (1994). Leicester: Centre for Urban History, University of Leicester

Trinder, B., *The Industrial Archaeology of Shropshire* (1996). Chichester: Phillimore

Trinder, B., *A History of Shropshire* (2nd ed., 1998). Chichester: Phillimore

Trinder, B., *The Industrial Revolution in Shropshire* (2nd ed., 2000).Chichester:

Phillimore

Trumper, D., *Shrewsbury in Old Photographs* (1994). Stroud: Sutton

Trumper, D., *Shrewsbury: a Second Selection* (1995). Stroud: Sutton

Trumper, D., *Shrewsbury: the Twentieth Century* (1999). Stroud: Sutton

Trumper, D., *Britain in Old Photographs: Yesterday's Shrewsbury* (2002). Stroud: Sutton

Trumper, D., *A Glimpse of Old Shrewsbury* (2003). Stroud: Sutton

Tucker, D.G., 'Electricity Generating Stations for Public Supply in the West Midlands 1888-1977', *West Midlands Studies*, vol.10 (1977)

Turner, K. and S., *The Shropshire and Montgomeryshire Light Railway* (1982). Newton Abbot: David & Charles

Victoria History of Shropshire. Volume 2 (1973). Oxford: Oxford University Press

Victoria History of Shropshire. Volume 3: County Government (1979). Oxford: Oxford University Press

Victoria History of Shropshire. Volume 4: Agriculture (1989). Oxford: Oxford University Press

Wadlow, E.C., 'Shropshire was an important lead-producing area a century ago', *Shropshire Magazine*, April, May, June 1959

Walker, W.B., *Salop & County ABC Railway and Omnibus Guide* (1947). Shrewsbury: Walker

Walley, D.M., *Images of England: Around Shrewsbury* (1999). Stroud: Tempus

Walsh, V.J., 'The Diary of a Country Gentleman: Sir Baldwyn Leighton Bt. (1805-71)', *T.S.A.S.*, vol. 59 (1976)

Ward, A.W., *The Bridges of Shrewsbury* (1935). Shrewsbury: Wilding

Ward, A.W., *Shrewsbury of 1772* (1947). Shrewsbury: Shrewsbury Chronicle

Ward, A.W., 'The Stone (or East) and the Abbey Bridges, Shrewsbury, in 1765', *T.S.A.S.*, vol.53 (1950)

Watson, M. and Musson, C., *Shropshire from the air: Man and the Landscape* (1993). Shrewsbury: Shropshire Books

Watson, M. and Musson, C., *Shropshire from the air: An English County at Work* (1996). Shrewsbury: Shropshire Books

Watson, N., *A Family Business: Morris & Co. 1869-1994* (1995). Shrewsbury: Morris & Co.

Webb, Mary, *Gone To Earth* (1917). London: Constable

Wells & Co, *Wells's Directory of Shrewsbury, Ludlow, Oswestry, Wellington and Districts* (1890). Shrewsbury: Wells & Co.

Wells & Manton, *Directory of Shrewsbury* (1886; 1888). Shrewsbury: Wells & Manton.

White, R., 'Summary of fieldwork carried out by the Wroxeter Hinterland Project 1994-97', *T.S.A.S.*, vol. 72 (1997), 1-8

Wilding & Co., *Shropshire: a beautiful English county* (1914). Shrewsbury: Wilding

Wilding & Co., *Wilding's Directory of Shrewsbury &c.* (1896, 1899, 1903, 1906, 1910). Shrewsbury: Longworth Wilding

Wilding & Co., *Wilding's Directory of Shrewsbury &c.* (1916, 1922, 1925, 1928, 1931). Shrewsbury: Wilding & Co.

3. *Printed Maps:*

Baugh, R., *Map of Shropshire* (n.d., *c*.1808, reprinted 1983)

Hitchcock, A., *Map of the Borough of Shrewsbury as extended and settled by Act of Parliament* (1832)

Rocque, J., *Plan of Shrewsbury* (1746)

Speed, J., *A Plan of Shrewsbury* (1610)

Tisdale, T., *Town of Shrewsbury* (1850)
Tisdale, T., *Map of the Town and Borough of Shrewsbury* (1875)
Wood, J., *The Plan of Shrewsbury* (1838)

4. *Academic theses and dissertations:*

Frost, P., *Victorian Public Hangings in Shrewsbury*, Dip. H.E. dissertation, Wolverhampton Polytechnic, 1988
Jones, I.C., *The Industrial Archaeology of Coleham Riverside*, MSocSci dissertation, Ironbridge Institute, University of Birmingham, 1992-93
Macleod, M., Trinder, B. and Worthington, M., *Ditherington Flax Mill, Shrewsbury: a Survey and Historical Evaluation, a report for English Heritage* (1988). Telford: Ironbridge Institute
Smith, J.T., *Shrewsbury: Topography and Domestic Architecture to the middle of the 17th century*, M.A. thesis, University of Birmingham, 1953
Thomas, P.A., *A Study of the History of the Shrewsbury Lancasterian School 1812-1930*, Special Study, Certificate of Education, University of Birmingham, 1979

5. *Newspapers and periodicals:*

Chambers's Edinburgh Journal
Chester Chronicle
Eddowes Salopian Journal (sometimes *Salopian Journal*)
Hereford Journal
Salopian Shreds and Patches
Shrewsbury Chronicle
Shropshire Conservative
Shropshire Magazine
Wellington Journal

6. *Websites:*

www.darwincountry.org
www.historicaldirectories.org
www.kingslandgrange.com

Index

The index is divided into three parts: an index of personal names, an index relating to Shrewsbury, listing houses, streets and other features, and a general index of subjects and places outside Shrewsbury.

199

Shrewsbury index

This index is divided into the following categories: burial grounds, hospitals, house names, industries and commerce, parishes, places of worship, public houses, railway stations, recreations and recreational organisations, schools and colleges, streets, courts, localities and physical features

Places (outside Shrewsbury) and Subjects